"Take a super-high bandwidth Internet, add a healthy dose of Information Warfare, sprinkle in a few liberties with virtual reality, and you will find yourself immersed in Jefferson Scott's thoroughly absorbing world of a not-distant future I pray never comes to pass."

WINN SCHWARTAU
International Security Consultant and author of
Information Warfare: Chaos on the Electronic Superhighway.

"*Virtually Eliminated,* set within the worlds of cyberspace, international intrigue, national issues, and individual need, is a mind-expanding, spiritually stretching experience. For one who considers himself computer illiterate, I was caught up in the story's flow whether I understood the terminology and technicalities or not. This is great Christian leisure reading!"

BOB OLDENBURG,
Baptist General Convention of Texas

"*Virtually Eliminated* is a gripping thriller so filled with suspense that you can't put it down. While the storyline is intriguing, it also affords valuable insights about how to live the Christian life in a high-tech age. Although it is fiction, it deals with people realistically and compassionately as they grapple with true-to-life issues."

STEVE LEMKE
Associate Professor of Philosophy of Religion
Southwestern Baptist Theological Seminary

"Jefferson Scott handles well the difficult task of conveying to the general reader the subject of Virtual Reality. Today's video-game generation should find the story especially interesting. The computer/VR addiction raised is significant even outside the Christian theological framework."

VENKAT DEVARAJAN
Associate Professor of Electrical Engineering and
Leader of VR Research Group at the University of Texas (Arlington)

a novel

virtu@lly
.eliminated

jefferson scott

MULTNOMAH BOOKS . SISTERS, OREGON

MAI 404 445 N

This book is a work of fiction. With the exception of recognized
historical figures, the characters in this novel are fictional. Any
resemblance to actual persons, living or dead, is purely coincidental.

VIRTUALLY ELIMINATED
© 1996 by Jeff Gerke

published by Multnomah Books
a part of the Questar publishing family

Edited by Rodney L. Morris
Cover design by David Carlson

International Standard Book Number: 0-88070-885-9

Printed in the United States of America.

ALL RIGHTS RESERVED
No part of this publication may be reproduced, stored in a retrieval
system, or transmitted in any form or by any means—electronic,
mechanical, photocopying, recording, or otherwise—without prior
written permission.

For information:
Questar Publishers, Inc.
Post Office Box 1720
Sisters, Oregon 97759

96 97 98 99 00 01 02 03 — 10 9 8 7 6 5 4 3 2 1

For my Lord Jesus,

My wife, Robin,

And my daughter, Grace

I would like to thank the following people for their invaluable assistance to me in the preparation of this book. Robin, John, and Anne Gerke, Brian and Pam Walker, Sue King, Reba Hill, Paul Dickinson, and Jody Mapston. I must thank Winn Schwartau for his kind words and also for the inspiration behind the data sniffer scene in this book from Mr. Schwartau's *Information Warfare* (Thunder's Mouth Press). Thanks also to Bob Oldenburg, Dr. Venkat Devarajan, and Dr. Steve Lemke for their contributions and endorsements. Thanks also belong to Rod Morris at Questar for taking a chance on me as a writer.

virtu@lly
.eliminated

< virtually eliminated >

prologue

ONCE HE DECIDED TO KILL HIMSELF, the rest was easy.

He took a last look at the candle burning on the bedside table, then willed the interface open. The world he saw through the goggles was dark, as it always was at the beginning. But with a nudge of thought, a portal of light opened and he flew through, leaving his body far behind.

Back there, his name was Louis Parks. Here, he was called *Sentinel*. In a few moments, he would be neither.

Sentinel smiled as he soared into the familiar local hub. Below him was what looked like a tourist's map, oversimplified to pick out special attractions. There was a quaint school, a library, a public square, a city hall, a gymnasium, and a number of other buildings. These were representations of the different areas of interest offered by this network. The gym, for instance, was the area for interactive sports games. The schoolhouse was the site to take a short course on any and every subject. The library represented the storehouse of downloadable information.

He remembered the first time he had discovered this place, back when he was still in the clinic.

But one glimpse of this corny, splendid village, one exchange with the friendly school teacher, and young Louis Parks had been instantly

< jefferson scott >

charmed. Here, in VR, he was just like everybody else. It was the first thing he found he could do as well or better than "normal" people — even adults. He plunged into it with abandon.

Sentinel reached the border of the local net abruptly. The collision momentarily rendered his body visible to the eyes of other users. His stealth tools weren't perfect yet. He toggled himself back off, cursing softly.

This local net no longer satisfied him. He knew every node, every subdirectory — even every user — all too well. It confined him.

He hurried to the GlobeNet interface. There was the usual long queue. Sentinel wrinkled his forehead, and a collection of small three-dimensional objects appeared in the air before him. A computer-generated hand reached out from his invisible body to grasp something out of his inventory. It looked like a bullhorn. He activated it.

Every network had a system administrator. Every system administrator had some kind of priority access siren, which he or she used when there was a need for more system horsepower for such things as upgrades or overhauls. When the alarm went off, Netiquette dictated that every user not engaged in some kind of file transfer immediately log off the net.

Sentinel's bullhorn precisely matched this particular system administrator's siren.

Sheep, he thought, moving through the now-unpopulated net. He closed his bullhorn subroutine and sped invisibly through the interface.

He had existed as Sentinel for two years now: watching, listening, piecing things together. The inescapable conclusion grieved him, turned to stone what was left of his heart. It became clear that the time for sentinels — passive, quiet, and immobile — was past.

The turning point had been Senator Griffith's rebuttal. The lesser officials to whom Sentinel had divulged his findings had turned him away, but that had neither surprised nor discouraged him. If a full senator would turn a blind eye to the indisputable facts, however, America was in worse trouble than Sentinel had first imagined.

< virtually eliminated >

That was when Sentinel had left the beaten path. If the United States government was not going to combat America's invaders, then he was going to have to defend her himself.

Sentinel breathed more easily once inside GlobeNet proper. He lived for the freedoms offered here. Freedom of expression, of presence, of information. Freedom from all restraint: physical, monetary, legal, racial.

Moral.

GlobeNet was set up graphically — similar to the local network but on a much larger scale. If the local hub was a village, GlobeNet was a metropolis. The whole planet summarized in one stylized city.

Near the airport icon, he could see his young friend Freebooter harassing the InterAir Traffic Control computer. Beneath him, his trained eye spotted a group of cyberpunks trying to get into the back door of the World Bank. Much as he might like to, Sentinel had no time to play today. Perhaps never again.

He bounced around the city, laying an elaborate system of alarms and relays. Someone more tied to spatial distances might have been impressed that, though it took less than two minutes to set these precautions, Sentinel had circled the earth six times — electronically. If he was going to commit ritual suicide, there was no tolerance for interruptions by self-appointed net vigilantes or NSA patrols.

Hovering above the GlobeNet downtown, Sentinel called up his inventory again and selected a metallic-looking gridwork. He pressed with his mind, and the grid expanded around him to form a protective cube. An unseen pocket from which he could view his own demise.

He reached into his inventory again and grasped something resembling a crystal dagger. He rotated the blade lovingly, admiring its edge, its sheen — its perfection. He lifted it above his head with both hands.

"O happy dagger!" he quoted. "This is thy sheath; there rust, and let me die."

He shut his eyes.

Plunged the dagger through his grid.

< jefferson scott >

The blade sailed out from him for three seconds, then soundlessly exploded into hundreds of crystalline shards. The fragments dispersed, vanishing into the blackness of GlobeNet. Each particle was a modified *archie* data retrieval utility, altered to search thousands of databases for a very specific set of characters and, upon encountering those characters, to delete them.

In seconds it was accomplished.

He opened his eyes. And beheld a world suddenly fresh and sharp, full of promise. For officially — electronically — Louis Parks had ceased to exist.

"Moksha, at last," he said. "Release." He laughed then, a robust, cleansing laughter. Not since the accident had he felt so free.

"Henceforth," he boomed to no one, "Sentinel shall no more haunt this Earth. May he rest in peace. In his place am I — *Patriot.*"

He was free now. Free to do what had to be done.

< Part I >

It is your concern when the wall next door is on fire.

HORACE, EPISTLES

■

< virtually eliminated >

chapter.1

CHALLENGER DEEP. Deepest point on the planet. In the Marianas Trench, twelve hundred miles east of the Philippine Islands and twelve hundred miles north of New Guinea. Almost seven miles beneath the surface of the Pacific Ocean.

Julia Willis was studying for an exam.

Physically, she was sitting in her dorm room at the University of Nebraska, hooked up to an Ono-Sendai VR-Sport Head Mounted Display (HMD). Her body looked comical, sitting there in her wicker chair. The light-blocking goggles covered her eyes like a blindfold; her gloved hand reached out into the empty air in front of her. Her mouth gaped open. She looked like a blind woman begging for alms.

Her virtual presence, though, was on the ocean floor.

"Where is it, where is it?" She swiveled her head in Lincoln, and in the Marianas Trench her view spun around. "Okay, there's that offshoot canyon. Not deep enough." She tilted her head forward and plunged into the abyss.

Her Geophysical Phenomena mid-term was tomorrow, and she just knew Professor "Hang'em" Hier was going to ask about the fabled Challenger Deep. She thought she'd better have one more look at it.

< jefferson scott >

When she arrived at the spot, all murky and dark, someone was already there. She didn't see anyone, but that wasn't odd. Not much light made it this far down. Further, in virtual reality every user had the option of choosing or refusing an on-screen persona. But Julia could sense another presence, all the same.

"Is that you, Robert?"

"No."

The voice came from her right. She spun around, but saw no one. Something about the voice seemed strange, but she couldn't pinpoint it. "Well, who are you? You studying for Hier's GP exam?"

"No."

It sounded too close for a normal GlobeNet conversation — that's what was strange. It seemed to come from inside her head now, or perhaps from all around her.

"How did you get such a clear connection?" she asked. "You are going through the library computer, aren't you?"

"No."

"Look, Dr. No, either show yourself or amscray. I'm trying to study here. Wait a minute. I shouldn't be on your screen. I didn't choose a persona-thingy. How do you even know I'm here?"

"'The best of seers,' Euripedes wrote, 'is he who guesses well.'"

"Yeah? Well, I can't just guess on this test tomorrow. So, if you don't mind, I'm going to get back to my studying."

But Julia didn't feel like studying anymore. This guy gave her the creeps. Better to leave and come back when he wasn't around. Back in her dorm room, she raised her hands to take off the headset.

"Wait!" the voice said.

Julia hesitated. "What?"

"Very well. I shall show myself."

Seven miles underwater, at the earth's lowest point, Patriot emerged from perfect invisibility. He manifested himself as a tall man in a billowing black cloak, with a hood pulled over a shadowed face. He was upside down, above her, his feet pointing toward the surface. When he moved, it was with graceful inertia. It reminded Julia of a Zero-G plane she'd ridden in.

"There," he said. "You see."

< virtually eliminated >

"Well, what do you want?"

Patriot did a leisurely somersault, his black robes rippling in an unseen wind. "Actually, I wanted to ask you about your friend Kenji."

"Who?"

"Of course you know him. Do not deny it."

"I don't —" She cut herself off.

Patriot nodded. "Thank you. While we are on the subject of denials, do you wish to deny that this very semester you destroyed the symbol of the United States of America?"

"The what?"

"The flag, my dear. Do you deny burning the American flag at a recent demonstration?"

Of course she wished to deny it. Unfortunately, she couldn't. She was young and intelligent and in college. She wanted to feel a part of her world. Burning the flag was the most powerful thing she could think of to do. It had seemed like the right thing to do at the time. Now she wished she could take it back.

"Well, what about Kenji?" she asked.

The intruder chuckled. "Very well. You gave Kenji access to your father's home computer, did you not?"

Oh, so that's what this is about. "Are you some kind of lunchroom monitor for passwords or something?"

"Or something." He circled around her, descending. "Why was it again that Kenji needed the security password to your father's computer?"

"I don't know. Why don't you ask him?"

Black arms crossed. "I have. Unfortunately, your friend Kenji proved most uncommunicative. I would ask you to reprimand him if I thought you would be seeing him soon." The intruder chuckled — an unsettling sound. "Of course, depending on your belief structures, you may be seeing him very soon indeed."

"Who are you? And what do you want?"

"I want you to tell me why you gave —"

"Kenji wanted to send my dad a message, okay? They're buds. What of it?"

"Yes, bosom buddies, no doubt. Your father was exceedingly foolish,

< jefferson scott >

you know, to maintain a link between his computers at the airbase and at home."

"What is your problem, buster? This is the twenty-first century. People work from home, or haven't you heard? Besides, my dad gets sick and can't go in sometimes."

"In that case I have good news for you. Your father, Major General Willis, has been miraculously cured of whatever ailed him."

"What? How could you know?" Julia felt something like a trap door opening beneath her. She gaped at the intruder, knowing she should jack out right away.

"I understand why your father wanted to see his force deployment database from home," the black-robed figure said. "I even understand why your friend Kenji would want access to that database — certain research in Japanese surveillance technology would make such knowledge indispensable. What I do not understand, Julia, is why you would knowingly give out the passwords to your father's computer. Were you truly so ignorant of Kenji's motives?"

Julia wanted to say she was. Kenji's request had seemed benign enough — he said he just wanted to look for specs on the recently unclassified Stealth Bomber. In her heart, though, Julia had known there was something behind his innocent advances.

On the ocean floor, the black-hooded man raised something out of his robes. It looked like a golden box.

"What's that?"

"You should like it," Patriot said. "It will excuse you from your impending catechism."

"My what?"

"Julia?"

"What?"

"Don't ever burn another American flag."

"I —"

He pressed a button on top of the little box.

It took fifteen minutes for the custodians to come up with a key for Julia's dorm room. It turned out that there was no need to rush. When they did get in, they weren't even going to bother to call an ambulance,

< virtually eliminated >

but they finally did. None of them could force themselves to pick up what was left of Julia's charred body.

When Crowell's Patriot Air Defense System team met for their monthly meeting, none of the project managers left his or her office. The Crowell host computer manufactured a conference room — this particular design featured a long table, windows overlooking a computer-generated forest, and a large display screen at the rear of the room. The project managers donned VR helmets, logged in, and took their places around the artificial table.

The man at the head of the table addressed the other four. "Hello again, everyone. I trust you've all had a productive January. Without further dilly-dally, let's get to work. Alvin, why don't you get us up to speed on the PAC-28 upgrades."

"Yes, Mr. Vice President."

Alvin's persona rose from the table and moved to the presentation screen. The vice president and the other three project managers — two men and a woman — turned in their synthetic chairs. Alvin entered a code into the viewscreen's keypad and the Crowell Electronics's logo appeared on the screen.

"Since its introduction in the late 1980s," Alvin said, "the makers of the Patriot missile — first Raytheon Electronic Systems and now Crowell — have endeavored to make it the best ballistic missile defense system in existence."

Video of the Patriot missile in use from both the Persian Gulf and Latvian Wars played on the screen. Clip after clip showed the Patriot launch, close on an incoming missile, and detonate with great pyrotechnic display.

"Through its competitive upgrade program, Crowell has succeeded in positioning the Patriot Air Defense System at the forefront of anti-missile ordnance for over a quarter of a century. The Patriot Advanced Capability-28 — or PAC-28 — is the latest in a long line of scheduled improvements."

< jefferson scott >

A schematic of a Patriot missile appeared on the screen. The view zoomed in on the guidance system. "PAC-28 gives the Patriot a new gyromagnetic targeting device — a new brain, if you will — based on Motorola's new CENTAUR technology. This upgrade more than compensates for the alleged new capabilities of the TS-1108, the so-called SuperSCUD VII." The video screen cut to footage of the improved Patriot shooting down its improved adversary. Alvin returned to his chair.

"Most impressive, Alvin," the vice president said. "When will the upgrade be in effect?"

"New units are already being built with the upgrade, of course. Kits will be available to preexisting customers by the end of the month."

"Excellent. Now let's hear from Launch Systems. Judy?"

"Not just yet, Judy."

The project managers looked at each other. "Who said that?"

"I did. Out here."

The man next to Judy stood up. "Look! Outside the glass."

"Don't be a fool, Jacobs," the vice president said. "The glass is just an illu —"

A hooded, black-robed figure stepped through the glass into the conference room. "An illusion, Mr. Osborne? Perhaps. Be careful not to part with your illusions, however. For as Mark Twain reminds us, 'When they are gone, you may still exist, but you have ceased to live.'"

"Alvin," Vice President Osborne said, "I thought this was a secured site."

"It is, sir. I mean," Alvin said, looking up at the intruder, "I thought it was."

"Get rid of him, will you, so we can get back to business."

Alvin stood and faced the hooded figure. "This is a private meeting, sir. You'll have to leave. If you'd like, I can get you in touch with our customer relations people. They'd be more than happy to —"

"I will leave, Alvin Kissler, when I have completed my purpose here." He crossed to the video screen and called up Alvin's presentation. As the first Patriot missile impacted the incoming SCUD, he paused the playback.

< virtually eliminated >

"There is no more purely American defensive system than the Patriot missile. The name itself arouses images of George Washington, minutemen, and Paul Revere." He pointed to the screen. "Rockets' red glare, bombs bursting in air. Marvelous! The element of self-sacrifice inherent in its design makes one feel almost virtuous for using it. How wonderful to be an American, wouldn't you say?"

The vice president was losing patience. "Look, kid — and I'm assuming you're either a snot-nosed kid or a hacker bucking for a lawsuit — we all know how great the Patriot is. We build it! Now get out of here before we call your parents."

"I loved the concept of the Patriot system so much, I even took it as my final appellation."

The vice president stood up. "Okay, that's it everybody. We'll take a break then reconvene at another site in an hour." The personas' hands rose as, back in their offices, the project managers reached for their headsets.

"But then I began hearing rumors about the Patriot's true effectiveness," the intruder went on. "Rumors that perhaps it wasn't as potent as we Americans had all been led to believe." The five Crowell employees paused, leaving their headsets on. "Reports surfaced suggesting the missile had failed on many occasions, that the on-board radar/software package had trouble distinguishing between a SCUD's warhead and its fuel tank. Thus an incoming missile might be intercepted, but its warhead would then fall upon whatever — or whomever — was underneath. I read one report that said there had never in the history of the Patriot program been a confirmed successful hit."

The vice president spun around. "That's a lie! We sued the writer of that article for ten million. He settled out of court and retracted his statements."

"Yes, you bought him off. I understand. What else could you do — admit the truth? How would you explain that to the U.S. Army come reordering time? Oh, by the way, I understand congratulations are in order. Has Vice President Osborne not told the rest of you that Crowell's just been awarded a $62.2 billion contract? You should all be proud; you'll be helping to rearm one of America's most bitter enemies, Japan."

< jefferson scott >

"Japan's had Patriot missiles since the '90s," Judy said.

"Sobering, is it not? Does it not alarm you the rate at which Japan's military might has increased over the last five years?"

"That's ridiculous," the vice president said. "Japan's constitution only lets them spend one percent of their GNP on defense."

"So what is one percent of the highest GNP of any nation on the planet, Mr. Osborne? Anyone? Something on the order of fifty billion dollars annually. Japan's defense spending exceeded that of France in 1992, the United Kingdom in 1994, and has been second only to the United States ever since."

"Thank you for the economics lesson, Mr....?"

"He said his 'appellation' was Patriot," the fourth program manager said.

"Is that your real name or do you maybe think you're a missile?" Alvin asked.

All at once, gravity seemed to lose its hold on Patriot. Gently he tumbled up to the synthetic ceiling, pushed off, and floated around the conference room. "Would it surprise you to learn that the Japanese know how to defeat your vaunted Patriot Air Defense System — that your Patriots would sail past their new line of ballistic missiles like so many butterflies?"

"Is this true, Jacobs?"

"We had one unconfirmed report, sir, but —"

"When were you going to let me in on it?"

"Don't be so hard on him, Mr. Osborne," Patriot said. "After all, you've known about those same weaknesses since the beginning."

"I don't know what you're talking about. Come on everybody, let's go."

"Yes, go. You would not want to hear that the company to which you give your livelihoods is responsible for purposely sabotaging the very thing you produce."

"What is he talking about, sir?"

Patriot went on. "From the first day Crowell acquired Raytheon Electronic Systems to today, your Patriot missiles have been designed to fail. Haven't they, Alvin? The missiles must work well, so as to impress the prospective buyer, but not too well, so as to allow for improved —

< virtually eliminated >

more expensive — versions through the competitive upgrade program. What are you on now, upgrade twenty? Thirty?"

"That's a lie, mister. Take your slander back or —"

"Or you'll pay me ten million dollars? Nice try, Mr. Osborne. But I'm afraid the price for my silence is far more dear."

"What do you want?"

"I want you to cancel the contract with the Japanese. They must not receive the PAC-28 upgrade. For now, at least, they cannot defeat it."

"Cancel the contract?" the vice president said. "Kid, we've already spent the money."

Patriot didn't speak for a moment. "That is disheartening."

"Look, Mr. Patriot, Japan is just a customer like any other. They have as much right to our product as the U.S. Army. If you've got a problem with that, then you've got a problem with every major company in America."

"Well said, Mr. Osborne." Patriot touched down lightly atop the simulated conference table. He drew a yellow orb from the folds of his cloak. "I do not begrudge the Japanese their economic success. Nor do I deny the pure capitalism in your upgrade program. I have only small grievances with you, actually. Almost two thousand of them. Granted, the number is only a rough estimate."

"Estimate of what?" Alvin said.

"Of how many civilians have died as a direct result of your intentionally flawed Patriot missiles."

"But we didn't know!" Judy said.

"Yes, it is a shame that the innocent must die because of what the guilty have done. Isn't that true, Mr. Osborne? Mr. Kissler?" He held the yellow orb aloft with both hands.

"We —"

"Say hello to George Washington if you should happen to see him." The orb flared.

Crowell Electronics was suddenly hiring in five key positions.

The barbarian came down the staircase carefully. He was huge: barechested, blond hair flying, with only a trace of luminosity at the edges

< jefferson scott >

of his chiseled face. He held a battle-ax in both hands.

"Out, ye black villain," he said. "Show thyself that I may remove thy foul head from thy body." He reached the bottom of the stairs and looked around.

The gameworld he was exploring was sparse and dark. Surrealistic obstacles — colored platforms, school buses, burning hoops, World War I fighter aircraft — dotted the computer-generated landscape randomly. The stairway behind him poked out of the ground, ascending into nowhere. As the objects receded into the distance, they became less distinct, until at last they lost all form and merged into a pixelated horizon.

His adversary was nowhere in sight.

"I knowest thou art here, foul knave. Show thy cowardly face to Rhatok, Barbarian Prince!"

He headed for a row of giant video screens. Each displayed a different moving image. He stopped to stare at one of the screens.

Behind him, a black-clad figure flitted from one simulated shadow to another.

The blond barbarian reached a hand out toward the screen. His hand passed right through. "I thought so," he said in a most unbarbarous voice. He backed up a step, then walked forward, disappearing into the monitor. He soon reemerged, but continued to walk back and forth, in and out of the video screen.

Behind him, a black-gloved hand raised something at the barbarian's back. A computer-rendered thumb hovered over a gold button.

"This needs to be fixed." He headed for the exit.

"Not so fast, Rhatok," the hooded man said.

The barbarian spun around. "There you are, thou fiend." He hefted his battle-ax and took a step toward the black-hooded figure. "Well, I don't know about your other victims, but you won't get me without a fight." He shouted a war-cry and charged toward his dark enemy.

Too late.

The thumb came down. The virtual battlefield lit up in an all-white negative image. A tremendous bolt of energy sprang from the black

< virtually eliminated >

hand. It struck the barbarian in the chest, landing with a sickening thump. He dropped his ax, fell, then faded out.

The black figure picked up the fallen ax and vanished.

< jefferson scott >

chapter.2

"DAD! ARE YOU OKAY?"

Jordan Hamilton was only nine years old, but already he had a barbed sense of humor. He pushed the TacBack box aside and set his VReam-20 HMD on the wooden desk. "I fried you big time. I got your weapon, too."

"I was distracted," his father said.

Ethan Hamilton was thirty-five, complete with a widening bald spot, but everybody said he acted more like twenty-five. He still loved cartoons, comic books, and a good game of Go Fish. His metabolism hadn't changed since his twenties, either. Even on a balanced diet of peanut butter cracker sandwiches and Payday candy bars, he stayed at a trim 170 pounds. His wife hated his metabolism.

His ancient PowerGlove sat, mostly un-Velcroed, in his lap, along with his NASA Ames HMD. "I walked right through that video screen. Guess somebody forgot to turn on the clipping." Ethan cracked his knuckles. "Time for a little programming."

He slid out a keyboard from below the desk and began peck-typing at a remarkable speed. He accessed the programming code of the

< virtually eliminated >

gameworld they had just been playing in and paged through it with the efficiency of a surgeon performing a routine procedure. His thumbnail rose to his teeth for its habitual chewing.

Jordan watched his father with declining interest. It didn't seem strange that his dad was fiddling with the source code of a brand new $150 virtual reality game. Didn't everybody's dad do that?

The Hamilton game room had been designed with hours of virtual reality gaming in mind. There were no windows, no posters, no wallpaper or fancy light fixtures. Just a desk to hold the computers, a ceiling fan to keep the players and equipment cool, brown carpet to hide spills, lots of power outlets, a one hundred-watt bulb on a dimmer, and a sound-damping sliding door. If Ethan or Jordan had ever bothered to notice, they would have seen that the walls were off-white.

The game room door slid open. An eighteen-month-old girl wobbled in, a fountain of blonde hair shooting straight up from her head.

"No, Katie, you can't come in here," Jordan said. "Mom! Katie's in here again."

A gray and white cat pranced in on long, elegant legs. Jordan grabbed the cat into his arms. "You're okay, Wizzy. But the brat has to go." Wysiwyg, accustomed to such privileges, only purred.

Ethan looked up from the computer screen blankly. "Hmm?"

Sometimes Jordan wondered if his dad would escape with his life if the house caught fire while he was programming. Not that Jordan was any different.

Ethan's face brightened when he saw his daughter. He spun around in his chair. "Come to Daddy, baby girl."

The little girl half ran, half staggered forward, laughing, but stopped when she saw the wire snaking off her father's right arm. Her brow wrinkled up.

Jordan knew what that meant. "Take cover!" He tried to cover his ears without dropping the cat. As if on cue, Katie opened her mouth and screamed.

Wysiwyg bolted from Jordan's arms and out the door.

< j e f f e r s o n   s c o t t >

"What's wrong, Katie?" Ethan said.

"It's your glove, Dad," Jordan shouted irritably, examining his scratched forearm. "She thinks the wire's a snake."

Ethan yanked at the PowerGlove's last Velcro strap. His helmet fell to the floor with a crash. Katie cried louder.

The "soundproof" door rocked aside, almost off its tracks. A slender woman with light brown hair rushed into the game room and swept the little girl off the floor. "What is going on in here?"

"O Kaye," Ethan sighed. "Save us."

"There, there, Katie." Kaye patted her daughter's back. "Are these mean old boys picking on you again?" The little girl's wail faltered, then trailed away completely. She turned and looked for the PowerGlove. "Did she fall?"

"Nope. Dad scared Katie with his glove again. And Katie scared Wizzy."

"Well, no wonder," Kaye said. "That thing scares me, too. Why can't you get one with no big button-do-dad on the top and no wire sticking out? Or get a tacky-thingy, like Jordan has?"

Ethan picked up the PowerGlove lovingly. "This is sacred."

"Humph." Kaye's disdain carried a hint of laughter.

Jordan caught his mom as she turned to take Katie out of the room. "I toasted Dad big time, Mom. You should've seen it. I snuck up behind him and blasted him with my psi pistol. *Pow!*"

"Bow!" Katie echoed.

"No, Katie. Pow! P- P- P-."

"Puh puh puh," she said seriously. Then she giggled and wanted down.

Jordan turned back to his mom. "After I shot him, he kind of glowed a little. Then he poofed out. I got his ax, too."

"That's nice, honey," Kaye said. "Put some first aid cream on that arm." She shut the door behind her.

< virtually eliminated >

Out on the hallway's wooden floor, Kaye allowed herself a sigh. She really did try to care about Jordan's games — and for that matter, her husband's — since it seemed important to them. To tell the truth, though, she didn't care one iota about it all. She would never understand what it was about those computers that so captivated the males in her home. And the violence! Why not spend the time doing things as a family instead?

She hadn't mentioned that to Ethan yet. Nor had she told him that his affection for his computers was beginning to bother her. It was so much easier just to wait and hope that it would go away by itself. But sometimes it seemed as though Ethan would rather spend time with his machines than with his wife and children.

Come now, Kaye. Jealous of a machine?

She spotted Katie about to attempt the stairs. Kaye left her thoughts behind and hurried over to play lifeguard.

In the game room, Jordan watched his father peck at the keyboard. It seemed to him that his dad just pounced on the keys randomly, like Katie on the piano. But the parade of white letters that marched across the blue screen was always letter-perfect. Even if the words didn't make much sense to Jordan.

"Why'd you choose the ax-guy, Dad? He doesn't even have a long-range weapon. I could fry you all day long from across the world."

"True," Ethan said, half rising from his chair, turning to his son. "But don't let him get too close to you!" He grabbed his son and tickled. Jordan liquefied and collapsed on the floor in a pool of delirium. "Gotcha, now, thou black villain!" his father growled. "Gotcha, gotcha, gotcha!"

The door slid open again. Kaye clucked and rolled her eyes. "Boys."

< jefferson scott >

She held out a section of newspaper to her husband. "Here, it's another review of your book."

Ethan kept one knee on his son's ribs, giving a little dig now and then, and took the newspaper. "Did you read it?"

"Most of it. Don't you know the guy who wrote it — Ronald Dontwell? That sounds familiar."

"Ron wrote this?" Ethan stood up, all fun and games concluded. Jordan scrambled under the desk.

"Isn't he that man at Intech?" Kaye asked absently, checking behind her for Katie.

"*Im*Tech, honey. *Im*Tech. Yes, that's him." Ethan sat down and examined the article. "He's just the brain behind ImTech's new M7 Reality Engine, that's all. I wonder how he found time to read my book." He slapped his thigh with his palm. "I knew I should've cited his book in my introduction."

"Oh well, he liked it." Kaye leaned down and gave Ethan a kiss. "My famous author." Then she walked to the door. "I'm going to give Katie her pill and put her to bed."

When the door slid shut, Jordan crawled out from under the desk. "Dad, let's play again, okay? This time I'll be a UFD Marine and you can be a NarcoNinja."

"Not now, son. You go ahead."

"But Dad! It's no fun alone. The AI's stupid—you said so yourself." His father wasn't listening. "If you're not going to play, can I at least play on the Net? I'll see if Thomas wants to play."

"Hmm? Oh, all right, all right."

Jordan took his place in the padded chair and logged onto Venue Texas, a local VR network. He didn't bother to remind his dad that Mom had said no Nets after dark. It wasn't his job to remember that kind of thing—he was just a kid. He put on his HMD, slid his hand into the TacBack, and was at once engrossed.

"But only until nine," Ethan chided. "It's a school night."

Now it was his turn to be ignored.

< virtually eliminated >

Ethan poured himself some Sprite in the kitchen and peeled open a Payday bar. He took his snack carefully through the living room and into his study.

When they had built this house, Ethan's contribution had been to pay for it and Kaye's had been to decorate it. And decorate it she did. He wasn't joking when he told her it looked like a model home. She called his study her masterpiece.

A carved oak desk dominated the office. A leather executive chair stood behind the desk, brass studs up the edges. A green banker's lamp poured out a pool of warm light. Matching high-backed chairs faced the desk, angled just so, for those history-shaping negotiations he was supposed to be having. Broadleaf plants, a bookcase with brass curios, and a cherry wood bureau stood strategically around the room. It looked every inch the office of a powerful executive.

Unfortunately, the effect was lost on Ethan. As long as he had table space, light, a chair, two phone jacks, and lots of electrical outlets, he was happy.

He had brought four computers into the room and linked them all together in enigmatic and somewhat devious combinations. Two computers sat on the oak desk, one on the floor beside the desk, and the fourth on a filing cabinet. The other filing cabinet supported a combination laser printer, copier, fax machine, answering machine, and vidphone.

On top of the leftmost monitor was a little cross, whittled from two pieces of wood and held together by a leather thong. Jordan had made it at a church camp the previous summer. Ethan's leather Bible lay on the desk, ready for his daily quiet time.

Cables writhed around the room, only barely out from the middle of the floor. Programming magazines languished in lazy stacks, along with a few of Jordan's comic books.

It still looked like a powerful executive's office, but one in which a

< jefferson scott >

vagrant had taken up residence. That image was enhanced since Wysiwyg had taken a liking to the leather chair. She was careful to leave a few gray or white hairs behind every time to mark her place.

Ethan sat in the chair and flipped the computers on. There wasn't anything specific he wanted to work on; he just felt most comfortable with them on, awaiting his instructions. There was probably something a little strange about the behavior. It was almost as if he needed the computers on in order to feel complete. He chuckled, wondering if Oprah would ever do a show on computer codependents.

What was the big deal? Some people couldn't sit in their car without the radio on. He couldn't sit in a room without a computer on. That didn't mean he had a problem.

Ethan took out scissors and clipped the book review from the newspaper.

It was a strange thing, he realized, to have written a book. Suddenly people all over the country felt entitled to an opinion of him and his work. He believed in what he had written, even if it was a dry, technical manual on the nuances of virtual reality programming. He was gratified that at least one other reviewer, a man whose work Ethan respected, agreed.

He read the last line of the review one more time: "No matter what the public response will be, Hamilton's new book is already a *virtual* success." Ethan winced. "Oh, Ron, Ron, Ron. Don't quit your day job."

He went to the bureau and opened the left side door. There was a corkboard on the inside of the door, with several other newspaper and magazine reviews tacked up. Ethan moved these aside so he could make a place in the very center of the board. When he went to pin it up, though, the article was backwards.

On the reverse side of his review was part of a headline: "— ASKA STUDENT KILLED IN VR ACCIDENT." He scanned the part that wasn't cut off, then went back to his desk to put it with the rest of the article.

Kaye came in and sat in one of the high-backed chairs. "Whatcha doing, honey?" When Ethan didn't answer, she went over to the bureau and closed the cabinet door. Then she busied herself around the study, restacking magazines, dusting everything — including the plants — tucking cables out of sight. Ethan looked at her and made a helicopter noise with his lips.

"I am *not* hovering!" Kaye said. "I asked you what you were doing, and I'm still waiting for an answer."

"Okay, okay. I'm sorry." Ethan pulled her to him. "I was reading this article. This girl at the University of Nebraska got electrocuted while she was in a VR session. They all think it was some random power surge."

Kaye pulled away a little. "But you don't think it was a random power surge. You think it was," she paused melodramatically, "Mr. Computer Psycho!"

"It could be, Kaye. It's just the same as the others." He opened a desk drawer and pulled out a file of newspaper clippings. The articles dated back almost a year. He flipped through them.

"People all over the world are getting electrocuted on-line — all in virtual reality — and nobody puts anything together. They're just scattered enough to look random, I guess. Even the press people haven't caught on. You'd think the *Crusaders* show would do an episode on it, or something. But every time, the officials just say, 'It was some random power spike through the phone lines.'"

"All right," said Kaye. "You win. It *was* Mr. Computer Psycho. Can we go to bed now?"

Ethan pointed a finger. "You should be nice to me. I'm a famous author. Ron Dontwell said so."

"I know. I'd better watch it or you'll write a book about me and say nasty things, won't you?"

"That's right."

Kaye sat in his lap and looked into his eyes. "If you really think there's something to this, honey, maybe you should call someone."

Ethan kissed her cheek. "I've thought about it. But who do I call? The electric company? Psychos Anonymous?"

"Can't you just call the police?"

< jefferson scott >

"Oh, I can just hear myself." He spoke in a cartoon voice. "Uh, yes sir, you don't know me, but I think I've figured out a conspiracy of international proportions. Would you like to hear about it?"

Kaye giggled, then tried to sound unamused. "Very funny." She kissed him passionately.

"Wow," he said.

"There's more where that came from, too." She went to the doorway and looked at him seductively. "You know, I've always wanted to make love with a famous author."

"Now's your chance, sweetheart." Ethan leapt out of his chair.

Kaye shrieked and bolted for the stairs. "Shh!" she said between giggles. "Jordan will hear."

"No, my little radish, no one can save you now." Ethan chased his wife up the stairs to their bedroom.

Life was good.

< virtually eliminated >

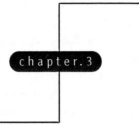

chapter.3

ETHAN CALLED HIS OFFICE THE PIT. It was only a slight exaggeration. If the office had been only two high-rise windows wide instead of three, the name would have been more than deserved. But with an office size reserved for a select few, there was enough room to just shove everything against the walls and still have plenty of clean floor in the middle to give the illusion of neatness.

Motion detectors turned on the lights while Ethan shut the door behind him. "Power up," he said. Those computers and monitors that didn't stay on at all times came on at his command. The hum of cooling fans made an effective ambient noise mask.

Ethan walked over to the eighth-story windows and looked out over the unending corporate suburb that glued Dallas and Fort Worth together. Directly below him, Highway 183 was clogged with people on their way to DFW Airport or late to work in Dallas. Fall was upon the Metroplex, but the land along this stretch of highway remained consistently brown. Ethan could see six hotels — all competing for the frequent flyers' business.

There were eight computers in The Pit, supported by two desks, a

< jefferson scott >

counter, and a once-beautiful conference table. Monitors ranged in sophistication from a 21-inch flatscreen 1.2 billion-color Sony to an ancient 10-inch amber monochrome beast that Ethan kept alive just for bragging rights. Cables snaked off everywhere.

Little plastic crabs hung from an air duct, leftovers from some forgotten software promotional.

But the real centerpiece of the room was over against a window, in the corner farthest from the door. It was a blue metal cube the size of a small refrigerator. The cube was a turbocharged Sun Microsystems ANDI 3112-F, until recently the most advanced Reality Engine available in a minisupercomputer.

Digital Environment Specialists wasn't the most prestigious virtual reality company in the world, but they were determined to become players, at least. They did not hesitate to buy the best equipment. Ethan foresaw the day, in the very near future, when DES would graduate up to supercomputers.

Virtual reality input devices of all kinds lay out on the conference table: flying mice, data gloves, wands, tactile- and force-feedback devices, and various other 6DOF tools. The name 6DOF stood for Six Degrees Of Freedom, the six elements of an object's position and orientation in an artificial world. The first three referred to the object's *position* on the x-, y-, and z-axes. The last three degrees referred to the object's *orientation* in relation to that world: pitch, yaw, and roll.

On the blue-gray carpet beneath the table was a collection of VR headgear — three helmets, two late-model HMDs, shutter glasses, and one pair of cardboard and cellophane 3-D glasses. On top of the Sun ANDI computer, a toy tarantula stood guard, a Bart Simpson action figure perpetually clamped in its mandibles.

Ethan selected an old Michael Card CD from his collection and put it in a disk drive. As the first notes of "I Will Bring You Home" poured from the speakers, Ethan sat in his chair and logged on to his primary terminal.

But instead of his usual no-nonsense text interface, Ethan saw a bright yellow smiley face.

< virtually eliminated >

"Uh-oh."

Michael Card's voice cut off in mid-lyric and was replaced by the sound of a lit fuse.

"Oh, great." Ethan typed into his keyboard but got no response. He turned to other keyboards, with the same result. The fuse started sputtering. Then the fire alarm went off, a clanking, shattering klaxon. Ethan remembered the fire extinguisher down the hall. He opened the door and — thirty people screamed, "Congratulations!" They all wore party hats and silly grins. A pudgy young man with untamed brown hair came forward and grabbed Ethan around the neck.

"Ha, ha, Curly," he yelled. "Gotcha!"

Ethan tried to sound unperturbed — he still had plenty of hair, after all. "Yes, Camillo. Yes, you pack of goons, you got me."

Camillo released Ethan's neck. "Somebody turn that alarm off! It's in the phone room." He shook Ethan's hand. "Congratulations on the book."

"Thanks."

The fire alarm went silent.

"Yes, congratulations." The DES employees made room for the speaker — a gray-haired man wearing a suit. The only one present with either peculiarity. The others, mostly males in their twenties, wore jeans, T-shirts, and sneakers.

Ethan accepted his employer's hand. "Thanks, Larry."

"Well, we all knew your book would do well," he turned to the crowd, "didn't we?"

The crowd cheered.

"Come on," Larry said. "There's cake and punch in the lounge. Denise has been setting up since seven."

The crowd herded down the hall. Ethan fell in on one side of his boss, Camillo on the other.

Larry Tarkenton had formed Digital Environment Specialists ten years prior, with only himself, his wife, and his brother as employees. Back then the enterprise was primitive, only one step above the garage

< jefferson scott >

workshop level. Things soon improved. Ethan was employee number four.

With the company's first major success, Mrs. Tarkenton left to become a full-time housewife. Over the years, employees were added as needed to handle the expanding client list. Larry's brother retired two years ago. Now, with Larry handling all the executive duties, Ethan was the senior programmer. Though hierarchies shifted from project to project, whenever anyone had a problem, they all knew whom to ask.

Larry was talking about Ethan's book. "I'd been wanting to do something for you ever since I read your last proof, but I didn't really know what. Then, when Dontwell went on and on about it like that in the *Star Telegram*, I figured I'd better get busy. So I called this character," he slapped Camillo on the back, "and asked him to plan something for you. Were you surprised?"

"Was he surprised?" Camillo said, "Did you see his face? For a minute there, I thought I was going to have to clean up a wet carpet."

Ethan laughed self-consciously. "I was surprised."

"Willy broke into your office and I did your computer — Mr. Tarkenton said it was okay. The fire alarm was Denise's idea."

"Well," Ethan said as they arrived at the lounge, "looks like I'm going to have to rethink the security on my system, doesn't it? I'm going to make durn sure nobody can ever hack my computer again."

It was probably no accident that the party didn't die out until lunchtime. Laborers the world over have always possessed the ability to dissipate large blocks of otherwise useful time. Mr. Tarkenton justified it by throwing in a state of the company address.

Ethan sat alone in The Pit, with only a cake plate and a plastic fork as evidence of the celebration. He had to smile at his co-workers; the goodwill was flattering — though he could have done without the "Congratulations, Dear Curly" dreadfully sung to the tune of "Happy Birthday to You." He wasn't hungry for lunch just yet, so he set about

< virtually eliminated >

making his computer as impenetrable as he knew how.

Camillo had simply sat down at Ethan's terminal and found a way to gain access. Ethan would have to think of some appropriate payback later. For now, he just changed his keyboard password. Then he devised a cunning security algorithm. To successfully navigate it, the user had to insert a certain CD into a certain recordable-CD drive. Ethan kept that disk on his person.

Then he addressed the threat of a break-in from an outside computer. There were seventeen possible ports of entry into Ethan's system. The phone lines, the network cables, the host computer, hardware circuit boards inside his computer, the software — even the memory inside the keyboard itself — all offered potential doors to an intruder. He used an array of firewalls, public/private key systems, and simple passwords to defend, not only his computer, but the entire DES network from attack.

Then he added something extra at his own machine, just to reward anyone for getting through all the rest. He knew some of the programmers at DES were very clever — too clever, perhaps, for their own good. If they were that determined, he reasoned, they ought at least to be heckled for their efforts. In addition to ridiculing potential hackers, the program would call his mobile phone if anyone got to this, his last layer of security.

It was 12:45 when he finished. He rocked back in his chair and stared at the plastic crabs hanging from the ceiling. In the background, Michael Card sang "The Death of a Son."

Ethan thought about his Theory of Mr. Computer Psycho, as Kaye called it. It was probably false, the product of an aging programmer's overactive imagination. But what if he was right? His eyes strayed to a phonebook CD.

Who would he call, anyway? Serial Killers R Us? He popped the CD in and accessed the Tarrant County Blue Pages. He scrolled past the city, county, and state sections and turned to the listings for United States government offices. He found the number he was looking for and

< jefferson scott >

opened a vidphone window on one of his monitors. He selected audio only — he didn't want to look like a fool as well as sound like one — and entered the number.

"Thank you for calling the Federal Bureau of Investigation," said a recording. "If you know your party's extension, you may enter that number now. Or if you would like to hear other options, please press '1' now."

Maybe I can just leave a message and hang up, he thought. He pressed '1.' The pleasant voice went on, listing more choices. Ethan heard none that said, "If you would like to report a suspected misuse of virtual reality technology and fiber optic cabling resulting in the electrocutions of innocent victims, please press 4." Finally, he just pressed zero to speak with an operator.

Liz Hinnock had been a receptionist for the Fort Worth FBI office for seven years. She saw herself as a kind of guardian, shielding the good men and women who served out on the streets. Often she was the first person to hear of some new criminal activity. At her word special agents sprang into action, sometimes risking their lives.

She also got her share of bizarre calls. Kids, crazies, and paranoiacs called almost daily. Living in the Dallas/Fort Worth area, she still got a disproportionate number of calls from people who claimed to have figured out the Kennedy assassination. In one week last year she got calls from three people who all claimed to have spotted Jackie Onassis at Hulen Mall. She had almost been ready to believe it herself.

The phone icon blinked on her monitor, and the display showed her it was audio-only. *Great, that usually means a maniac.* "Federal Bureau of Investigation, may I help you?"

She listened as a man on the other end of the line began to clumsily spell out what he thought was a connection between some widely separated accidents — which he, of course, claimed weren't accidents at all. He thought someone was intentionally sending electric charges through

< virtually eliminated >

the phones in order to kill people. It had something to do with that virtual reality thing, like in the malls.

Liz's first thought was just to disconnect. It was too weird. Next he was probably going to say that space aliens were behind the "accidents" and were preparing for an imminent invasion. But there was something in the man's voice that wouldn't let her hang up. An earnestness maybe. A self-consciousness that seemed to say he knew how ridiculous his idea sounded but believed in it anyway. *All right, just get his name and number — then hang up.*

After she switched the phone off, Liz looked at the information the man had given. Ethan Hamilton, chief systems analyst, Digital Environment Specialists, Riverwalk Office Tower, Irving. Didn't sound like the résumé of a psycho. But then, she'd been fooled before.

Liz typed up a summary of the call and walked over to the message board. She thought about pinning it under Agent Rickshaw's name, since Ann was into high-tech stuff. But she left it for Agent Gillette, since he was duty agent for the day. She wasn't allowed to admit it, but she thought Agent Gillette was kind of cute.

Special Agent Mike Gillette returned from lunch an hour later. He was in his mid-thirties, slightly taller and broader than average, though with a little extra ballast across the middle. He had short brown hair of a nondescript shade. He dressed plainly, with an affinity for cowboy boots and Wranglers. He was intelligent, patient, and observant. Those who met him thought him fairly good-looking, but altogether forgettable. He was the perfect undercover agent. Until he spoke.

"Afternoon, darlin'," he drawled to Liz. "Gonna get you some lunch?"

"I thought I would, now that all the agents are back."

"Angelo's has their brisket sandwiches, remember now," Gillette said, with a look of ecstasy. "All the sliced beef you can push past your teeth."

"Thanks, Mike." Maybe you could take me there tonight, she wanted to say. "I'll, uh, see you in an hour."

"Be good now."

Liz grabbed her purse and headed for the door to the reception room, trying to hide the flush on her face. "Oh." She stopped in the doorway. "I put a call under your name on the board. Some guy says he's onto another serial killer."

"I'll give her a look. Bye, now."

He watched through the glass window as Liz walked to the elevators. She looked back just as the elevator arrived, and Gillette thought she smiled. "Play your cards right, Mikey boy."

He took the message from the bulletin board and read it. Then he swaggered down the tile hallway. "Hey, Jerry," he said through an open door, "you're not going to believe this one!"

< virtually eliminated >

chapter.4

FEODOR IVANOVICH SLIPPED through cloud cover six thousand feet above the English Channel.

At least that's where he seemed to be. His body was in his flat in Odessa, on the Black Sea, hooked up to a Sony VR-Man portable VR deck. He was playing a multiplayer World War II game called *Battle of Britain IV*, a new VR flight simulator.

Ivanovich flew for the British, of course.

He dipped his Supermarine Spitfire out of the clouds for a moment to check for German aircraft. None. He thought he saw something at the edge of his vision, but when he looked, it was gone. Great, now his real-life paranoia was invading his VR games, his last refuge. He pulled back up into the clouds.

Ivanovich worked for the CIA. He'd been placed in the Ukraine twelve years ago, in the chaos following the collapse of the Soviet Union. His cover was to be an up-and-coming young bureaucrat from St. Petersburg, working his way to mid-range political office. Along the way, he was to keep an ear open for rumors of the movements of the

< jefferson scott >

powerful Black Sea fleet — and pass the information along through his contacts back to the U.S.

But Ivanovich hadn't really worked for America for ten years. Soon after he'd arrived, a stateside leak had exposed his true identity to Ukrainian intelligence. Rather than eliminate him, however, they made Ivanovich a deal. He could choose either to be executed or to live in opulence while providing the CIA with the most precious commodity in the world of counterespionage — believable misinformation.

Ivanovich, whose real name was Ken Jacobson, continued to collect his CIA commission. Part of it went to his mother in San Diego, and the rest went to help put two nephews through college. The money — not to mention the other luxuries — provided by the Ukrainians was pure profit.

The little Sony deck he was using now didn't provide total immersion into the artificial world. He needed a full setup for that. But to just relax a moment at his lunch break, the VR-Man was perfect. The visuals through his LCD goggles were passable, and the three-dimensional sound in the little plastic and foam headphones was actually quite good.

One of his wingmen broke radio silence. "Bandits at four o'clock, Cap."

Sure enough, Ivanovich spotted a flight of Messerschmitt Me-109s escorting three Heinkel He-111 bombers on their way to English targets. They hadn't seen the Spitfires yet.

Ivanovich pulled the microphone to his lips. He spoke in Russian. The host computer in Seoul would translate it into whatever languages his co-players had selected. "All right, *malchiki*, here's the plan. Planes three and four, maneuver around to the east. Plane two and I will draw the fighters off, and you two go in and splash those bombers. Got it?"

"Right, Cap."

Planes three and four had just faded out of sight in the cloud when Ivanovich felt himself being watched.

Of course it could have been his restless imagination. A few years ago, when he'd first agreed to the Ukrainians' deal, Ivanovich's mind

< virtually eliminated >

had been relentlessly haunted. But after the first few contacts with the CIA came and went without a hitch — and after a few months of ultra-privileged life — he'd started to relax.

Lately, however, he'd begun having the nightmares again. And, as always, troubled sleep left him jumpy. Which explained why he almost yanked the headset from the VR-Man when he heard the knocking.

He didn't identify it as knocking right away. It sounded like machine gun fire pelting his canopy. The game had a very limited vocabulary of sound effects, and gunfire was the closest thing it could come up with for the sound of someone knocking on the glass of his cockpit. Which was what someone was doing.

Ivanovich had a moment of vertigo when he saw the black-robed man.

Many people had problems interfacing with virtual reality. In the early days of VR, people got seasick because of the delay between a movement made in the physical world and the corresponding move in the artificial world. Expectant mothers and people with heart conditions were warned about the incredible strain brought on by VR's realism.

Some primitive VR goggles were shutter glasses, which gave the left eye one image for a microsecond, then blocked that eye while giving the right eye another — slightly different — image. The brain resolved the two pictures into a single three-dimensional image. But in some people, the flashing lights set off epileptic seizures. Others lacked the capacity to resolve the disparate images. For one reason or another, fully 10 percent of the world's population could not use virtual reality.

But none of these caused Ivanovich's disorientation. What affected him was the incongruity of what he saw. A huge dark form floated like black cumulus above his airplane. The rippling cloak stretched almost to the horizon.

But it was the massive face that disconcerted Ivanovich most. Cold eyes stared down at him, each pupil large enough to swallow ten Spitfires.

The black form tapped on Ivanovich's canopy with a golden pin.

[47]

< jefferson scott >

"Kenneth." The tapping was machine gun fire, the voice was thunder.

"Who — Who are you?"

The voice of Ivanovich's wingman crackled back. "Who is who, Cap?"

"You have been very naughty, Kenneth." The giant eyes blinked, too slowly.

"You've got the wrong man. My name is Feodor Ivanovich. Who are you, anyway? Get out of our game."

The wingman answered again. "I can't leave now, boss. Planes three and four are in position. Let's get those fighters."

"Right." Ivanovich forced his mind back on the game. He nosed his plane toward the enemy ME-109s, gaining immediate separation from the black-robed cumulus. He fixed his eyes on the German planes, fired his machine guns.

His concentration was blown, though. He missed everything. He flew through the enemy formation, then banked to make another pass. But there was no need; two of the fighters were on his tail. He hoped the other two had gone after his wingman. Planes three and four could now make their run at the unprotected bombers.

Then suddenly he was moving backward. He turned around to see what was going on. Black fingers grasped the tail section of his plane like the legs of a giant squid. The Messerschmitts passed Ivanovich abruptly, the pilots' digitized faces incapable of showing astonishment.

Then Ivanovich's Spitfire dangled upside-down before a huge mouth. He looked up — or was it down? — through his canopy into monstrous nostrils. "Let me go! What do you want?"

"Let me first admire your choice of zeitgeist. Ah, the Battle of Britain! It reminds me of my favorite Prime Minister. Have you read Churchill, Kenneth?"

"What do you intend to do to me?"

"Come, come, Kenneth. Play along. Churchill was a staunch advocate of democracy, as you no doubt will remember. 'No one pretends,' Churchill once said, 'that democracy is perfect or all-wise. Indeed, it has been said that democracy is the worst form of government except all

< virtually eliminated >

those other forms that have been tried from time to time.' You are an advocate of democracy, are you not, Kenneth?"

"I favor anything that will help my motherland. If my government believes democracy will —"

"Posh, man. You may dismiss with the subterfuge." Huge eyes rolled. "I can see conversation is out of the question." The eyes snapped back onto Ivanovich. "We are called by similar names, you and I."

It occurred to Ivanovich to jack out. Just take the headset off and put the deck away. This was only a game, after all. But first, get this hacker's name. He would make a few phone calls and teach this intruder a lesson. "Your name is Ken, too?"

"Perhaps. But I was referring to the name by which you will be remembered. You see," the cavernous mouth said, inching the plane closer, "I am called Patriot. A good name, don't you think?"

"Of course. And I'm a patriot too, is that it?" Ivanovich hardly stammered at all.

"Not precisely."

When Patriot spoke, Ivanovich could see what looked like a golden tooth deep inside the mouth. Strange, he thought, why deliberately portray a physical imperfection in a perfect, synthetic world?

Patriot went on. "Actually, I believe one of the names they call someone like you," he brought the plane to his lips, "is expatriate."

The game tried to pick an appropriate sound effect for what happened next. But it had no good alternate for the sound of chewing. It finally settled on the sound of a plane exploding. It sounded just right to Patriot.

Ethan pressed the snooze button on his alarm, but the chiming didn't stop. Kaye put her head under a pillow and rolled over. It was still dark outside. Ethan clobbered the clock again. "Stop it!"

Kaye lifted the pillow. "It's the phone, honey."

"Oh."

< jefferson scott >

The vidphone chimed again.

It was Ethan's opinion that mornings should be banned. He peeled the covers aside and staggered to the monitor in the corner of their bedroom, matting down what was left of his hair. It was one of the great injustices of life that a balding man should have terrible morning hair. He swiveled the monitor/camera away from their king-sized bed to shield Kaye from the light.

He was just about to pick up when the answering program kicked in. Animated caricatures of the Hamilton family cavorted around the screen, cheerfully instructing the caller to leave a message. Ethan pressed a button on the keyboard and said, "Override." The message screen vanished. "Answer," he ordered the phone.

Ethan didn't know the man facing him on his monitor. He was about Ethan's age, white, a day-old beard. He wore a suit coat and tie, with perhaps a southwestern flavor. Something about the man's expression reminded Ethan of what he himself looked like after an all-night programming session.

Ethan opened his mouth once, but nothing came out. He cleared his throat and tried again. "Hello?"

"Ethan Hamilton?" There was a twang in the man's voice.

"Who's this?"

"You Ethan Hamilton?"

"That's right. Who's this?"

"Mr. Hamilton, I'm Special Agent Mike Gillette, FBI."

Ethan felt suddenly more alert. "Yes, sir."

"Sorry about calling so early, Mr. Hamilton."

"It's all right."

"Got that message you left yesterday."

"Yes, sir."

"Like to talk at you about it, if I could."

"Okay. Shoot." He heard himself give in to the man's cowboy speech pattern.

"You know the Ol' South Pancake House on University?"

< virtually eliminated >

"I think so."

"Meet you there in half an hour?"

"You mean now? Today?" Ethan had never gone from-bed-to-presentable in thirty minutes in his life, never mind traveling across town. "What time is it, anyway?"

Gillette looked offscreen. "Ten till five. Okay, tell you what. Meet you at Ol' South at five-thirty. That'll give you about forty minutes. All right, Mr. Hamilton?"

Ethan rubbed his stubbled cheek. "I guess so. I don't have to be at work until eight."

"Taken care of. Talked with your boss, Mr. ah…" He checked a legal pad in front of him. "Mr. Tarkenton. Looked worse than you — no fooling. Anyhow, we explained everything to him. As of today, you're on an indefinite leave of absence from your job."

"I'm what?"

Kaye sat up. "What is it?"

"I, uh, called the FBI yesterday, Kaye."

"But don't worry," Gillette went on. "Mr. Tarkenton's agreed to keep your paycheck coming. Mr. Hamilton, the Department of Justice respectfully requests your presence at this meeting. We might ask for your help, too, if you're of a mind."

This was too much for five in the morning. Ethan just scratched the bald spot on top of his head.

"Ol' South Pancake House, Mr. Hamilton," Gillette said. "Five thirty."

"Five thirty. Right." Ethan sighed. "Well, I guess it's taken care of, right? Okay, I'll be there as quick as I can."

"Good. Oh, one more thing, Mr. Hamilton." Gillette reached for something outside the camera's field of view. He held up Ethan's book. "Did you really write this?"

"Yes, sir." Despite his drowsiness, Ethan felt a surge of pride. "I wrote it."

Gillette turned to a page and read. "'Adding the 7106 is relatively easy. Just apply the potentiometer value to gate D of the 86505.'" He put

< jefferson scott >

the book down and shook his head. "If all this means something and ain't just horseapples, then maybe you can help out, after all. Well, we'll see. Good-bye, Mr. Hamilton."

"I'm not really—" Ethan protested. But the screen was already blank.

Kaye was still sitting up in bed. "Was it the real FBI?"

"Yes." He walked to the bed. "Kaye, the federal government wants to buy me some pancakes."

"You're just saying that so I won't worry."

"Taxpayers' money at work, yes sir."

"Stop it. You always do that when you're nervous about something. It only makes me worry more."

Ethan affected seriousness. "You're right, Kaye. I didn't want to tell you. They want me to go to Nigeria and assassinate their president."

Kaye smiled despite her best efforts not to. "What do they really want you to do?"

"Don't know. I didn't think the girl I talked to yesterday even took my idea seriously. I guess somebody did."

"What did you call them about?"

"Mr. Computer Psycho." They said it together.

"Just tell them you made a mistake. Tell them you don't want to get involved."

Ethan stroked his wife's hair. She looked singularly beautiful to him this morning. "Kaye, I have to at least go and hear what they have to say. Besides, they're the FBI. I don't really have a choice, do I?"

"Okay," she allowed. "But just one thing." Her face softened. "Please be careful."

"Of course I'll be careful." He lowered her down to the bed. "I'm a professional. On special assignment with the Federal Bureau of Investigation."

"I suspected it all along."

< virtually eliminated >

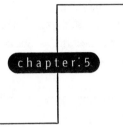

chapter: 5

ETHAN PARKED HIS MINIVAN next to one of three police cars in the lot. Ol' South was a favorite launching-off place for Fort Worth police, and dawn usually found at least one officer finishing up coffee and biscuits. Usually the police presence made Ethan feel safe. But today, since he still wasn't sure exactly why he'd been called here, the patrol cars gave him visions of being taken Downtown to the Stationhouse.

He grabbed his file of clipped articles from the passenger seat and got out of the van. He faced the minivan's door and activated the alarm system. The headlights flashed once. From a hidden speaker, an accented voice quoted an old Schwarzenegger film, "I swear I will not kill anyone." He pocketed the keys and headed for the restaurant.

He stood at the "Please Wait To Be Seated" sign, looking around blankly. Ol' South Pancake House was just what the name claimed — an old, southern restaurant, serving breakfast twenty-four hours a day.

The walls were paneled in the same brown wood that the tables and chairs were made of. The booth seat cushions were maroon with tan backs. An old glass case stood beside Ethan, noisily rotating a selection of salads and desserts. The whole place smelled of maple syrup. Ethan

< jefferson scott >

spotted the police officers — four of them at a table in the center of the room. There were, perhaps, fifteen other patrons.

A waitress approached Ethan, a pencil stuck through her bun of red hair. She picked up a menu and smiled wearily. "Just one, darlin'?"

"I'm supposed to be meeting —" Suddenly he saw Gillette, waving from a booth in the corner of the restaurant. "There he is," he said to the waitress. "Thanks."

Mike Gillette wasn't alone. A powerful-looking black man was sitting across from him.

Gillette extended his hand to Ethan. "Mike Gillette. This here's Special Agent Gerald Tubbs, my supervisor, over from Dallas."

Tubbs attempted a smile when he shook Ethan's hand, but the expression seemed closer to constipation. "Mr. Hamilton."

"Have a seat, Mr. Hamilton," Gillette said, indicating a spot beside Tubbs.

The Supervisor? Curly, baby, what have you gotten yourself into now?

The waitress approached their table. She peeled a sheet back on her pad and pulled the pencil from her hair. "Can I get you some hotcakes, sugar?"

"No thanks." Ethan saw that Gillette and Tubbs had coffee. "I could use something to get me going, though."

"I'll get you some coffee, then."

"Uh, actually, could I have a Coke?"

"Sure, hon." She left.

There was a moment of uncomfortable silence as they waited for the waitress to return. Ethan saw his book on the seat beside Gillette. He put his file folder on the table in front of him. Gillette had taken his coat off and loosened his tie. Tubbs sat still, mountain-like. His grey tweed coat hung on him awkwardly, as if someone had dressed a mannequin hurriedly. At last the waitress came with Ethan's Coke, refilled the agents' coffee mugs, and left.

Gillette took a sip of coffee, then leveled his eyes at Ethan. "Mr. Hamilton, I've got to admit I didn't think much of your message when

< virtually eliminated >

I read it. Sounded dumber than a five-legged mule, if you want to know. If I hadn't been duty agent, I don't suppose I would've given it a second thought. But it was my day, so I would've called you eventually. This is just speeding things up a bit, if you know what I mean. I mean, normally, the duty agent —"

"Mike," Tubbs interrupted. "Cut to the chase."

"Right. Sorry. Anyhow, Mr. Hamilton..." Gillette took another drink. "Something's come up to make us take your idea a little more serious-like. And the FBI's not the only ones interested." He shot a glance at Tubbs, who gave an almost imperceptible shake of his head. "Special Agent Tubbs and I were wondering if you could tell us how you came to this theory of yours."

"Well, that's all it is, really, a theory." He swallowed, trying to make himself say the next words. "You know, you guys don't really need me. Who you ought to talk to is Ron Dontwell, over at ImTech, in Dallas. He's the real local expert."

There. He'd said it. It was important, somehow. Dontwell was, after all, one of the country's top three or four VR entrepreneurs. But now that he'd gotten it out, Ethan suddenly wished he hadn't. Something inside him desperately wanted to be involved with this.

Tubbs nodded to Gillette, who produced a pen and wrote Dontwell's name on a napkin. The black man looked at Ethan. "Go on for now."

"All right." Ethan opened his folder. "As you know, I'm a computer programmer. I specialize in certain kinds of virtual reality applications. Can I assume you both know what virtual reality is?"

Tubbs didn't look too sure.

Gillette interlaced his fingers. "You know, boss, like at the Galleria, they've got that room set up with all those booths. It's a kick. They give you this helmet and gun, and you stand in this little ring about the size of a phone booth. There's twenty or so other folks in there, too. And you're all in this underground maze together, but in different spots. And you have to find the other fellas and blow them all away. And all the

< jefferson scott >

time there's these zombie things coming after you." Gillette's eyes gleamed. "Definitely a kick."

"But virtual reality's much more than games," Ethan said. He was touchy about that. "With virtual reality or telepresence or immersive remote control, things are possible that have never been possible before. Astronomers can explore a three-dimensional model of the universe without ever leaving the lab. We can operate robot vehicles in places humans can't enter — like inside a volcano, on the surface of the sun, or even inside a human body. We can project images of ourselves around the world or out into space."

Ethan looked at the FBI agents. Despite their apparent fatigue, they were tracking his words eagerly. "Most of the advanced stuff is done for the government or the military. I thought you guys would know all this."

Gillette snickered.

"The government is compartmentalized," Tubbs said. "Information is restricted. We can't tell other agencies what we know, except in special situations. They can't tell us."

"Yeah," said Gillette, "that's if they even know about any of this."

Ethan nodded sagely, as if he understood what they were talking about. "Anyway, since I program VR, I'm naturally interested in anything I hear about it." He pulled out a yellowed article from the bottom of his file. "About a year ago, I guess, I saw this article in the *Star Telegram*.

"It's just a little story about a guy in Euless whose computer got fried while he was in a VR session. He wasn't hurt, but his computer was destroyed. Nobody thought much about it. The story wouldn't even have made the paper if the guy hadn't been subcontracting for Bell Helicopter. All his work was lost.

"I thought it was strange, though. Virtual reality networks are no more dangerous than normal ones. The systems are designed to resist power spikes like that. The guy had a pretty good surge protector for his own system, too. Those are supposed to clamp down when they sense high-voltage surges."

< virtually eliminated >

Ethan took a sip of his Coke. "Ever since then, I kept an eye out for similar stories. It wasn't long before I saw this one." He pulled out another article. There was a photograph of a corpse, blackened at the temples.

"She was a nuclear chemist working in a NASA lab. She used VR to examine models of special electrons — I don't understand it all. It had something to do with nuclear fusion. The officials said a 'random power spike' overloaded her system and electrocuted her. They didn't understand why the normal protections didn't work.

"It didn't take too much imagination to link these two together — at least I didn't think it did. But no one else seemed to notice. Probably because they happened in different places."

As he explained his theory, Ethan gathered confidence. His far-fetched theory didn't sound so foolish, after all.

"Over this year, I've collected everything I could find that resembled these two." Ethan indicated the thick file. "Still nobody's caught on, as far as I know. It never happens in the same place twice. But they are happening, and they're happening all over the world. There are articles in there from France, Israel, Australia, Argentina… There's even one in space — if you recall that shuttle mission earlier this year."

Gillette sat forward. "I thought that was some glitch with the on-board computers."

"That's right. But if you read carefully, that Chinese astronaut who got electrocuted was in VR when it happened, piloting a drone."

"I remember," Tubbs said.

"But in each instance," Ethan went on, "even the one on the shuttle, the authorities always say it was just some 'random power spike.' But I don't think so. It's too much of a coincidence." He shut his folder. "That's why I called you."

Ethan wiped his sweaty palms on his jeans. He picked up his Coke and saw that his hand trembled. He took a drink and put the glass down quickly.

Gillette reached for the file folder. "Have a look?" He paged through

< jefferson scott >

the newspaper and magazine clippings.

Tubbs looked tired. He rubbed his forehead and the bridge of his nose. "So, Mr. Hamilton, you think there's one individual behind all these incidents?"

"Or a group." Ethan sat on his hands to try to steady them. "If there is someone behind it all, he's very good. To break into all these VR sessions, trigger some kind of electric shock, and get out without being noticed. I don't even know if I could get into some of these protected systems, much less do the rest." *Careful, Curly.*

Gillette shut the folder and sighed heavily. "What now, boss?"

Muscles rippled along Agent Tubbs's jawline, betraying clenched teeth. He pulled back a tweed cuff and looked at his watch. "In a couple of hours we can call the U.S. attorney's office, get us a prosecutor. Then we'll have to assign someone to the case." He looked at Gillette wryly. "Don't tell me, Mike — you want it?"

"Wouldn't be so bad." Gillette picked up Ethan's book. "Maybe I could get Einstein here to explain some of this nonsense to me along the way."

"Excuse my ignorance," Ethan said, "since most of what I think I know about the FBI comes from TV and movies. But don't you have people and equipment for this sort of thing? Supercomputers and such. I mean, who investigates computer crime like this for you guys?"

"Truth to tell," Gillette began quietly, "we're still trying to catch up in this area. In some high-tech areas, the FBI is on the cutting-edge. Our crime lab's the best in the world. But in other areas, like catching hackers or crackers or whatever you call them, we're still way behind.

"Now, we do have a squad of computer experts up at HQ. They do some of this kind of thing. Don't be surprised if we end up in D.C. before this is all over. Or they'll come down here, one. But I don't think they're set up for this vir-tu-al re-al-i-ty." He said the words like an octogenarian saying, *newfangled.* "Who knows, we might have to call us an expert consultant." Gillette looked at his supervisor, who gave a miniature nod.

< virtually eliminated >

Gillette leaned forward and smiled. "What do you say, Ethan Hamilton? Will you help us out?"

Ethan swallowed. "How?"

"Who can say?" Gillette said casually. "Give us advice. Help us poor old federal agents out. Poke around inside that World Net thing. Maybe do some undercover work. Who knows?"

"Are you serious? Undercover work?"

"No prostitution rings or drug cartels, Scout's honor."

Tubbs faced Ethan in the booth. "If you feel you or your family is in danger, you can quit. We'll protect your identity."

Ethan looked from Tubbs's black eyes to Gillette's easy smile. "What about Ron Dontwell at ImTech?"

Gillette opened his hands. "Why should we look for someone else when we've got you right here? Besides," he said, settling back in the booth, "you come highly recommended."

Recommended by whom? Larry, probably. "Can I have some time to pray about this? Ask my wife about it?"

Gillette's left eyebrow went up; he shot an inscrutable look at Tubbs.

"That's fine, Mr. Hamilton." Tubbs pulled his coat sleeves down. "We need a few hours to get things going on our end, anyway. Can we take your file?"

"Sure, fine."

"Do you know where the Fort Worth FBI office is, Mr. Hamilton?" Tubbs asked.

"No, sir."

"Special Agent Gillette will give you directions." Tubbs looked at his watch again. "Could you be there by nine with your answer? A prosecutor should be assigned by then, and you and Mike can get started with the investigation."

"I think so."

< jefferson scott >

chapter.6

"FATHER, THIS ALL SEEMS KIND OF UNREAL to us, like a movie. We don't know if I should work with the FBI or not. So, Lord Jesus, please guide our discussion. Lead us to Your answer. Amen."

Kaye looked up at her husband, her man of prayer. "Amen."

"Well," Ethan said, a gleam in his eye, "what do you think?"

She knew that gleam. It was a spark of childlike joy. One of the things, in fact, that first attracted her to him. But sometimes it scared her, too.

She remembered a moment in their courtship. They were walking through a parking lot on their way somewhere. He wanted to go faster, she wanted to slow down. So she hooked a finger through his belt loop. He went faster than she wanted, but not as fast as he would've liked. And she got him to slow down, but ended up being sped up a little herself. They balanced each other out.

"Well, what would this mean to your family?"

Ethan shrugged. "Don't know. My guess is I'll just go into their office and tell somebody else what I know, and they'll take it from there."

"That's not what you said when you got home. You said you would

< virtually eliminated >

be doing undercover work. I'm not sure —"

"I said I *might* be doing that."

"— how I feel about you doing undercover work for the FBI! I married a computer programmer, not James Bond."

Ethan nodded. "Maybe computer programming is all they'll want me to do. They said they weren't really up to speed on computer crime yet."

"I don't know, Ethan. You know how I feel about those people on the Internet and GlobeNet. Strangers coming right into our house, talking to you, talking to Jordan. I heard another story yesterday about a girl getting lured out to meet some 'friend' she'd made on GlobeNet — she ended up dead."

"How is it that you are afraid of all the crazies on GlobeNet but you don't believe in my Mr. Computer Psycho?"

Kaye didn't answer. It made perfect sense to her, but trying to explain it to him would probably be a waste of time. "Why can't we just be anonymous? Couldn't we just wrap ourselves in our little cocoon and live happily ever after?"

Ethan smiled and rubbed her neck.

"How long would you be doing this?" she asked.

"Don't know. Maybe just today, maybe longer. I guess it could work out to where I'd be working for them instead of DES."

"Can you be away from your job that long? Don't you only get two days for jury duty?"

"I don't know, Kaye. This is the government. They made the rules. I guess they can break them when they need to."

"Well, do you trust them?"

"The FBI? Sure, why shouldn't I?" Ethan sighed. "You don't want me to do this, do you?"

Silly question. If it were up to her, Kaye would ban computers altogether. They frightened her, threatened her. She saw her husband spending more and more time on machines she didn't understand, doing things she couldn't see a need for, for people who ought to be

< jefferson scott >

spending more time with their families. It wasn't any better when Ethan came home. He spent half his time in the study working on the computers there, and the other half on the computer in the game room with Jordan. The worst part was that Jordan was starting to act just like his daddy.

The other thing that scared Kaye about computers was GlobeNet. The weirdos on GlobeNet, to be more accurate. Not a week passed in which she didn't hear of some new crime or obscenity taking place online. GlobeNet was to Kaye the domain where all the rapists, child pornographers, and pimps of the world got together to compare notes. As far as she was concerned, they could have it. Now her husband wanted to go looking around on GlobeNet for a killer. She was sure he would find one — he probably spoke to them every day without knowing it. Of course she didn't want him to do this.

"Tell me what *you* want to do."

He smiled. "I want to do it. You know that without asking. If I said it didn't sound fun, you'd know I was lying, wouldn't you?"

"Mmm-hmm."

"It does sound fun: the FBI, undercover work, a big national — maybe international — crook on the loose."

Kaye fought the inclination to veto the whole affair simply because Ethan thought it sounded fun. It sounded more fun to Kaye to have Ethan home, away from all the computers and psychos of the world.

"Well," she said, "I guess what we really should be asking is what do you think God wants you to do?"

Ethan brought his thumbnail to his teeth and chewed. "I'm not sure. I guess I'd have to say that there's no way I could've noticed this pattern of accidents on my own. I'd like to think that it was God who revealed it to me in the first place. And if He really has — and the FBI wants to go with it — then, well..."

Kaye pushed down her fears and completed his sentence. "You have to see it through."

< virtually eliminated >

Ethan buzzed the button at the glass window, and an attractive woman in her mid-thirties came forward.

"May I help you?"

"I'm here to see Mike Gillette."

"All right," the receptionist said. "Let me check." She stepped away from the window.

Ethan peered through the glass into the office area. He tried not to look overeager, but he'd never been inside an FBI office before. He half-expected to see an armed Iraqi terrorist running down the hall, chased by federal agents.

But nine o'clock at the Fort Worth FBI office looked pretty much like nine o'clock at any other office. Professional-looking men and women milled around, drinking coffee, talking on the phone, reading faxes. Photocopy machines and the cooling fans of dozens of computers whined loudly enough to be heard through the glass. Tile hallways extended away to either side of the entrance. Ethan thought he smelled doughnuts.

On second glance, however, Ethan noticed one thing that separated this office from others. Most of the workers here wore automatic pistols beneath their suit coats.

The receptionist appeared at the window. "Mike's not in the office just now. You can have a seat there," she pointed behind him to a chair and sofa in the little waiting area. "I'm sure he'll be back soon."

"All right, thanks."

Ethan was glad to have a minute to collect himself. He didn't like going into situations where everyone else was comfortable and he was the only new person. When he was a kid, he used to make his mom get him to school half an hour before classes started. He felt it gave him a kind of squatter's rights.

He sat down in the high-backed chair to wait. The door out to the elevators was at his back. The wall in front had the glass window and

< jefferson scott >

the door to the offices beyond. Another door, designated "Interview Room," was on the wall to his left, along with an almost poster-sized photo of President Connor. The wall on Ethan's right was dominated by America's Ten Most Wanted. Murderers, bank robbers, and drug traffickers gazed on Ethan with frozen malevolence.

Ethan looked away. He took a recent copy of *The Law Enforcement Bulletin* off the glass coffee table and flipped through it. He was examining the insignia patches on the back cover when Gillette arrived.

"Sorry I'm late," he said. He was across the room and through the door to the offices before Ethan could even put the magazine down. Gillette held the door and turned around, a mischievous gleam in his eye. "Come on, *partner*."

Ethan hurried after him. Gillette tipped an imaginary Stetson at the receptionist. "Morning, Liz, darlin'."

He led Ethan past a wide room with tables lining the windows. The FBI office was on the sixth floor of a building just off downtown Fort Worth. The windows offered a magnificent view of the skyline. It was a beautiful September morning, but it was going to get hot.

"Sorry I'm late," Gillette repeated. "Had to make an arrest this morning in Dallas."

"No problem."

They reached a row of wooden doors. Gillette opened one, labeled "Conference Room," and motioned Ethan inside. "Get you some coffee?"

"No thanks."

"That's right — you like Coke in the morning. Well, pardon me while I get me some." He smiled disarmingly. "It's the only thing from Columbia us feds are allowed to enjoy."

The conference room was small — enough room for about six people, though ten chairs crowded around the table. Ethan sighed, and for the umpteenth time since he and Kaye had agreed he should do this, he prayed for inner peace.

Gillette returned a minute later, carrying a coffee mug, file folders,

< virtually eliminated >

and a doughnut. The latter was stuffed in his mouth. He placed a glazed pastry in front of Ethan, along with a cold can of Coke pulled from his jacket pocket.

"All right, let's get started."

At least that's what Ethan thought he said; the jelly-filled doughnut garbled the transmission. Ethan popped his Coke and took a drink.

Gillette swallowed the rest of the doughnut and wiped his mouth with the back of his hand. "We're in business. We've got us an assistant U.S. attorney on the job, and my super assigned me to the case."

Gillette started to open the top file folder, then closed it again quickly.

"What I'm about to show you is highly sensitive. This folder contains classified material. If asked, I will deny I showed it to you." Gillette pulled his coat back, revealing his holstered pistol. "If you ever share this information with anyone, Mr. Hamilton, I will be forced to shoot you on sight."

Ethan sat perfectly still.

Gillette burst into laughter. He reached across the table and slapped Ethan's shoulder. "Ease up, Hamilton." He covered the weapon, still snickering. "Just a little FBI humor."

Ethan tried to smile.

Gillette tried to stop laughing and failed. He raised his hands in a placating gesture. "It's all right, now, really. Quit looking at me like that, Hamilton. You look like you're backing away from a rattlesnake."

"Is this why you brought me here, Mr. Gillette?"

"No, no. I'm sorry." Gillette wiped tears from his eyes. The corners of his mouth quivered. The laughter escaped again.

Ethan smiled in spite of himself. "Are you sure you're really a federal agent and not some undercover comedian cop?"

Gillette affected a wound to the heart. "Fidelity, Bravery, and Integrity all the way."

"More like Funny Business Incorporated."

Gillette's eyes widened. "There you go, Hamilton. There's some fire.

< jefferson scott >

I knew you had it in there — just had to coax it out is all. You look so serious."

Gillette, his chuckles receding at last, opened the top file folder. There was a photograph of a dour-looking man along with several densely typed pages. "Like I said at Ol' South, I would've gotten in touch with you anyway about this theory of yours, sooner or later. But something's happened to make us speed things up." He slid the photo to Ethan.

To Ethan, the man in the picture looked Slavic — heavy forehead, dark eyebrows, black eyes, stocky. An older woman was in the photo with him. His mother?

"This man's a CIA operative," Gillette said. "Guess I should say *was* a CIA operative. Anyway. You don't get to know all the dirty details, but he was a spook for us in Russia."

When he didn't go on, Ethan prompted. "But now he's not?"

"Now he's not. Not a spook. Not in Russia. Not an operative." He paused dramatically. "He's dead, Jim."

Ethan nodded thoughtfully. But even with a photograph in front of him, the whole thing seemed a little unreal. A dead CIA agent — so what? He'd already seen it five or six times that week on TV. Ethan had to keep reminding himself that this was reality — not the artificial world he worked in all day long. Sometimes the line between real and unreal got a little blurry.

Gillette was going on. "We still don't know the whole scoop. But apparently this guy was playing a vir-tu-al re-al-i-ty" — *newfangled* — "game on his lunch break, when he was electrocuted."

Ethan's haze vanished.

Gillette read from one of the typed pages. "Emergency personnel on the scene reported that it appeared the victim had been struck by lightning. Officials at the local phone company are calling it 'an unfortunate accident' caused by 'faulty old Soviet wires.'" He looked at Ethan expectantly. "And you know what that means?"

"A random power spike?"

< virtually eliminated >

"Exactly. Sound like your guy?"

Maybe this was another trap — in the name of FBI humor. Ethan shrugged. "Could be."

"We thought so. My supervisor did, anyway. So we got busy on it right away, last night." Gillette blew a sigh through puffed cheeks. It made him look like a blowfish.

"You wouldn't believe how hard it is to get information from the CIA. Or the NSA, for that matter, or the Secret Service. You'd think the FBI would have access to their stuff. Sort of the same club, you know? But, no!" He shook his head. "Anyway, they didn't want to, but they finally faxed us a copy of that report you just read."

Gillette opened the other file folder. "Now, this other stuff is different."

Inside the thick folder Ethan saw copies of the articles he had clipped, along with many others he didn't recognize.

"I haven't looked at these," Gillette said. "Liz just handed this to me when I was getting your Coke. She's a pretty sharp cookie. Not a bad looker either, huh?" He pushed the file across the table to Ethan. "Why don't you take that home and read it."

Ethan didn't take the folder. "All this is assuming I've agreed to help you guys out."

Gillette's mug halted halfway to his lips, sloshing his coffee. "I just thought — I mean, since you're here, I thought —" He put the coffee mug down. "Well, Hamilton, are you going to help us, or what?"

Ethan savored his moment a little longer, then relented. "Relax, Gillette. Just a little civilian humor." He smiled innocently.

Gillette called him a name.

"Yes, I'm going to help you," Ethan said. He reached for the folder in front of him. "Did you get these from *ArticleCat* or something?"

"Something like that. I don't really know that computer stuff. I just asked Liz to find out everything she could on other cases that might be like the ones you found."

"You just want me to read it?" Ethan asked. "Then what?"

< jefferson scott >

"See if you can find something that makes them all stick together. A pattern, something that happens every time. You know."

Ethan looked at the file. As long as he was on extended leave from DES, he might as well just plunge into this new role. "All right. I'll look at it."

"Then maybe you could, I don't know, poke around a little on that Global Network."

"Poke around?"

"Yeah, you know. Can't you do that? Talk to people, leave messages, ask questions? Some of that computer nonsense. See if anybody knows anything. Detective School 101, Ethan."

Ethan hadn't remembered giving Gillette permission to call him by his first name. "I'll see what I can do, *Micky*."

Gillette laughed. "There's that fire."

< virtually eliminated >

chapter.7

ETHAN SAT IN THE GAME ROOM, staring at his VR helmet.

His own words echoed in his head. *Sometimes the line between real and unreal got a little blurry*. He could affirm that from experience.

His headset of choice was a NASA Ames helmet, only a year old. It combined stereoscopic video, spatiated 3D sound, and a comprehensive voice input system. LCD monitors in the helmet gave each eye its own offset image. With a 120° horizontal and 100° vertical field of view and 1280x1024 resolution, it was still state-of-the-art.

Not quite the same as being there yourself. Not quite real. But close. Virtually real.

The helmet's 3D sound came from a Crystal River sound card, based on NASA Ames Convolvotron technology. Like the eyes, the ears receive slightly different information from one another, at slightly different times. The brain uses these discrepancies to localize a sound source.

Using this knowledge, VR researchers discovered how to synthesize sounds which could be "placed" in different spots above, below, in front, behind, or to the left or right of the listener. The speakers in Ethan's helmet told him where a sound was, in which direction it was moving, and

< jefferson scott >

how close or far away it was.

Add voice input, a PowerGlove, force/tactile feedback, and a virtual body provided by the software, and the result was complete immersion. Electronic escape into a convincing virtual realm. For some, it was better than the real world.

Much better.

Ethan studied the little plastic clock on the table. The clock was real. The table was real. He was real.

He had to keep reminding himself, had to get a firm lock on the distinction, because every time he entered cyberspace he felt more and more at home. The real world seemed less real — less vital, somehow. As if all its blood was seeping out, transfusing, perhaps, to the synthetic world inside the computers.

The thought crossed his mind that maybe Kaye was right about him spending too much time on the computers. It was conceivable that somewhere Ethan had crossed that blurry line, that he was attempting to live in two worlds at once. If so, both worlds had a strong claim on him.

It's not true. I can quit any time I want. I just don't want to, that's all.

Ethan forced himself to focus on the clock — 2:45. Kaye and Katie were due back from the pediatric urologist around four. If he was going to do this thing, he'd better get started.

He decided to stall a moment longer, just to prove to himself that he liked the real world, that he enjoyed spending time there.

Wysiwyg was sleeping on the other chair. Ethan picked her up and held her in his lap while he flipped the FBI's file folder open again and leafed through the clippings. Out of the fifty-odd articles in the file, most seemed different from whatever pattern Ethan had unconsciously begun to sense. But there were probably fifteen that felt right.

One article, cut from the in-house newsletter of a defense contractor, was an expanded version of a short article Ethan had clipped almost a year ago. Four project managers and one vice president of this corporation had been electrocuted at once. No survivors.

< virtually eliminated >

Ethan shook his head. What could he do to stop this pillager, if there really was some central personality behind these incidents? There were no living witnesses to these crimes, if they were crimes at all. No evidence. No fingerprints. No bullets to send to the famous FBI lab. No murder weapon found at the scene of the crime. How could Ethan solve anything when even the scene of the crime didn't exist?

Or did it?

He reached for his PowerGlove and pulled it on his right hand. He dumped the cat to the floor and pulled Jordan's TacBack toward him with his left hand. The TacBack was a box, roughly the size and shape of a shoebox. Ethan inserted his hand deep into the molded foam. With his right hand, he pressed a button on the side of the box, and the foam inflated around his left hand. It always reminded him of having his blood pressure taken.

By pressing his hand toward the back of the box, he could move himself forward in a virtual world. By rotating his hand clockwise or counterclockwise, he could roll. Other hand motions caused his virtual presence to pan, tilt, elevate, sink, and move backwards or sideways.

These were standard 6DOF features. But where the TacBack came into its own was in tactile and force feedback. When the user's presence came up against a wall in the virtual world, the TacBack presented resistance in that direction. When the user jumped off an artificial cliff, the pressure to the bottom of the hand fell away. In this way a third sense, touch, was added to the virtual reality user.

And the line got a little more blurry still.

The current state of tactile feedback technology, though quickly improving, was rudimentary. The TacBack user could feel only certain things, such as the difference between a flat or uneven surface. Developers promised refinements in the near future. One company in Canada claimed to be perfecting a glove that could simulate the feel of such textures as silk and burlap.

Canada's real, he thought.

He pulled his helmet on.

< jefferson scott >

A beautiful live oak tree towered over him, rotating slowly in a simulated clearing. Ethan had downloaded the 3D photo from an artist on
GlobeNet. It was a computer image of an actual tree somewhere in
Louisiana. Ethan thought it was a good symbol for him, somehow, having existence in both the real and virtual worlds.

This was Ethan's home page.

He lowered the microphone arm to his mouth. "Comm." The
image of the tree dimmed but kept spinning. In the air in front of it
appeared an array of three-dimensional tools. There was a fax machine
icon. It repeated a little animation of a piece of paper going into the
machine and a flash of pixels flying out. There were similar icons for
vidphone calls, modem transfers, telepresence, audio messaging, telnet,
ftp, and web-browsing.

Ethan didn't want this session interrupted. He thumped on the vidphone icon with a computer-rendered hand. This temporarily disabled
call waiting, relaying all incoming calls directly to the messaging software.

The ninth icon floating before him resembled a nerve cell or perhaps a tumbleweed. An intricate mesh with hundreds of major arteries
and thousands of branching capillaries. This was the symbol for the networks.

"Nets."

The icons from the communications menu were replaced by those
from the network menu. Three icons hovered in Ethan's vision, one for
each network to which he had purchased access. There was GlobeNet,
Venue Texas, and DESquirk (his company's network). Of course, all
these networks were part of GlobeNet, but the icons represented direct
access to the particular subnetworks.

"GlobeNet."

The network icons disappeared. The image of the live oak brightened again and gracefully spun to a halt. A hole opened up at the base

of the tree. Ethan moved toward it.

Ethan had written this tree-and-portal routine to make his daily drudgery a little more like fun. Once he stepped into the hole, though, he passed out of the world of his own making.

Just inside the hole a skeleton appeared, blocking the way. Bones creaked hollowly. "Identify yourself," it moaned, "or join the ranks of the undead."

Ethan smiled. This was a new one. The security people on GlobeNet designed what little protections there were for the net. They were notorious for their clever user-identification schemes. Last week it had been the genie from an old Disney movie.

Ethan gave his username and password. After a transient pause, the skeleton seemed to smile. "At last, at last!" Then it came apart at the joints, collapsing to the ground with a groan. Ethan stepped over the pile of bones and plunged into the black orifice.

GlobeNet. The world's only unified network, connecting literally billions of computers from all over the planet, in earth-orbit, and on the moon, Mars, and Venus.

The graphical interface was deceptively simple. He seemed to be standing on a raised platform, overlooking a digital cityscape. The city was laid out in a flat square, ringed by snowcapped mountains. Tunnels plunged into the rock on every side, indicating passages to other areas. The sky was orange, representing either dusk or dawn. The city seemed to live eternally poised at the moment between one thing and another.

This was the GlobeNet home site, the launching pad for points known and unknown.

At the center of the square were icons for the general functions of the network. There was a simulated bank; a post office with a satellite dish on the roof; a convention center; a university; a library; and a low, plain building universally recognizable as a government office. Each icon represented a subnetwork — or network of subnetworks — employing anywhere from one to one thousand host computers.

The city seemed deserted. There was no traffic — no pedestrians,

< jefferson scott >

no airplanes, no trains. But this was misleading.

Normal users saw the Net personas of the thousands of other users going about their business in the hub. A popular feature of some GlobeNet software was the option for each user to customize his or her appearance in the Net. When Ethan was first exploring the nets, he had given himself the appearance of an old Oriental wise man. Named Bubba.

But that was a long time ago. And Ethan was not a normal user.

He soon learned to program his software to toggle the images of the other GlobeNet users on and off. He called it a Bozo Filter. It wasn't exactly the correct usage of the term, but he liked the idea. He always left the filter on.

Ethan looked down on the city from his platform. "'Poke around.' Humph." He moved to the center of the platform. "I need my helpers."

Instantly, a pack of colorful creatures floated around him, watching expectantly. They were all smaller than Ethan, roughly pet-sized, with the beautiful too-clean appearance of computer-generated objects. One — resembling a chrome ball — reflected all the other helpers on its surface. A second helper was a purple rabbit-thing with massive rear legs and an exaggerated nose. A third looked like a chameleon. Even as Ethan watched, it faded into the color of the background and became almost invisible.

Others were like fluid or cloud, or were only two-dimensional, or shaped like a fireplug. They had giant ears or ten arms or fur. Some made noise — one sounded like a cricket with the hiccups. Others were silent. But they all looked to Ethan with the same doglike loyalty.

These were Ethan's artificial children. In the GlobeNet vernacular, they were infobots, spiders, wanderers, and gopherbots. As of yet, he lacked the wherewithal to bestow sentience upon them. They were essentially tools, each designed to fulfill a specific purpose or set of purposes. The chameleon, for example, was designed to wait, undetected, until a given set of conditions was met, then proceed to its next instruction.

He reached out a digital hand to the purple rabbit-thing. Its nose

< virtually eliminated >

twitched with simulated excitement. He commanded the rest of the creatures to disappear, then leaned into the rabbit's purple ear.

"All right, Thumper, listen up. Search all Veronica servers."

Veronica was the name for a database, or catalogue, of gophers. Gophers were databases, or catalogues, of information on GlobeNet. Thus Veronica was a database of databases. An effective place to begin a search.

At this point, Ethan was having trouble seeing this search as any different from the hundreds of others he had done in the past. Merely an academic exercise. A research project. Funded by the FBI, though.

Ethan held his helper at arm's length. "Find: virtual reality *and either* death *or* electrocution *or* assassination *or* execution *or* shock *or* CIA." Purple legs pumped the air. "Thumper, go!"

The rabbit sped away from him across cyberspace. It bounded over the post office in a purple flash and vanished into a mountain tunnel on the far side of the city.

"Well, that'll probably get us a big ol' pack of nothing."

Most GlobeNet searches produced massive amounts of off-target results. He predicted he'd get several findings accidentally, simply because they used some of his keywords. He remembered a search he'd recently done on artificial intelligence that had turned up a whole genre of e-books about the dating habits of single adults in California. It seemed everybody wanted to hook up with someone of *intelligence*; someone who was genuine, not *artificial*.

Ethan smiled at the memory. "Oh, well," he said aloud. "Let's see what we can find until he gets back." He launched himself off the elevated platform and plummeted toward the post office.

Of course there was no gravity in cyberspace. Nor did the ground exist, nor the buildings around him, nor the mountains. These were all conventions designed to ease the transition between the real world and the virtual one. Ethan had read somewhere that it was possible to turn off the simulated physics in the system. One day he'd have to look into that.

< jefferson scott >

The post office doors swung open as Ethan approached, and he went inside. The first thing he saw was a digitized bulletin board on the wall, America's Ten Most Wanted Fugitives. It made him smile. The criminals looked slightly less frightening on a simulated wall than they did in the Fort Worth FBI office.

The post office looked like one he might find in a small town in rural America. There were copy machines, stamp collector kits, rows of PO boxes — even an overfilled trash can. Absurdly tranquil music permeated the place.

But this colloquial image was deceptive. The electronic mail system on GlobeNet processed messages for close to two billion customers — approximately twenty-five billion e-mail messages every day.

A clerk sat behind the counter, smiling blandly, his eyes tracking Ethan's movements. Ethan smiled. He always liked coming here.

"Why, hello there, Ethan Hamilton," the clerk said. "Hot enough for you out there in Texas?"

Though 3D animation had come a long way since the twentieth century, some of it was still based on polygons. Every now and again the clerk's face went oddly angular. But for the most part it was a convincing representation.

"Too hot, Harry."

Harry nodded knowingly, geometric planes in his face glinting momentarily. "Guess what, Ethan Hamilton? You have mail!" He seemed very excited, as if Ethan had just won a sweepstakes. "I'll get it."

"Thanks, Harry."

The mail clerk made an about-face and walked away in a straight line. When he got to the wall he made a sharp right-angle turn and disappeared into the back offices.

It didn't bother Ethan that Harry wasn't real. Some of Ethan's best friends were synthetic.

Ethan felt that probably 40 percent of real-world jobs could be better handled by computer-controlled pseudoanthropoids. He had only scarcely managed to restrain himself from mentioning that thought to

< virtually eliminated >

the cashier the last time he had driven through at McDonald's.

Harry reappeared, did a crisp left-face, and approached the counter. He placed Ethan's "letters" on the countertop, smiling the same bland smile.

"Hope it's good news," Harry said, indicating the letters.

Ethan picked up his envelopes. "Listen, Harry. Can I ask you a question?"

"Of course, Ethan Hamilton."

"I've been wondering about something." Ethan debated how to proceed. "Does the post office ever find, you know, strange mail passing through? Threats, maybe?"

"You mean flames? Every day, Ethan Hamilton."

"No, not flames. More like people saying they're going to kill somebody else, or bragging that they already did. You ever catch things like that?"

Harry froze. Ethan knew his question was outside Harry's purview. Somewhere a mailhost computer was searching its files for an appropriate answer. Until something happened, Harry's animations were disabled.

Ethan examined the inert postal clerk. Who was to say Harry wasn't real, in the philisophical sense? What were the qualifications for reality, anyway? Permanence? Displacement? The ability to be sensed or perceived? Height, width, depth? Or was it something else entirely? Something eminently more subjective. Must someone believe in you for you to be real? If so, for Ethan at least, Harry was thoroughly real.

A woman's voice came through Ethan's helmet speakers. "Hang on. I'm coming in."

The image of a tanned woman in her twenties flickered into existence behind the counter. But only in two dimensions. Ethan recognized the flat image as telepresence. This was a picture of a real person projected into the artificial post office.

Was this woman real? He tried disbelieving her existence, but when he opened his eyes, she was still there.

< jefferson scott >

"Can I help you, sir?" she asked.

"Did you get my question?"

"Yes, sir. Something about threats of violence?"

"That's right. Do you ever get things like that?"

"May I ask why you want to know?"

"I'm, uh, doing some research."

"May I ask the purpose of your research?"

Ethan thought about saying he was working for the FBI, but thought she'd probably want some kind of proof. He could give her Gillette's name and number, but he knew how vulnerable certain computers could be to prying eyes and ears. It might get Gillette into trouble, maybe even danger.

It suddenly struck Ethan that he hadn't been too bright about his whole investigation so far. If there really was a killer out there, he or she might prove a bit sensitive to the kinds of things Ethan was doing. The nature of his Veronica search, the questions he was asking in the post office. The GlobeNet host computers would record his path. Anyone with an ounce of programming savvy could retrace his every move.

Oh well. Too many fingerprints on too many doorknobs to worry about it now.

"Mr. Hamilton?"

Ethan jumped. "What?"

"Mr. Hamilton," the woman repeated. "The purpose of your research, please."

He headed for the door. "Never mind."

< virtually eliminated >

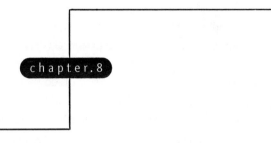

chapter.8

THERE WERE MORE PLACES in GlobeNet than any one person could ever know. Directories were available for the major sites and networks, but not even the most comprehensive listed all the minor nets, much less every interest group, home page, and server. Scores of new sites opened every day, and just as many closed.

It was as if GlobeNet was an uncharted world. Certain major land masses had been mapped, but the rest was *terra incognito*. And like a black void on an ancient map, cyberspace appealed to certain kinds of people. There were those like Magellan, Columbus, and Amerigo Vespucci, explorers questing for discovery. Then there were the plunderers — the progeny of Leif Erikson, Cortez, Ponce de León. Those whose deeds required a certain degree of anonymity.

Patriot aligned himself with neither pioneer nor conquistador. He preferred another paradigm. Years earlier, when he went by another name, Patriot had fancied himself a dark superhero: The Shadow, Batman, The Shroud. Predators with a touch of the supernatural — putting fear back into the criminal element, where it belonged.

< jefferson scott >

It was astounding, really, what possibilities fell within reach with only a change of metaphors.

Patriot emerged from an uncharted pathway and looked around. He appeared to be in some kind of store. Artificial walls displayed various products related to health care. He dissolved up through the ceiling.

By now the CIA would know of their operative's death. Ivanovich's betrayal clung like cheap candy inside Patriot's mouth. Why, if he was cleansing America of her enemies, did he feel so contaminated? He consoled himself with the knowledge that he had singlehandedly eradicated twenty-two traitors, infiltrators, and sympathizers — insidious enemies of his beloved nation. Not a bad year's work. He decided to take his nausea over Ivanovich as a favorable omen — at least such acts of treason still made him ill.

He headed home.

Ethan raced for his entry/exit platform, imagining cybernetic wolves on his heels. He reached the landing and looked back down at the city.

What had appeared open and friendly when he first arrived now felt dark and sinister. It wasn't a lovely alpine village anymore, but an evil outpost cowering in the mouth of a questionably dormant volcano. Shadows he hadn't noticed before now seemed to consume half the net. The tunnels piercing the mountains were no longer portals to adventure, but black netherworlds where hordes of murderous demons lurked, thirsting for human blood.

He decided the orange sky portended coming night, after all, not coming day.

"Come on, Thumper, come on." He took a step back from the ledge. "I need my helpers." He felt a little better then, encircled by his colorful friends. They gave him a sense of fixity. He did mute the hiccuping cricket, however.

The seconds passed without incident. Some of Ethan's bravado began to come back. And with it, his reason.

< virtually eliminated >

"If there really is a VR killer," he lectured his familiars, "he must be very good. An expert — no, a *master* — in virtual reality. And an expert in GlobeNet. It's probably a hacker, which usually means male and young. A programmer, an innovator, a genius. To pull off that many murders and still have no one suspect anything." Ethan whistled in admiration.

His synthetic progeny watched him closely, waiting for an instruction they could act on. They formed a bizarre tableau, if anyone had cared to notice. One man, talking aloud, standing on a platform, surrounded like Saturn by a ring of floating oddballs.

"If I were this guy — or this group — how would I work? What would I be interested in?" He chewed a simulated thumbnail.

Ethan's eye caught a flash of purple on the other side of the dark metropolis. "There he is. Come on, Thumper!"

But something was wrong. Thumper was moving slowly, erratically. Ethan dove from the platform, his manufactured friends right behind. He bounded over the municipal buildings and down toward his purple helper.

Out of the corner of his eye, high above the synthetic floor, he thought he saw movement — a flash of black. Impossible, of course. He'd toggled everyone else off.

He fell to his knees and caught Thumper up in his arms. "What happened to you, little friend?"

Thumper looked at him helplessly. His ear was torn and one of his front legs was missing. The purple rabbit opened its mouth and a little pouch fell out — the results of his search.

"Was it a trap, Thumper? Did you trigger a trap? An alarm? Who did this to you?"

Ethan knew very well that Thumper couldn't answer him, that he wasn't a real animal, and that he wasn't in any pain. But it hurt Ethan just the same.

"All right, little fella." He stroked his purple companion's back. "Let's get you home."

< j e f f e r s o n   s c o t t >

Ethan led his entourage back up to the platform and called up the exit portal. But there he paused. "Wait a minute!"

He opened the pouch Thumper had brought back. It contained the names and electronic addresses from the search. Ethan would have to read through these later. But what he was looking for now was in the fabric of the pouch itself.

He had designed his infobots with an automapping feature. The record of Thumper's search was encoded into the pouch. Ethan could retrace Thumper's every step. After a moment's examination, he found the GlobeNet address where Thumper had been injured.

He called his chameleon forward. It floated in front of the green fireplug helper and immediately began to turn green.

"Listen up, Meely. I want you to go to these coordinates" — he fed in the address — "and wait for someone to check on his traps. When they do, I want you to use this."

He called up an inventory subwindow and pulled out what looked suspiciously like a dynamite plunger taken straight from the arsenal of Wyle E. Coyote. Ethan put the plunger into the chameleon's mouth, then put his helper down.

"All right, Meely. Go! Do your worst," he said, watching the chameleon scamper away. "For Thumper."

On the way to his home page, Patriot paused for a moment over GlobeNet's main hub. There was the usual mob. He could never understand, with all the possibilities offered on the nets, why people still flocked to the post office icon. As if e-mail was the only thing GlobeNet was good for.

He was just about to leave the cityscape behind when a blur of motion caught his eye. Someone jumped down from one of the entry platforms, followed by what looked like a pack of brightly colored dogs.

Patriot paused in mid-flight, momentarily engaged. Whoever this was, he was certainly in a hurry. Patriot watched the user cross the

< virtually eliminated >

entire city. He saw something else coming the other direction. It was purple, whatever it was. It looked like another one of his dogs. Maybe a rat.

Patriot watched the happy reunion. "I think I could turn and live with animals," he quoted, "they are so placid and self-contained.... They do not lie awake in the dark and weep for their sins; they do not make me sick discussing their duty to God; not one is dissatisfied, not one is demented with the mania of owning things."

Five seconds later, Patriot was at his outer perimeter, represented by a white picket fence in front of a house right out of the American Dream. This was his home page. He stepped through the swinging gate and called up his defensive menu.

The display that appeared in the air before him was a simple two-dimensional square. Since his rebirth, Patriot no longer felt the need to make everything flashy. To whom could he show it off?

The display used a simple bank of green lights to communicate all its information at a glance. Each light represented a point of vulnerability in Patriot's information fortress. There were traps or sentries at every point, should anyone get a little too curious. To date, no one ever had. These days he checked his menu only by force of habit.

He was so confident no one was onto him that he almost failed to see the red light at the bottom of the display. He punched the zoom button to get a closer view.

That's when Meely struck.

~

"What was that?"

Willy Stanton put down his paperback thriller. He checked all the meters and dials, but they looked normal again. Surely it wasn't his imagination. True, he was only a rookie med-tech, and yes, this job was just to pay for school so it wasn't permanent or anything. But he still thought he knew what he was doing. At least he knew all the dials in his panel shouldn't just max out suddenly, then go right back to normal.

< jefferson scott >

He punched a button on the wall and spoke into the intercom. "It's Willy. My panels are freaking out. Could you come take a look?"

Moments later a white woman with cropped salt-and-pepper hair came down the hall from the living room. She entered the patient's room and passed Willy without even a glance at him or his instruments. She never looked at Willy if she didn't have to.

Willy chose to interpret it as yet another persecution of the black man. But neither was he without humor about such things. He had fantasized once about dying his hair orange just to see how long it would take her to notice.

Willy leaned forward in his chair furtively, straining to hear a snatch of their conversation. The woman was leaning down over the bed, listening to the patient. Wispy brown hair flowed over the pillow and onto the sheet. Why didn't they get somebody in to cut the dude's hair once in awhile?

Willy wanted something juicy to tell his homeys in class — and Tuleesha Middleton, of course. He loved the attention, the power, he commanded when he told them a good one. But with home care jobs there were rarely good ones.

He was disappointed again. After another moment, the woman straightened up and headed for the bedroom door. Willy sat back guiltily.

"It's all right, William." She refused to call him Willy. "Just a bad dream. Everything's all right now."

"But my instruments." Willy tugged at his ear. "They ought to be checked or something. They shouldn't do that. What if something really did go wrong, how would I know the difference?"

"Then get them checked," she snapped and marched back down the hall.

Willy sat back down and picked up his book. "Witch."

Kaye jabbed the "off" button, folded up her phone, and dropped it back into her purse. That was the third time she'd tried to call home, and the

< virtually eliminated >

third time she'd been sent straight to the answering program without so much as a ring. Ethan was on-line, she knew, probably working on the FBI thing. *And so it begins.*

"Not home?"

Kaye looked up at the nurse. "No, Janie, he's home all right. He's just on the computer, and he's got the phone switched off." She probably should have tried a little harder to conceal her frustration. She adjusted Katie in her arms.

Janie guided Kaye to a padded bench beside the scales. They were in the little hallway outside the examination rooms, waiting for results of a urine culture. There was only the minutest trace of rubbing alcohol in the air. Kaye laid Katie down on the bench, and the little girl went promptly to sleep. Janie sat down beside Kaye.

"Is there something the matter, honey?"

Despite her best efforts, Kaye felt her eyes begin to water. Janie had seen Kaye cry many times in the past year, sometimes from fear or despair, sometimes from joy. Now she was seeing it from something else. And always Janie was there, like a mother, offering compassion.

"Do you know much about computers?"

Janie smiled and tossed her head back. "Honey, I couldn't program a computer if my life depended on it. I'd be lucky to even figure out how to turn the thing on."

"I just thought," Kaye surveyed the hallway, cluttered with medical gadgets, "that with all this stuff you'd have to know something."

"Oh, I know how to use it all, but don't ask me how it works. And heaven help us if anything breaks. Yesterday I thought the blood analyzer was broken, but it turned out I just didn't have the little screen turned on."

Kaye laughed. It always felt good to talk to Janie. "That's the way I am, too. Ethan's got me set up on one of the computers at home so I can print out my shopping lists. All I do is turn it on and choose the thing on the screen that says, 'Use me, Kaye!'"

"That's what I need." Janie leaned into Kaye's ear conspiratorially.

< jefferson scott >

"I'm surrounded by computer experts here. But I'm too stubborn to ask one of them to teach me. People have lived on this planet for thousands of years without computers and done just fine. I can last a few more without them, too."

"Well, at least you can leave your computer experts behind when you go home," Kaye retorted. "I'm married to one!"

Janie laughed. "Poor thing. Say, how's that book of his doing?"

"It's doing fine, Janie." Kaye hesitated. "Janie, you know something about addictions, don't you?"

"Some, dear. Do you think you may be addicted to something?"

"No, not me. It's Ethan."

They paused as another nurse led a mother and baby past them into an examination room.

"Janie," Kaye said, "do you think it's possible for somebody to be addicted to computers?"

There. She had broached the subject, given voice to it. Now that it had been heard by someone else's ears, it seemed to come alive, to take shape in the air in front of them. Before it had just been a theory. Now it had become an Issue. Theories could be ignored. Issues had to be dealt with.

Janie's forehead wrinkled. "Hmm."

Dr. Sinkolit came around the corner. He was a young doctor, in his late twenties, but he was supposed to be the best at treating cases similar to Katie's. He carried a sheet of paper.

"Mrs. Hamilton, have you been able to get in touch with your husband?"

Kaye stood up. She always felt that formality was required around him. Katie stirred a little but didn't wake up. "Not yet, Doctor. I think he's got the phones...that is...no, not yet."

Dr. Sinkolit watched her expressionlessly. When she fell silent, he glanced at the paper in his hand. "The antibiotic hasn't had the desired effect. There's still bacteria in her urine. It's beginning to look like we might want to consider that procedure I was telling you about."

< virtually eliminated >

"Surgery?"

"What we'd do is just go in and reimplant the ureter into the bladder. In most cases, say 95 percent, this clears up the reflux completely. We've had good results with it."

"If we did this surgery, then she'd be fine?"

"Probably."

"No side effects, no more medicine, no other surgeries down the line?"

"We'd keep her on antibiotics for two to three months after the procedure. Then we'd bring her back in and run another voiding cystourethrogram to make sure everything's okay. If so, no more medicine, no more surgery."

"How long before we need to do this? I mean, does she need to go there right now, or are we all right so long as we do it before she graduates from high school?"

Dr. Sinkolit chuckled. "I don't think that would be advisable. Bacteria doesn't belong in the kidney. It can cause renal scarring, severe hypertension, and perhaps end-stage kidney failure. But I don't see a need to rush her to Cook's right now, either. There's no immediate danger, but I wouldn't recommend waiting more than a month or two."

"All right, thank you, Dr. Sinkolit."

The pediatrician handed the paper to Janie. "Why don't you make a copy of this for her?" He looked down at Katie, then winked amiably at Kaye before turning to go. "Bye, now."

Janie brought the copy to the front counter, where Kaye was paying for the office visit. "I'm sure Ethan will be fine."

"Oh, I know."

"Every recovery program I know of that doesn't rely on drugs relies on a Higher Power to get the help the person needs. And I know you both have a good relationship with the best Higher Power there is." She squeezed Kaye's hand. "I'll be praying for you," she whispered.

< jefferson scott >

Kaye set four plastic grocery bags on the kitchen table. "Ethan."

"Hi, honey." His voice barely reached across the house.

She knew that meant he was still on his computer. "Could you come help with groceries?"

"What?"

"Come help!"

She was headed back in from the garage with another load before Ethan appeared. He gave her a quick kiss and swept by.

"I'll get Katie."

"Okay." *Why not help me with these bags?*

Ethan followed her into the kitchen and put Katie down. "Did you ladies have a nice trip?"

"Sure, if possible surgery sounds like your idea of a good time."

He looked at her strangely. That last comment had been a little sharp, she had to admit. "Go play, Katie." When the little girl was gone, Ethan took Kaye's hand. "Let's go sit down and talk about it."

She pulled her hand away. "I've got to get these cold things put away."

"All right. Well, I've got some things to do, too. We'll talk about it over dinner."

"What are you working on?"

"The thing for the FBI. You know my helpers, my little infobots who help me on GlobeNet?"

No, not really. "Oh, uh-huh."

"Well, one of them got attacked today."

She put away some frozen broccoli. "Really?"

"And I know where, too. I'm trying to patch him back together, find out what happened to him before I go take a look." With every word he inched farther out the kitchen door.

"How long will that take?"

"Shouldn't take more than an hour or so. If I'm not done by the

< virtually eliminated >

time dinner's ready, I'll just take a break from it."

How generous of you. "I was thinking we could go out tonight."

Ethan shut his eyes. He sighed tragically. "Kaye, I was hoping to spend the evening working on the computer."

"And I was hoping to spend the evening with my husband."

"We still can. I'll be here and you will be, too. We'll be together. Maybe we can watch a movie together, or something."

"Okay."

He smiled at her, but there was anger mixed in it. "That's not enough for you, is it? You still want to go out."

"Mmm-hmm."

"Kaye, it's not like I'm playing a game. I'm working for the FBI. The federal government. I'm doing important things. I have to get back to it."

"Since when does going out with your wife not count as an important thing?"

He wisely chose not to answer that.

"Am I in your way?" she said.

"What?"

"It just seems like I'm in your way. Like you wish your children and I would just go away and leave you alone to play on your computers. Our baby has to have surgery and all you want to do is go play."

"I asked if you wanted to go talk about it. But all you wanted to do was put away groceries. What do you want from me, Kaye?"

"I want you to be my husband and their father!"

Ethan blinked at her. "Kaye, you're upset about what the doctor said. Let's go sit down and talk about it."

Kaye hated that she cried at moments like these. A part of her mind wondered if the crying was an unconscious ploy to get sympathy. It had worked for her in the past. But surely she wasn't so manipulative, was she?

She slammed the freezer door. "You spend all day long on…on…that computer! And when I want to do something with you…or

< jefferson scott >

just talk…or go out to dinner…you act like it's such…a burden to you. Well, I'm sorry I'm such a nuisance! Maybe I'll just go away. All of us will. That would make you happy, wouldn't it?"

"I don't want you to go away, Kaye." Ethan rubbed his face. "I'm a computer programmer, Kaye. That's what I do. Now you want me to stop working on the computer? What am I supposed to do for money?"

"I don't want you to stop being a computer programmer. I just want you to be my husband, too. First! And a daddy. " He could make her so mad. "I feel like one of those plates that man on TV spins on sticks. He goes around spinning his plates just enough to keep them from falling. I'm just another one of your plates, aren't I? Not even the most important one."

"That's not true."

"Oh, really? Name the times — awake times! — you and I have spent alone together in the last month."

He thought for a second. "We were alone last Friday night."

"Last Friday night? Last Friday night we went to a new ComputerLand store. You spent the whole time talking to the manager about microchips."

"But we were alone together on the drive out and the drive back."

Words refused to come to Kaye.

"Okay, okay," Ethan put his arms around her. "Bad example, sorry. You're right, we haven't spent much time alone together lately." He sighed. "Okay, what do you want to do?"

She lifted her face out of his shoulder. "I don't want it to be up to me. What do *we* want to do?"

"I thought dinner sounded good. How does Pepper's sound?"

She snuggled. "Sounds wonderful."

"Where are we going to get a babysitter so late?"

"The Hutchins girl is usually available."

"She makes more per hour than I do."

She gave him the "Do you want to fight about it?" look.

He raised his hands. "Okay, okay. You call the babysitter and I'll go

< virtually eliminated >

get things to a stopping point on the computer."

The atmosphere in the car on the way to the restaurant was strained. The easy dialogue she and Ethan usually shared was gone. In its place was a brooding silence. Ethan didn't give her more than a two syllable reply until they got a table and ordered their food.

When Kaye began telling him about the visit to the pediatric urologist, however, she commanded his full attention. When their daughter was born, she had a severe case of jaundice. The Rh factor in Kaye's blood didn't match that of little Katie's. The hospital discharged mother and daughter only thirty hours after the birth. The doctor's only instructions were, "Keep an eye on that jaundice."

So they did. They watched their baby girl sleep more and more, wet diapers less and less, and grow more and more yellow. What were they supposed to be watching for? After four days they went in to the pediatrician. Katie was admitted into Cook Children's Medical Center the same morning.

Ethan and Kaye — and even seven-year-old Jordan — began learning all sorts of new terms. Bilirubin. Jaundice. Rh factors. There was the distinct possibility of brain damage.

After an agonizing three days at Cook's, Katie's bilirubin levels fell from twenty to less than ten. They sent her home. Kaye made sure they left armed with better instructions than "Keep an eye on her." After a year had passed, Katie showed no signs of brain damage.

Then there came a new problem. Katie began having pain urinating. Their pediatrician said Katie had developed a urinary infection. That didn't sound too serious to Kaye and Ethan, but the doctor was concerned. He ran some tests, which led to more tests, which ultimately confirmed his suspicion. Katie had vesicoureteral reflux.

In a healthy person, urine flows from the kidney to the bladder in two tubes called ureters. A valve prevents urine from flowing the other way. One of Katie's valves was not working. Urine and the bacteria it carried were getting back into one of her kidneys.

It tore at the parents' hearts. Why did such a little girl have to suffer

< jefferson scott >

so much? Kaye was still waiting for her answer from God.

On recommendation, they began taking Katie to a specialist, a pediatric urologist, who had had success treating vesicoureteral reflux. Dr. Sinkolit. He put her on an antibiotic to treat the infection, hoping the reflux would cure itself with time, as it sometimes did in small children.

The appointment today was to see if, after three months of treatment, the medication had had any effect. It hadn't. When urinary infections continue despite antibiotics, surgery is often recommended.

Ethan's hamburger sat cooling on the plate before him. "How long before they have to do it?"

"He said we could wait a month or two."

Her husband looked off into space. "I wonder if God would consider letting me switch medical conditions with my daughter."

Kaye reached across the table and stroked her husband's cheek. "If He did, I know you would do it."

He kissed her hand. "So would you."

They ate their dinner then, talking easily. Kaye sighed. It felt so good to be "back" with him. But would one of their children always have to be in pain in order to hold them together?

There was something malignant growing between them. Most of it had to do with Ethan's preference for his computers over his family. She felt that in her heart. They had to either get the malignancy out once and for all or pay the painful consequences of leaving it alone.

O Father, please... Even in silence her prayer faltered. *Please...help!*

She didn't know how or when, but she knew He would.

< virtually eliminated >

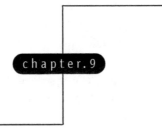

chapter.9

THE CHAMELEON'S AMBUSH had done no real damage, Patriot could tell. Now that he had calmed down. It had hit like a grenade, though. The bright, searing light; the screaming alarm that distorted his speakers; the swift stab in his mind.

For a moment he had thought he might actually be dying.

Now he saw he was all right. He almost even smiled. Someone had punched him in the eye. That had not happened in a very long time. He was almost giddy as he re-entered GlobeNet. Now he would have some fun.

Finding who had stung him was child's play. The hide-and-strike routine that bit him had an embedded date stamp and creation signature. It was almost embarrassingly easy to decode. Whoever this Ethan Hamilton was, Patriot deduced, he was not accustomed to writing malicious logic.

Even if the traitor had not left his signature in the chameleon program, Patriot would have been able to trace him. This Hamilton had been so careless, so reckless, in his trip through GlobeNet that it almost looked like he wanted to be found.

< j e f f e r s o n   s c o t t >

His quarry had entered the net at 15:47:33, eastern standard time, from somewhere in the southwestern United States. Patriot could tell that much from the GlobeNet access log.

At 15:49:06 Hamilton had initiated a search. The nature of the search arrested Patriot's full attention. *Find:* virtual reality *and either* death *or* electrocution *or* assassination *or* execution *or* shock *or* CIA.

This Mr. Hamilton was asking some discomforting questions.

Next, Hamilton had visited the post office, where he foolishly maintained a mailbox under his real name.

Amateur.

Patriot ran the usual workup. He detoured into the World Bank to run a credit check on this man, and into MedLine Plus for medical records. He launched a gopher search on the newspaper and magazine databases. As always he charged it all to credit card codes from his private cache.

Hamilton appeared quite the model citizen. Excellent credit. Two cars, both paid for. Insurance — current. No recent accidents or traffic violations. No overdue loans or bounced checks. No discreet hotel bills that might indicate an illicit affair. No dry-out clinics or emphysema or AIDS or anything else someone might interpret as a sign of vice. The family had magazine subscriptions to *Artificial Worlds*, *Woman's Day*, *GameTips*, and *The Christian Reader*.

Wonderful, he thought, vanquished by Mr. Rogers.

The only unusual find was a cluster of medium to large medical bills beginning about eighteen months ago. Admission into a children's hospital. Daughter's name, Katie; wife's name, Kaye. Several unusually high invoices from a Dallas pediatrician.

Possible sickly child.

Possibly from Texas.

Possibly Christian, active or laxed.

Ethan Hamilton seemed entirely out of profile for the type that might assault anyone on GlobeNet, especially someone like Patriot.

"What's this?" He examined the results of the gopher search. "A

< virtually eliminated >

book, Mr. Hamilton? Do wonders never cease?" He scanned the reviews for the book's title. *An Investigation into the Efficacy of Interphasic Telephony on Manufactured Environments.* "A VR man, eh, Mr. Hamilton? Good."

Judging by what he had found so far, Patriot had begun to think Hamilton might be a monk of some kind. He was relieved, therefore, to find he was dealing with an adept in virtual reality.

"Correction, I was not bested by Mister Rogers. I was bested by *Cyber*-Mister Rogers!"

His embarrassment was further assuaged when he accessed Hamilton's direct-deposit paycheck information. Chief systems analyst, Digital Environment Specialists. The company, DES, even sounded familiar to him. Something about event splicing.

This Hamilton deserved investigation.

Patriot found Digital Environment Specialists through the on-line equivalent of the Yellow Pages. Within seconds, he hovered over a street of simulated office buildings in the high-tech district of GlobeNet.

Each artificial building represented a corporation and was designed to convey something of the character of the firm within. These were the de facto logos of the companies they depicted. Customers in VR need only select the desired building to be transferred inside.

Patriot recognized the upward arrow architecture of a Japanese communications subsidiary, the Hindu temple motif of an Indian bio-genetics firm, and the miniature mountain peaks of an American game/communications alliance.

He had been flying in a prone position, like Superman. But when he arrived at DES, Patriot righted himself and descended to the synthetic ground. He never cared much anymore for his apparent relation to the simulated world. But this time he wanted DES's image to have its full effect on him.

It left him flat.

The DES storefront was a three-dimensional line graph — a hollow cube, set at an angle, with two walls cut away so the viewer could look

< jefferson scott >

in. Blue, green, and red lines zigzagged across the chart. And it was small. Much shorter than the neighboring buildings. Hardly twice as tall as Patriot.

Disappointing.

At least the chart showed an upward trend. Decidedly up, in fact. Little animated figures crawled along the surface of the line graph, walking like lemmings forever toward the future.

Patriot reached into his jet-black cloak and pulled out what looked like a river rock, round and flat. Perfect for skipping. It was actually a utility program used to probe the defenses of a target computer. In the hacker/phreak vernacular, it was an ICE-Pick. Conventional picks had a tendency to trigger certain alarm systems and get snared in a system's defenses. So Patriot had made his a poke-and-run probe. A skipping stone.

He flipped it at the DES building with a negligent toss. The stone sped away from his hand as if jet-propelled, accelerating until it struck the invisible boundary of the DES bar graph. Where it struck there was a quick spherical glow, like a bottle rocket exploding underwater.

The stone disappeared.

It took a moment for Patriot to realize what had happened. He still held out his hand, waiting for his probe to bounce off the image and return to him. But the stone was gone.

He was not concerned, really. Even he left out a line of code now and then. Maybe that pick was just a dud. He pulled out another from his void cloak and tossed it at the DES building.

The same quick globe of light at the point of impact. The same result.

Patriot felt his self-control detach a notch. Had outside eyes been able to see it, they would have observed Patriot's body come untethered from GlobeNet's simulated gravity. He lifted from the ground and began a lazy cartwheel.

This was not going to be the simple invasion he had at first imagined. Patriot had never seen a defensive array so quick that it could erase

< virtually eliminated >

one of his skipper picks. Not even Nanotech. He could immediately see how it was done, of course. He recognized the flaw in his design and saw at once how to correct it. But that was beside the point.

The point was DES was hiding something. They had a secret they were serious about keeping to themselves. Why else this elaborate security system? Now the dull line graph motif began to make sense; they were loathe to draw attention to themselves. Working for the government, were they? Whose government?

Patriot was suddenly very interested in DES in general and Ethan Hamilton in particular. He put his entire to-do list for the day on hold. There were few things Patriot detested worse than secrets in the possession of others. He recited Levy's famous Rules to himself: 1) Access to computers should be unlimited and total; 2) All information should be free; 3) Mistrust authority and promote decentralization.

Patriot, as it happened, had never read *Hackers*, the book from which Steven Levy's famous Rules were drawn. But he trotted out Levy's commandments whenever they served his purposes. As a result, Patriot felt vaguely righteous as he prepared to rob DES of its dearest secrets.

The first thing he did was create a pocket of adjusted linearity. His presence was hidden, as always, but he needed to set up a field workshop of sorts, and he wanted no one to see his activity, either. So he created a cyber-bubble, invisible to VR visuals, in which to work.

Within minutes, he was ready to begin his assault. His hunt for Ethan Hamilton, the memory of the blinding sensory overload, even his desire for retribution — all faded for the moment into inconsequence. Now he was after a bigger fish. He was convinced DES was up to something patently un-American. And if exposing — and thwarting — such activity was not the job of a Patriot, whose was it?

He proceeded methodically, scientifically. Gently, so as to not be further detected, Patriot probed at the DES host computer. First he tried to log on to the computer as a visitor, as if someone had dialed in innocently, by accident.

A holographic image appeared in the air before him — Abraham

< jefferson scott >

Lincoln, sitting on his throne in the Lincoln Memorial.

Patriot was mildly disappointed. If this was the simple password system Patriot thought it was going to be, it was as good as defeated. Lincoln would probably begin one of his famous sayings — probably "You can fool some of the people all the time"—and the user would simply have to complete the quotation to gain entry. Patriot was more than qualified for the task.

"What is the word?" Lincoln's voice boomed.

Patriot wrinkled his forehead. Lincoln had no known quotation that began thus. Perhaps this was going to be more difficult than he imagined. What is the word? There were a hundred ways to attack that problem: Logos, the word of God; words, the great foes of reality; words, the most powerful drug used by mankind.

"The word, Mr. President?"

"The password, son. I can't let you in here without that." Lincoln's body was the same pale white as the stone in his memorial.

"Pardon me, sir. It seems I have reached this exchange by mistake. I was attempting to reach Dental Ergonomics Systems."

Lincoln's image disappeared and the link was disconnected.

Patriot tried a new approach. He scanned for tele-links. The data lines flowing in and out of DES were relatively inactive. Only six remote connections. People getting in some late night work. He thought he might piggy-back onto one of those.

Types of gooks? What kind of a stupid question is that? Earl Dekk wondered. *Who cares?* As far as he was concerned, they were all the same.

But that wasn't good enough for Jerry Jack Wilson or old Bill Gunn. They wanted to know types. Chinese, Japanese, Vietnamese, Korean, Laotian, Burmese, Okinawan, and whatever else.

Why they wanted to know this was beyond Earl, but he didn't really have a choice. The Grand Cyclops had made a decree, and it was his task as Nighthawk to carry it out.

< virtually eliminated >

Not that there were that many gooks of any kind in Wallonia, Kentucky. Lexington was supposed to be crawling with them, according to reports. Earl didn't even want to think about how many might live in Louisville. But there just wasn't that much ethnic diversity in Wallonia; a fact which suited Earl and his klavern just right.

So why did he have to have categories of gooks?

He entered his wood-paneled office at his house and shut the door behind him so Ellen wouldn't see what he was doing. Ellen didn't approve of going too far with this kind of thing.

She hadn't always been like that. But something the preacher said last spring had put a bee in her bonnet. Now if Earl ever spent too much energy on his Klan work, she would let him have it. Something about Jesus and some Samarian woman or something.

Boy Preacher's gone from preachin' to meddlin'.

Earl turned his computer on. He turned the speaker volume down so Ellen wouldn't know he was working. He called up his database files and browsed his racial categories. He kept most of the klavern's business data on his service provider's computer, but he did have a few choice files on his own PC.

Here he had the name, address, and ethnic identity of every non-white resident in Trigg County, as well as the probable ancestral nation of origin of every non-Protestant. Earl even kept a secret file of every non-Baptist.

When you got down to it, it was amazing how few people could actually be considered approved.

He was going to need some help on this one. His "Gooks" sub-directory had about seventy names, but Earl had no way of knowing who was Taiwanese and who was Cambodian and who was whatever else. He was fairly sure Rick Mantrell over at the Klan Web Site would know. What was the national headquarters good for if not to help out with things like this?

He initiated a GlobeNet link. He used the same graphical Web browser he'd used on the Internet back in the nineties. He'd never

< jefferson scott >

gotten into that virtual reality garbage. Some of the brothers down in Tennessee had, and they swore by it. But frankly Earl was a little suspicious of anybody from out of state. So he stayed strictly two-dimensional, his feet firmly planted in reality.

His service provider window came up like normal. But instead of dissolving into Earl's home page, a message window appeared. "User *BattleHymn* please contact network administrator."

Earl stared at the screen. He tried to swallow. What had they discovered? He was reminded of a note he'd once received summoning him to the principal's office. He clicked on the indicated electronic address and entered his password. Shortly, a message printed to his screen.

> DATE: SEPTEMBER 22, 2005
>
> TO: USER BATTLEHYMN@PUREEARTH.ORG (EARL WYLIE DEKK)
>
> ON SEPTEMBER 12, 2005, AT 2:18 A.M., YOUR COMPANY: PURE EARTH INTERESTS, EXCEEDED ITS ALLOWABLE DISK SPACE ALLOTMENT BY:783.64 TERABYTES.
>
> PLEASE REMOVE THIS OVERAGE BY 11:59 P.M. SEPTEMBER 22, 2005. FAILURE TO RETURN YOUR COMPANY'S DISK CONSUMPTION TO THE ALLOTTED 10 TERABYTES BY THIS TIME WILL RESULT IN PUNITIVE ACTION INCLUDING, BUT NOT LIMITED TO, ERASURE OF OVERAGE, IRREVOCABLE TERMINATION OF SERVICE, AND FINES NOT TO EXCEED $10,000.
>
> ED PEÑA, SYSTEM MANAGER, CYBERNET

Earl stared at the message dumbly. 783 terabytes? 783 terabytes! Only last month had his files even achieved the 100 gigabyte level. He couldn't imagine ever having even *one* terabyte's worth of information, let alone seven hundred. There had to be some mistake.

The system manager agreed. Ed Peña — *Spic*, Earl silently repeated — was none too happy about having over half of his chief storage unit

< virtually eliminated >

suddenly gobbled up by Earl's massive download. But when Earl continued to plead innocence, Peña got his permission to read the directory tree of the offending files.

"Pitstop Nums?" Earl repeated Peña's last words. "Freenet Nums? I don't know any of these names." He read the list from a window on the monitor. "Daemon Acs?"

"You're telling me you don't know what these files are, Mr. Dekk?" Peña's face, in another window on the screen, showed open distrust.

"No!" He was getting a little tired of Peña's spic face. "I don't know anything about them."

"Then may we erase them?"

"You gonna bag us for that?" *Do it, and I know who'll be getting a pretty burning cross in his yard.*

"No sir," Peña said. "We'll just get you back to your September 21 level and call it even."

"Do it."

Access Denied, Goober.

Patriot shouted, and for a moment GlobeNet spun out of control. Artificial buildings seemed to float around as if someone had shaken a glass globe. Patriot sneered at a passing pedestrian, a user who had taken the form of something once called a Power Ranger, and the image poofed out of sight. In Charlottesville, North Carolina, a GlobeNet user found herself inexplicably kicked out of the system.

Patriot turned back to the task at hand, his rage temporarily appeased. Try as he might, he could not penetrate the DES network.

Access Denied, Goober.

It was not Abraham Lincoln who now called him names. Patriot had encountered other personae as he probed diverse facets of the computer's defenses. Humphrey Bogart, Joseph Stalin. Mr. Ed.

But for the last hour, Patriot had been dealing with an animated finger puppet. A simulated thumb rose and fell beneath an index finger,

< jefferson scott >

informing Patriot in a man's falsetto that he could not proceed. And that he was a goober.

Now Patriot was mad again. Now he remembered how he had been so unfairly attacked. He remembered the searing pain, the blinding light, and the sonic overload.

Now he remembered the name Ethan Hamilton.

< virtually eliminated >

chapter.10

THE PRESIDENT'S STAFF VEHICLE was under attack. The human army had managed to beat back the alien offensive, but the chief of staff was not out of danger yet. Not by any means.

Jordan Hamilton and his fellow squad members surveyed the situation from a digital hilltop. "Why didn't she stay underground?" one of the marines whined. "She was totally safe."

Jordan turned to his comrade-in-arms. "Why didn't you stay underground when you were president?"

The marine pulled out a digital pistol and shot Jordan's persona in the foot.

"Hey!" Jordan hopped around, fumbling with his inventory. "I'm almost out of health-packs."

"Cut it out, both of you." Their squad leader wasn't in a very good mood today. "They'll hear us."

Jordan's grey battle armor bore a tactician's green V on the front and back. The squad leader's armor had a blue stripe down the middle, indicating his rank. Besides these, Hugo Squadron was left with only a plasma launch specialist (red circle), two battle chemists (yellow zigzags),

< jefferson scott >

and one electronic warfare engineer (black square). The Buklavian invaders had eliminated over half their squad.

"Tac-Op," their squad leader said, "magnify image — vehicle AA-1."

"Yes, sir." Jordan accessed his recon subdirectory.

A pane appeared in the air in front of them, showing a magnified picture of the president's armored vehicle. It was a huge thing, a virtual fortress, rolling on four sets of tank treads. It was half tank, half Mayan step-pyramid. Turrets on each of three levels swept the battlefield with an unending sweep of purple laser fire.

But it wasn't enough.

Buklavian soldiers threw themselves at the vehicle with mindless abandon. They blocked the turrets with their bodies so their comrades could advance in safety. They cast themselves under the treads to slow the vehicle's progress. And they fired weapons: huge, earthshaking cannons; quick-firing armor-piercing rockets; even pop-gun projectile weapons.

Jordan and the rest of Hugo Squadron had no problem predicting the near-future. Unless something happened immediately, the president was doomed. Worst of all, the game would be over.

"We've got to help them," the squad leader said. He turned to his squad. "Options."

The plasma launch specialist, who had shot Jordan in the foot, raised his cannon. "Let's just go get them!"

"We've got about thirty canisters of mustard gas left," said one of the battle chemists. "That should slow them down, at least."

"But then I can't use my stun-pulse," the electronic warfare engineer protested.

"All right, all right," said the squad leader. "We need everybody's weapons. Don't worry." He turned to Jordan. "Tac-Op, any ideas?"

"We could try a diversion, maybe."

"Like what?"

Jordan called up a blip-map of the area around the president's vehicle. "Michael could come over this hill here," he pointed at the map

< virtually eliminated >

on the floating pane, "and open fire with his plasma cannon. That should pull some of the aliens away from the car."

One of the battle chemists cut in. "Why don't I just shoot this at them." He held up an evil-looking projectile.

"Hey," the other BC complained. "You said you were out of napalm."

"Good," said Jordan decisively, as if he wasn't really nine years old after all. Thanks to his on-screen persona and voice-augmentation software, Jordan looked and sounded like everyone else.

He spoke to the battle chemist with the napalm. "You go with him. Try to get them to come to you. When you pull them to this point," he indicated a spot on the map, "let them have it." To the other BC, he said, "You stay with us. We need your mustard gas."

"Sounds good, Tac-Op," the squad leader said.

The squad leader liked Jordan. Of course they had never met in person. But he'd played multiplayer games with him for months and had come to rely on him. He had no idea Jordan wasn't an adult. His mental image of Jordan was as a junior executive at some high-tech firm somewhere.

"What do the rest of us do?" he asked his tactician.

"The rest of us will come around this hill here," again Jordan pointed at the map, "and wait for the aliens to go after you two guys. Then you," he said to the second battle chemist, "will use your mustard gas on the ones that stay at the vehicle. And you," he pointed at the electronic warfare engineer, "can use your stun-pulse. That should take care of most of them."

The squad members listened to Jordan respectfully. When he finished, the squad leader clapped his hands once. "Right. Whatever's left we can pick off with small arms or hand-to-hand."

"But what about us?" asked the plasma launch specialist. "We'll be toast."

Jordan shrugged. *Maybe you shouldn't have shot me.*

"No you won't," the squad leader said. "You two make your way

< jefferson scott >

back around to the president's car. You'll be all right."

"I still say the stupid girl should have stayed underground. The computer always stays underground when it's president."

"All right, button up." The squad leader touched the floating pane, and the picture changed back to the image of the president's armored car. "They've jammed the tracks. We have to go now or nothing will save her. When we secure the car, we'll have to clear the treads, then make a run for the caves. All right, Hugo Squadron, you know your duty. Move out."

The two sent out as bait descended to the bottom of one hill and sprinted behind another. They appeared now and again as they skirted around to get into position. The rest of Hugo Squadron started off the other way, hugging the base of a low hill.

As he jogged along behind his squad leader, Jordan detected some interference on his helmet speakers. He tapped his helmet distractedly.

"Time for bed, sport," boomed a hideous voice.

"Wha—?"

Then his world was ripped from him.

Jordan found himself in a brightly lit room. Off-white walls, brown carpet, no windows. The game room.

His dad stood over him, holding Jordan's VR headset.

"Come on, it's late."

Jordan shook his head, still a little disoriented. The babysitter should have warned him his mom and dad were back from dinner. "But Dad! Please let me play just a little longer. I made up this great plan and everybody thinks I'm old and we're going to save the president from the aliens."

Ethan grinned. "What're you playing?"

"*Earth Wars.* Can I, huh? They need me. Can I play just a little longer? Please, please, please?" He clasped his hands together as if he were praying.

"Oh, all right. But not long. Your mother's taking a bath, so you've got about ten minutes. Don't tell her I let you play."

< virtually eliminated >

"Give me my helmet back," Jordan snapped, suddenly demanding. Then he saw the look in his father's eyes. "I mean, 'Could I please have my helmet back?'" He smiled sweetly.

It bothered Ethan how much his son craved the games, the immersion. It was like a drug — with withdrawal, fixes, high cost, and all the rest. He knew how addicting computers could be. He realized he and Jordan might have to have a talk about this soon.

It also occurred to him that *he* had about ten minutes, too. He gave Jordan his helmet back and skulked down to the study.

Jordan's plan was working.

Almost half of the aliens had gone after the plasma gunner. The BC must have just launched his napalm, because aliens burned all over the face of the hillside. Through his helmet speakers Jordan could hear the gunner taunting them.

Around the president's car, the mustard gas had partially neutralized the remaining attackers. The electronic warfare engineer aimed his stun-pulse.

"Now!" the squad leader shouted.

The pulse fired out, frying all but the largest aliens.

"Great shot!"

The squad leader grabbed Jordan. "I thought you deserted us, soldier."

"Yeah. My d— I mean, I, uh…Someone was at the door. But I'm back now."

"Good. You ready for a little hand-to-hand?"

"Yes, sir."

"Then let's do it." The squad leader raised his shock-rifle defiantly. "For Earth and man!"

"For Earth and man," Jordan echoed. He followed his squad leader in a run toward the president's besieged vehicle.

And found himself in darkness.

< jefferson scott >

"Hey!"

Jordan looked all around. His voice was swallowed by the void around him. At first he thought his dad was playing a trick on him, had snatched the helmet away and turned the lights out. But he felt at his face with his free hand and found he still wore the headset. His body was artificially illuminated, too, as if he were painted in florescent paint. Definitely still in cyberspace.

So where was he? What had gone wrong?

"Ethan Hamilton?"

The voice scared Jordan. A man's voice. His 3-D speakers failed to localize the sound. It was as if he were inside the voice, somehow.

"Ethan Hamilton?"

Jordan spun around, trying to catch a glimpse of the speaker. "He's not here." He rotated slowly but didn't see anything. "Who are you?"

No answer.

"If you want to play you'll have to start a new game. This one's almost over."

Silence. Maybe the man had left.

"Can I go back to my game now? I'm supposed to go to bed before Mom gets out of the bathtub."

"What is your name, then?"

"Jordan. Ethan's my dad."

Jordan seemed to remember something his mom had said that might apply here. Something about talking to strangers. But he was pretty sure that was just about strangers on the street.

"How old are you, Jordan?"

"Nine and a half."

"Where do you live?"

"North Richland Hills." It occurred to Jordan that he could just take his helmet off and be done with this. "I have to go now, Mister. Bye." He reached for his headset.

< virtually eliminated >

"Wait, Jordan! I have to ask you something."

The man's voice carried a note of authority, of force. Jordan didn't move. "What?"

"Could you put your dad on for a second? I want to talk to him."

Jordan thought he saw something in the gloom. A flash, a streak of yellow or gold. Like a firefly. But when he turned to look at it, it was gone.

"Jordan?" the voice asked.

"What?"

"Your dad. Can I talk to him?"

"Okay. I'll look."

Jordan pulled his headset off.

He blinked in the light of the game room. His dad had left the sliding door open a crack. "Dad!"

"Jordan?" His mother called from the bedroom. "Go to bed."

"But Mom! Where's Dad?"

"Your father's giving Katie her pill. Get into your room this minute, Jordan Hamilton. You're not still playing that game, are you?" Her voice was getting louder, as though she were coming toward the door to her room. She seemed pretty mad.

"No, Mom! Okay, I'm coming."

Jordan turned back to the VR equipment. His headset lay on the desk — just plastic speakers and a visor. No power of its own. He didn't have to put them back on. He considered simply turning the machine off and running into his room. Yet it drew him somehow.

He thought he heard the floor creak softly.

He grabbed the headset and jammed it on.

Darkness.

"Ethan Hamilton?" the voice asked.

The man sounded different, less friendly. Jordan almost took the headset off again.

< jefferson scott >

"No, it's me. I can't talk now, my mom's coming. Dad's busy. You can talk to him tomorrow night. Or call him on the vid."

"Jordan." Again the voice immobilized him. "When can I talk to *you* again?"

Jordan heard his parents' door open. His mom's slippers flapped on the wooden floor.

He took the headset off, then quickly raised just the microphone to his lips. "Tomorrow after school." He set the headset on the desk and turned off the machine.

Just as his mother slid the game room door open.

< virtually eliminated >

chapter.11

● LAO TZE CLUNG TO HIS JOB BY A THREAD.

Lao worked at Victoria Power Station #12, on Singapore's lower west side. *Asleep at the switch* might be a railroad term, but it was particularly applicable to Lao in reference to his recent blunder.

Last week, on his graveyard shift, he had actually fallen asleep at work. Lightning struck a power pole on the east side, knocking out the electricity to over five hundred homes. Lao slept through all the signals and warnings his system gave him. No amount of flashing lights or highlighted text on a monitor could arouse him.

It was the telephone that finally woke him up — some irate citizen using a candle to read the phone book. At least it wasn't his boss. Lao immediately got up and began rerouting power.

As far as he knew, no one had gotten hurt as a result of the power outage. His first thought was simply to forget the whole incident. But his supervisor hadn't given him that option. In an impressive display of managerial pyrotechnics, he had all but scalded Lao.

When the dust settled, however, Lao found he still had his job. He thought it probably was because his supervisor also happened to be his

< j e f f e r s o n   s c o t t >

brother-in-law. Lao's sister would have absolutely devoured him if he'd fired Lao. But Lao knew that no family tie could save him if he blundered again.

Which was why he didn't hesitate to pick up the phone now when he saw the power surge developing.

"Chuan-Mei? Lao. Instruments are detecting a large buildup. Don't know why. Maybe you come see."

"Coming."

Tomorrow after school, the kid had said.

Patriot checked his internal clock. Hamilton was in the central time zone. Jordan would probably be home around four, his time. Nineteen hours.

The more he thought about it, the more Patriot liked the idea of exacting his revenge on Ethan Hamilton through his son. Nothing permanent, of course, just a reprimand for attacking him.

In the meantime, the electrical surge he had generated to punish Ethan needed to be discharged. He was never careless about such things. One reckless move could jeopardize his entire plan.

He extinguished the lightless sphere he had created and found himself high above the GlobeNet floor. Maintaining the appearance of normalcy was such an inconvenience for him. He preferred the boundless fluidity of cyberspace.

He righted his relative position and activated a macro he had programmed for this very situation. Seconds later, he knew the "address" of a little-used payphone in Adelaide, South Australia. He sent the electrical spike there.

No one was hurt when the phone detonated.

He was not a murderer, after all.

< virtually eliminated >

Ten seconds before Chuan-Mei arrived from his office, the massive surge Lao Tze had detected suddenly disappeared from all instruments.

"Where is this buildup, Lao?"

Lao saw the look in his brother-in-law's eyes. "I don't know where it is! It was here! Big buildup. No cause."

"Maybe you were asleep, Lao? Maybe you were dreaming of this big buildup."

"No, Chuan-Mei, I swear. Not this time. Lao is always awake now. I learned from my mistake."

Chuan-Mei regarded his brother-in-law carefully, perhaps weighing the consequences of his next action. How much family honor would it cost him — or, more immediately, how mad were his wife and mother-in-law going to be?

"Lao Tze," he said formally. "You are fired."

Naturally, Chuan-Mei never reported the mysterious rise and disappearance of the alleged power surge.

Tomorrow after school. Nineteen hours of waiting. It at once irritated him and thrilled his epicurean soul.

Patriot decided to pass the time sensibly. His sentry system would alert him if anything important arose. Martin Grant, the arch-betrayer, wasn't going to sell his country out for another three weeks, and Chairman Yasunari had not even returned from vacation. He would deal with their treachery in good time. Right now, though, there was nothing Patriot needed to do but wait.

He returned to the matter of Hamilton's work computer. It was beginning to become something of an obsession for him. If it had never been refused him in the first place, he would not want it at all. But it had been refused him. And it chafed him.

That and the *Goober*.

Patriot never bothered himself with geographical location anymore. He loved the ability to go to any place on the planet with the press of a button or, in his case, a press of thought. He did not even like to be reminded that GlobeNet was not the way the world actually was.

But this was a special situation. Much as it irked him to admit it, Patriot knew he could not get into Hamilton's computer by traditional information warfare tactics. By no means was he conceding defeat. He simply needed to escalate this little war to the next level. What he needed now was for a living person to go to an actual street address and physically do something for him.

The real world revolted him. Horrible things awaited him there.

Patriot sped through the passages of the Net. He had to speak with a young friend, and he knew the precise *alt.group* to visit. He also knew his friend would still be up, still on-line.

His friend just happened to live in Dallas.

Ethan came down the stairs to his study and picked up his morning printout. He always got the front page news stories and the Dallas Cowboys section. In addition, his infobots were continuously on the alert for stories incorporating certain keyword-combinations, such as "virtual" and "accident" (for him), "VR games" and "hints" (for Jordan), or "child's bed" and "sale" (for Kaye).

He brought the small stack of papers to the kitchen, where Kaye was cooking turkey sausage and had some pastries in the microwave. Katie was in her highchair, thoroughly enjoying a bowl of oatmeal. Some of it even made it to her mouth. Wysiwyg sat under Katie's chair, more for shelter than for the droppings.

Jordan dragged himself in a moment later. His hair tended to do strange things during the night, and this night had been no exception. The Hamilton men were notorious for their morning hair. It was, in fact, a secret amusement to Kaye and Ethan to see who got the daily mane award. This morning the prize went to Jordan, hands down.

< virtually eliminated >

The hair on one side of the boy's head looked perfect, ready to face the world. The other side was doing something of an ocean spray imitation. It bobbed gracefully as he walked. Jordan plunked into his chair and stared uncomprehendingly at the steaming sweet roll his mother placed before him.

Ethan looked at his wife and winked. Things had been better between them after dinner.

"Let's pray." They joined hands and bowed their heads. Ethan decided to hold Katie's wrist. "Father, thank You for another morning. Thank You for this wonderful family. Thank You for this food. Thank You for whatever You've prepared for us today. Make us more like Your Son. We trust You, Jesus. Amen."

"Amen."

The microwave beeped and Kaye got up to get the last of the pastries out. Ethan looked at his son, who was blowing on his sweet roll.

"How did it go last night?"

Jordan looked up, his eyes suddenly wide. "What?"

"*Earth Wars*. How did your plan go? Did you save the president?"

"Oh, that." The boy slumped back down. "No. I don't know."

Kaye came back to the table. "I caught him still playing at ten. Maybe he didn't get to finish it."

"No," Jordan said peevishly, "that's not why I didn't finish it. This guy came on and took me from the game. It was all dark and I couldn't see anything except myself, and he didn't want to play the game. I did see this yellow flash of light or something — it looked like a firefly — but when I looked I couldn't see —"

Katie chose that moment to fling her spoon to the kitchen floor. Kaye got up after it. "Wipe her face, please, honey."

"I think I need a new napkin," Ethan said. "Katie, are you trying to tell us you're not hungry?"

"Yes, she is still hungry. Come here." Kaye scooted Katie's highchair closer and began feeding her with a clean spoon.

Ethan turned to his morning printout. The Cowboys were finally

< jefferson scott >

starting to do well again. "What were you saying, Jordan?"

Maybe the Cowboys would finally get their tenth Super Bowl appearance. The defense was recovering from the annual free agency fallout, and their new running back acquisition from Nashville looked like he might finally be playing up to his potential.

Jordan was saying something. "— said, 'No, wait.' So I did. But he didn't really want to talk to me…" Ethan nodded knowingly.

If that defensive coordinator would just take a few more risks now and then, we wouldn't have so many squeakers. Don't ease up when the other team's behind. You have to annihilate them.

"—after school. So I guess I'll see him again today. But I don't even know where to look, but I guess that's okay since he found me the first time, he can just do it again after school today. He'll have to."

Ethan looked at his son. "What are you talking about?"

"The guy!"

"What guy?"

"The firefly guy!"

The firefly guy?"

Maybe he should have been paying closer attention to his son. He opened his mouth to ask his son to start over, but a car horn interrupted him. Jordan crammed the rest of the pastry into his mouth, grabbed his bookbag, and scampered out the door.

Ray Feathers wasn't really a telephone repairman.

In the first place, he didn't work for the phone company — for anyone, for that matter. In the second place, he wasn't a repairman, though he certainly knew enough about electronics and communication technology to have been one. Nor was he a man, not yet. He was only sixteen. Greasy skin, facial blemishes, and the works. Ray didn't even like owning up to his real name — he preferred his GlobeNet alias, Pinion.

Nevertheless Ray Feathers appeared every inch the telephone repairman, albeit a young one, when he arrived at the DES building at

< virtually eliminated >

7:30 Friday morning. He wore the right uniform, the right helmet, the right beltload of tools around his waist. He was especially proud of his fake beard and mustache — he'd have to show his drama teacher. He even carried a coil of fiber optic cable over his shoulder to add the right something to the disguise.

He pressed the "send" key on his palmtop computer, transmitting the signal for Patriot to suspend phone service to the floor. Then he beeped the call button at the visitor's entrance.

"Good morning," the receptionist chirped from the vidscreen on the wall. "Welcome to Digital Environment Specialists. May I help you?"

Sneaking in cyberspace was a lot more covert than sneaking in reality. His fake beard began to itch. He tried to speak into the little microphone hole, but ended up only mumbling.

"I'm sorry," the receptionist said. "What was that?"

"I said, 'Are your phones out?' I'm here to fix them."

The receptionist's hand went to the thin headset on her head. "I don't think so. I mean, I haven't gotten any calls, that's true. But it's early yet. I just got in." She pushed a button and listened to the little speaker in her left ear. "Hello, hello?" She looked at the video intercom suspiciously. "How did you know they were out? Obviously we couldn't have called you."

Ray was ready for her this time. Her moment of confusion had allowed him to regain his customary feeling of superiority. "Our computers tell us whenever something goes down. Somebody at Central must've seen your lines go bad, because they called me to come fix them."

Ray tried out his imitation of a blue-collar worker infuriated at the ineptitude of his so-called superiors. "Wouldn't you rather have all this fixed before the boss gets in? He'd never even have to know."

She thought about it for a moment, perhaps imagining what she could or could not do without vidphone service. Then she reached off-screen. Ray saw a light at the top of the door turn from red to green. "Come on in."

Ray — now Pinion in earnest — twisted the knob and went in. It was all happening just like Patriot told him it would. The receptionist directed him down the blue-grey carpeted hall to the phone room. Ray flipped on the light and shut the door behind him. No lock.

The phone room was small, about the size of a walk-in closet. There was an old office chair inside, with one of four wheels missing. Phone books, orange extension cords, boxes of toilet paper, and florescent light bulbs lay on the floor or on the chair.

One wall of the room was virtually covered with a baffling tangle of cables — electrical, network, serial, parallel, video, modem, fax, wirephone, fiber optic, and "other." Even Ray couldn't identify them all, though he'd been phreaking since he was ten.

This was the routing center of the entire company. All DES data of any kind spent at least some time traveling through the tiny cables in this room. If the receptionist had known what a valuable resource she was letting him into, and if she had known she was the company's only defense against this kind of attack, she would never have allowed him in. *You just can't trust anyone these days.*

Ray took a moment to trace out the paths in the delicate bramble before him. He was hoping for a bit of luck in this. Sometimes the guys who wire these rooms put little labels on the ports to identify what's what. That way if Manager A moves to Manager Z's office, the rewiring here would be fairly simple — just swap ports. He identified the network cables and followed them out to the nodes.

Bingo. Labels. "Gonzo," "Sabre," "Goldilocks," "Curly," "Tex," "Mungojerry."

Ray couldn't decide if he was reading fighter pilot nicknames or watching *Universal Gladiators*. Either way, these labels were not going to help. There was no legend on the wall giving translations. He couldn't exactly go ask the receptionist what nickname Ethan Hamilton went by.

Plan A had been to plant a passive detection device, a sniffer, on the cable going straight into Hamilton's personal computer. That way Patriot

< virtually eliminated >

could record all data traffic going into and flowing out from Hamilton's office computer.

Plan B still used the sniffer, but since Ray couldn't identify which cables went into Hamilton's computer, he would have to plant it in a more general location. Patriot would still get the right information, but he would have to sort it out from everyone else's.

In the hall, Ray heard a muffled, "G'morning." People were starting to arrive. He would have to get out fast.

Ray wanted to do a good job here. Aside from the bragging rights this task would afford him on the Net, there was the reward to think of. In return for this dirty little job, Patriot had promised him the most precious substance to any computer hacker — the complete password and encryption key file to the computer network of Ray's choosing.

Ray had considered asking for the passwords to NASA or the U.S. Treasury, of course. There was no question that Patriot would have these. But he was beginning to lean more toward IPK Software, makers of the most popular VR games in the world. He didn't want to do them any harm — they were his idols, after all. He just wanted a peek into the development of the rumored new game.

In GlobeNet, such insider knowledge could be parlayed into almost immeasurable power. He was out to make a lasting name for himself, and this might just be the break that would do it for him.

The other thing Ray might gain from this mission was the chance to work with Patriot again in the future. He was drawn to Patriot like a child to a ghost story. There was something mysterious about Patriot. Something dangerous. He knew he should probably steer clear, but he couldn't help himself.

So, in the data locus of Digital Environmental Specialists, Ray Feathers looked for the ideal place for his sniffer. He finally decided on the main data cable feeding the network file server. Almost everything of import went through that wire. Patriot, Ray decided, would be pleased.

Ray took out a thin green circuit board, about the size of a baseball

< jefferson scott >

card. A single red wire dangled from it, with a tiny squeeze clamp on the end. He flipped a dipswitch on the board, and a green light blinked once.

Ray heard the floor creak a little out in the hall. Someone put a hand on the knob to the phone room. Ray crammed the sniffer back into his belt. He unslung his fiber optic cable and tried to look busy.

"The phones are down this morning, Wally," a woman's voice said.

"What? When will they be up? I need to send a patch out to Seattle by eight."

"That's what I'm going to check on now. The repair guy's in here." The knob turned. The door began to swing open. Ray pulled a pair of pliers from his belt.

"By the way, Denise," Wally said — the door paused — "Did I get a fax overnight?"

"I haven't checked the machine yet." The door bounced back and forth, opened a little, closed a little.

"Would you mind checking that with me?" Wally said. "If the phones have been down all night and I didn't get that fax, then I don't have the data I need for that patch."

The door paused, one-quarter open.

"Sure. Come on." The doorknob swivelled loudly, the door swung shut.

Ray sighed. He put the pliers away and brought the sniffer out again. He peeled the sheet from the adhesive, lifted the frame of the wiring web from the wall, and slid the sniffer behind it. When he was sure the adhesive was set, Ray connected the clamp to the bottom side of the file server cable. Unless someone was looking for it, his datatap might not be found until the entire floor was rewired.

Ray pulled the palmtop computer from his toolbelt. He pressed a few keys, activated a cellular link, and transmitted the message for Patriot to reactivate the phones.

It was done.

Patriot should have the phones back on in less than a minute. He

< virtually eliminated >

checked his watch; he'd been in the phone room only seven minutes. He hoisted the fiber optic cable on his shoulder and stepped into the hallway.

Ray passed a young-looking DES employee and tried unsuccessfully to contain a look of green-eyed envy. Pompous little twit, he thought. Why should he get a job like this, and I can't get a job anywhere?

He made a mental note to log on to the Young Programmers Online discussion group and drop an especially annoying Trojan horse virus he'd recently written. That determined, he felt a little better.

The receptionist, Denise, was talking to a fat man in his thirty-somethings. Ray adjusted his toolbelt loudly until she noticed him.

"Thanks, Denise," the fat man said, and walked away.

She looked at Ray skeptically. "Well?"

Ray pointed to her switching console. "Try it."

She put her headset on and punched a button. The Time and Temperature channel appeared. "Okay," she said. "Looks like we're back up again. Thanks."

Ray headed for the door. "No problem."

"Wait a minute," she called. "Aren't you supposed to give me some kind of invoice or something? Something to sign?"

Ray smiled at her, backing toward the door. "Nope. Central will see the lines clear again, and they'll know I was here. They'll mail it to you. And I'll call in when I get back to the truck," he stammered. "I'll report in."

The receptionist didn't budge. Ray thought he was going to buy it here, at the end, when the only thing separating him from freedom was a stupid magnetically locked door. Denise's eyes narrowed a little.

The phone rang. Neither one moved.

The phone rang again. Ray forced himself to meet her eyes, daring her to accuse him of wrongdoing.

The phone rang a third time.

Denise crumpled down into her chair and answered the phone.

< jefferson scott >

"Good morning. Thank you for calling Digital Environment Specialists. How may I direct your call?"

Ray watched her helplessly. She still hadn't released the lock. He felt panic rising inside. She couldn't possibly know anything. Nonetheless, he felt the urge to cry out, "Okay, okay, I confess! I did it! I tapped your data lines and we're going to steal all your secrets. Take me away!"

Instead he just stood there. Behind him the door chimed, and an employee let himself in.

Denise looked up in time to see Ray slip through the door.

< virtually eliminated >

chapter.12

IT WAS ONE OF THE FRUSTRATIONS of life in 2005 that the world's phone systems were overwhelmed. Fiber optic lines had been laid to increase the amount of data that could be transmitted. New technologies had increased the available bandwidth. Communication satellites went up almost weekly. Telecommunication companies all over the world vied for their share of the consumer market. A handful of cellular networks now boasted almost 90 percent coverage of the earth's surface.

But these measures were not enough for the world's needs. Every home had at least two phone lines, many had three or more. Every car had a cellular phone, and many downlinked with satellites in geosynchronous orbit for hyper-accurate maps. Virtually every individual carried some kind of personal communications device. Every business computer had at least one phone line.

Add to these cable television, movies on demand, interactive classrooms, direct TV, and satellite-linked teleconferences, and one began to get the picture.

Most of these devices were plugged into GlobeNet, which made the

< jefferson scott >

world's telecommunications grid a prime target for terrorism or sabo-tage.

But that was not why Ethan Hamilton could not log on to GlobeNet right now. He couldn't log on because his service provider, the company whose computers granted him access to GlobeNet, was having "techni-cal difficulties."

He had the house to himself today. Kaye and Katie were at the church, preparing for a friend's wedding, and Jordan was at school. Ethan had been eager to get on-line so he could visit the site where Thumper had been attacked. It was almost comical to him now; how many ways could he be prevented from seeing that site?

The last time he'd spoken with the FBI, Gillette had told him to stay at home, stay accessible, and be ready to move at a moment's notice. That suited Ethan just fine. Since he rarely had the house to himself any-more, Ethan decided to take some time now on a project of his own.

He was creating a world inside his computer. The ultimate world of his dreams. An artificial plane of existence. It was purely medieval, full of castles, forests, mock battles, beasts both kind and fierce, daring knights, foul necromancers, and an eternal war.

He had begun it almost a year ago as something to do one rainy Sunday afternoon. He knew all the programming tools by heart — they were the ones he used at DES — so he was able to work quickly.

The corner towers of a castle had gone up first, with their crene-lated walls and spiral staircases. Then came the ramparts connecting the walls. Next he had constructed the gatehouse, easily the most complex part of the castle. That first day, he had completed all the stonework for the castle and begun work on the wooden buildings within.

He called it Falcon's Grove.

He found himself visiting Falcon's Grove more and more often as the months passed. Every time he went, he built a new room, fashioned a new catapult, or created a new creature. As in GlobeNet, Ethan had his helpers in Falcon's Grove. They were sentries or princesses or min-ions of the Black King. The castle completed, he moved on to the sur-

< virtually eliminated >

rounding demesne and the lands surrounding that: mountain ranges, cave systems, cities, enemy empires.

As the world expanded, so grew its claim on Ethan. Falcon's Grove became his sanctuary, his refuge from stress, fatigue, or frustration.

He didn't want to leave his real life behind. That wasn't it. He didn't think he was using this new world as a drug to escape his life. Why should he? He liked his life. He loved Kaye and Jordan and Katie with all his heart. He enjoyed his job and was good at it. He'd written a book, for goodness' sake. Wasn't that a sign of commitment to the material world?

Still, he loved Falcon's Grove. And he didn't think he had to explain that to anyone. Except Kaye, maybe. But she wasn't around just then.

Jordan loved Falcon's Grove, of course. He had his own domain here, on a faraway island. He was designing it himself. Jordan was less committed to the medieval motif than was his father.

Ethan had even taken Katie in once as a short-term introduction to virtual reality — against Kaye's better judgment. Ethan looked forward to the day when they could have a family excursion into Falcon's Grove.

That was what he was working on now, the spot for their upcoming VR picnic. He called it Katie's Bridge — a picturesque stone bridge crossing a clear mountain river. At least that's what it looked like in VR. Right now it just looked like a bunch of white numbers and letters on a blue computer screen. Ethan was trying to fix a glitch. And for that, he preferred the keyboard to the PowerGlove. Some things were still done better in two dimensions, even in 2005.

When he had tried to cross the bridge for the first time, he had fallen right through. Apparently, he had forgotten to give the bridge the appropriate floor height, even though it looked right. The other problem was that when he had fallen through to the water he hadn't sunk. Somehow the water had lost its permeability. He had probably just forgotten to put a close parenthesis on a formula somewhere.

These were the details about programming that drove most people crazy.

< j e f f e r s o n   s c o t t >

It was almost 1:00 P.M. Crumbs from an inhaled tuna sandwich sprinkled the plate beside the keyboard. Ethan stared at the screen, deep in concentration, chewing on his thumbnail.

He didn't know how many times the vidphone had chimed before he finally became aware of the sound. He had the vague impression that it had been ringing for some time, maybe a full minute. An incoming call would normally cause a notice window to pop up on the screen, but Ethan had toggled all such warning flags off. He had kept his promise to Kaye, however, not to just shunt all calls to the answering software.

He pressed a few keys and the notice window appeared in the upper left of his screen. It read, "Mike Gillette is calling." A few more keystrokes, and Falcon's Grove was saved and closed. Ethan clicked a key, and Gillette's face filled the screen.

"Well, howdy, sleepyhead," Gillette said. "You taking a nap or something?"

Ethan shook his head. It sometimes took him a moment to reorient himself to the real world. "Hi, Mike. I was working on something and I...I kind of get in a zone. It usually takes a minor explosion to get my attention. Sorry."

"No problem. Dallas PD's responding right now to something we might need to check out."

"What is it?"

"A 9-1-1 call said a kid got himself fried jacking around with that vir-tu-al re-al-i-ty. Right here in Dallas, too. Carrollton. How soon can you meet me there?"

Ethan stared at the screen. "Is it okay for me to go? I mean, for me to be there? Won't there be police and an ambulance and stuff?" *And a dead guy.*

"I hope there's an ambulance," Gillette said, "because I ain't touching *nothing*. You ever seen an electrocuted body?"

Ethan shook his head. He seemed to have lost the ability to speak.

"Trust me — you don't want to." Then Gillette smiled. "But don't worry, I'll be there. The medics'll probably have the whole thing cleaned

< virtually eliminated >

up before we even get there. If not, I'll throw a sheet over the kid. It won't be too bad, I promise."

"All right, I guess. Where is it?" Gillette gave him directions. Ethan looked at his watch. "I could be there in about forty minutes."

"Make it more like twenty, will you? I don't want to be too late."

"You want me to speed, Special Agent Gillette? I'm shocked."

"It ain't you that's shocked, Hamilton."

What Gillette hadn't warned Ethan about was the smell. The acrid, smoky odor slapped him as soon as he got out of his minivan, even though he was two houses away. For a confused moment, Ethan's brain said, "Smells like mesquite."

He leaned against the minivan, clasping his mouth shut. His notebook computer dangled limply in his other hand. His phone, clipped to his blue jeans, bounced noisily against the vehicle.

An ambulance was there, fortunately, as were a fire truck, three patrol cars, and several unmarked cars. Even in daylight, all those flashing lights made the residential neighborhood look like an episode of *True Cops*. The sirens were silent except for the one in the fire truck — every now and again it gave a little *rrrrr*.

Channel 4's TV van careened around the corner, pulling onto the sidewalk in front of the house next door. Several police officers moved to block the reporters' entry, while others strung yellow "police line" tape around the well-trimmed front lawn.

The front door opened. Paramedics brought out a stretcher. Ethan watched as if paralyzed. Even from two house-lengths away, he could see how the cover sheet stuck to the body underneath. Police officers and firefighters accompanied the stretcher, clearing the way, carrying cases of medical equipment, or just following. One of the firefighters held a towel to his face.

As they lifted the stretcher into the back of the ambulance, the sheet fell back a little, and Ethan caught a glimpse of the dead boy's face. The

< jefferson scott >

temples were charred like blackened chicken. The stretcher jostled a little, and no mere sheet could hide the stiffness of the claws that had been hands.

"Poor thing," a voice behind Ethan said.

Neighbors stood around Ethan, watching, partly sympathetic, partly curious.

Channel 4's camera crew had elbowed its way to the front and was getting great footage for the five o'clock update. Perhaps they would get an award for their gripping journalism.

A policewoman approached the little cluster of people. "You folks are going to have to make way for the ambulance."

Ethan saw Agent Gillette come out onto the front porch and look around. Ethan walked up to the officer. "Excuse me, ma'am, but I think I need to get in there. I'm supposed —"

"No one in without a badge, sir."

He lifted his notebook computer to her, as if that was some kind of proof. "I know, but I'm working with the FBI as a —"

"Sure you are, sir. And I'm on special assignment for the pope, but you still can't get in." She had a hand on his arm. A mental image came to Ethan, quite unexpectedly, of this woman flipping him over her back onto the ground.

"It's all right, darlin'," Gillette said, arriving at a trot. He showed his identification. "He's with me."

As Gillette escorted him toward the house, Ethan stifled the impulse to give the policewoman a big wet raspberry. She was only doing her job, after all. He asked God to forgive his pettiness.

Then he asked God to give him strength.

The mesquite smell was much stronger inside the house. Police and fire officers paraded in and out. For the most part, though, it seemed the action here was over. The paramedics collected the last of their supplies, then drove the ambulance away — no siren. The police seemed on their way out as well.

Gillette took Ethan through the middle-class living room and down

< virtually eliminated >

a hall. They had to step in the kitchen doorway to let the last firefighter by. Ethan saw the man's face as he passed. He'd never seen the man before, but he nevertheless knew he was controlling some kind of emotion only with difficulty. He passed by quickly, carrying a portable fire extinguisher.

Behind him, Ethan looked across the kitchen and into the den beyond. A plain-clothes policeman sat on a couch with a middle-aged woman, filling out a report of some kind. A little girl, about six, sat in her lap. The woman looked up and met Ethan's eyes.

Ethan wanted to do something, to say something that would take away the dullness he saw there — or at the very least to shield himself from it.

"That's the mother," Gillette said from the hallway. "And the kid sister."

Ethan nodded, unable to break the eye-lock.

"Come on," Gillette said gently. "Let's take a look."

Patriot was in.

He had breached DES security with the help of data provided by the sniffer. He was now, as far as the DES file server was concerned, a trusted user. The company's entire directory structure lay open before him. Scant moments after he had been granted access, he had found the location of Ethan Hamilton's computers. He was ready to begin the final assault.

It was a pity about the Feathers boy. He had been a good resource. Patriot might yet have cause to wish for his services. The sniffer his late friend had planted brought in gigabytes of useless information for every meg Patriot could use. But Patriot had not eliminated Feathers for sloppy work. He simply could allow no possible avenue for anyone or anything to interfere with the Plan.

C'est la vie, he thought. Or should he say, *C'est le guerre*?

More than twenty cubes rotated in the air before him, like dice

< jefferson scott >

eternally tossed. These represented the directories and subdirectories of Digital Environment Specialists.

In the patient hours of the night and morning, Patriot had listened in on the "conversations" carried on between the computers on the DES network. He had managed to match most of the callsigns the programmers went by with their actual names. He had stopped playing this match game, however, when he had been certain he had identified Ethan Hamilton.

He selected the rotating cube labeled "Curly." The cubes vanished.

Patriot beheld his last obstacle. And faltered. The beast before him was hideous. Tall, brown, horned. Dark eyes peered through him. It was cruel, almost, how difficult Patriot knew this last security measure was going to be to defeat. This Hamilton, curse him, was going to pay.

It was Bullwinkle.

Gillette led Ethan to the room at the end of the hallway. The boy's room. An unmade bed, clothes on the floor in the corner, posters of heavy-metal bands on the wall, a computer on a desk under the window. Ethan wondered if this was what Jordan's room was going to look like in a few years.

Two people were in the room with them. A young man with a camera, capturing the room on video, and a fortysomething Hispanic woman with a notepad. The woman made measurements with a tape ruler, then wrote them down.

The videographer clicked his camera off and looked at Gillette and Ethan. His face was pale green.

"What's the matter, kid?" Gillette prodded. "Forget your smell-a-vision camera?"

"Shut up." His voice lacked conviction.

The woman looked up from her note taking. "Did you get the exit points, Chad?"

"Yes, I got the stupid exit points. I got the exit points, the entry

< virtually eliminated >

device, the fried computer, and the chair. I even got what was left of his stupid shoes after they got blown off his feet. May I be excused now, Miss Stomach-of-Steel? I have to go throw up."

"Chad." She spoke very softly. She still hadn't acknowledged Gillette or Ethan. "Turn the camera on and get one more shot of the exit points."

"Yes, ma'am." Chad turned the camera on and focused on the floor beneath the desk.

Ethan whispered to Gillette. "Who are they?"

"Ident Techs," he said, too loudly.

The woman looked up sharply. "Can I help you boys?" But her tone said, *When will you be leaving?*

Gillette had his badge out. "FBI, Miss…?"

"Espinoza." She looked disappointed that Gillette really did have a right to be in the room. She went back to her notes. "What's federal about this boy's death, Mr. Gillette?"

"Don't know yet, ma'am." He stepped into the room and knelt on the floor beside the photographer. "Take a look at this, Hamilton."

Ethan ducked below the computer, which had once been off-white, but now, thanks to smoke and fire extinguisher foam, was an oozing two-tone. On the carpet directly beneath the desk were two black burns. "What are they?"

Espinoza spoke without looking up. "Exit points from an electrical charge in excess of 100,000 volts." She indicated her notepad. "And, judging from the body and the fact that his clothes were blasted off, I'd say it was closer to a million."

Ethan looked at her. "How could his clothes be blasted off?"

"Weirdest thing you ever seen, man," Chad said.

Espinoza examined the edges of a poster on the wall opposite the computer desk. She spoke casually, as if she did this kind of thing all the time. Maybe she did.

"The heat generated by lightning converts any sweat on the body to steam, which instantly expands."

< jefferson scott >

"Oh." Ethan thought the room smelled less and less like mesquite.

"Blew his socks right off, man," Chad said.

"So those marks on the carpet…"

"Are where the charge exited his body," Espinoza said. "Exit points." She made a final, decisive mark on her notepad. "All right, Chad, I'm through. Let's get back to the office."

"About time." Chad grabbed his camera case and fled out the door. Espinoza followed, but not without favoring Gillette and Ethan with a stern look.

When they had gone, Gillette swept a hand toward the computer on the desk. "Go ahead."

Ethan peered around the back of the unit at the blackened connections and cables. Power cables were still plugged in to a perfectly operational multi-plug power strip. The plug's faceplate showed no damage whatsoever. *Strange*, he thought.

One shredded cable snaked around front to a VR headset. It looked homemade. "Was he—" Ethan began, but faltered.

Gillette was looking at the pile of clothes in the corner. "Yeah, he was wearing it when the spike came through. Made a handy little closed circuit, too. Poor chump never knew what hit him. Say, look at this." Gillette held up a one-piece uniform of some kind and a heavy toolbelt. "This kid some kind of plumber or something?" He pulled up a coil of fiber optic cable. "Maybe a cable TV repairman. Looks like he was into electronics, whatever it was. Went out like he'd a wanted to, I suppose."

For the first time Ethan noticed an overturned office chair on the floor against the closet door. An image came to his mind of this teenage boy hooked up to VR when the power surge hit. He saw the boy's paralysis, his smoking temples, his exploding sweat, the escaping charge. The body thrown across the room.

The image burned into his mind. He sat on the bed and squeezed his eyes shut, but still the image remained, chasing him behind his eyes into his subconscious.

Gillette was saying something. "— out what happened, what the kid was doing that got somebody this mad."

"What?"

"What's the matter, Hamilton? You in that zone again?"

"I guess."

"Well I need you to be the computer expert now. Can't you figure out what this kid was doing when he bit it?"

"What, on this?" Ethan looked at the burned-out computer. "I guess I could take the hard drive home and try to get something out of it. Take his CDs, see if he backed up anything." At the thought, Ethan's stomach, already sour, threatened to empty its contents on the carpet. "It looks like he was using his VR headset when the surge came in. Probably in some kind of VR application or game."

"Any fool can see that, Hamilton. What I want to know is *what* application or game, *who* he was doing it with, *where* they live, *why* this kid had to be knocked off, and whether it did or did not have anything to do with our investigation."

Ethan was about to tell this FBI agent that you couldn't ask questions of a fried computer any more than you could of a fried person, when his cellular phone rang.

He grabbed it off his belt and looked at the caller ID. It wasn't a regular caller, there was no name. Instead, a message began to scroll across the little display, B-O-R-I-S. Ethan watched, transfixed, as the letters marched by, A-N-D — N-A-T-A-S-H-A.

Someone was trying to break into his computer at work — had gotten, in fact, all the way to the last level. The program had only one defense left.

Ethan switched his phone to dial mode and made a call. This time, he was going to catch Camillo red-handed.

"Denise, this is Ethan. Is — fine, thanks. Listen, is Camillo around?"

Ethan looked up. Gillette wasn't watching; he was inspecting what looked like a theatrical makeup kit.

"How long has he been in the meeting?" He consulted his watch. "No, it's okay, thanks. Listen Denise, when they get out of their meeting,

< jefferson scott >

would you tell Mr. Tarkenton that somebody's trying to hack my computer there? Thanks. I'll see what I can find out from my end. Maybe we can catch this punk before he even knows we're onto him. Bye."

He smashed down the antenna and threw the phone on the bed. Then he ripped open his notebook computer and sat down.

Gillette looked up then. "What's gotten into you?"

Ethan didn't look up. "Somebody's trying to break into my computer. *Nobody* breaks into my computer." He initiated a GlobeNet link and put on his portable VR headset.

"Nobody."

< virtually eliminated >

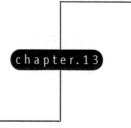

chapter.13

WHERE WAS ROCKY THE SQUIRREL when you needed him?

Bullwinkle stood in the center of his little stage, bound and gagged. If the situation hadn't been so serious, Ethan might have laughed. The sad brown eyes tracked Ethan as he approached.

"Who did this to you, old pal?"

Ethan scanned the dark theater; no sign of any intruders here now. He checked the door at the back of the synthetic stage. It was still locked. He walked back out to Bullwinkle.

"Couldn't get by you, could he? So he did this." Ethan inspected the ties. "A good job, too. Whoever it was must've been pretty —" He saw something white nestled between Bullwinkle's horns. "What's this?"

It appeared to be a note. But when Ethan plucked it from the antler, he saw it was the trigger for a video clip of some kind.

He activated the clip. The note icon flew from Ethan's hands and morphed into a little movie screen. It looked like the old canvas his dad used to show slides on.

A flickering black and white image appeared on the screen, file footage of an atomic explosion. Over the low rumble of the bomb and

< j e f f e r s o n   s c o t t >

the hiss and pop of old optical sound, a newsreel-style narrator spoke. "And then, in the summer of 1945, America blasted the sands of New Mexico with its first atom bomb."

ETHAN HAMILTON.

His name flashed on the screen, then off, mixing almost subliminally with the mushroom cloud.

WHAT ARE YOU HIDING?

The blast billowed and rumbled.

TRAITOR.

News footage of other famous disasters flickered on the screen. The Hindenburg, Challenger...

ETHAN HAMILTON.

...Mount Saint Helens, a Nazi death camp, the Oklahoma City bombing....

I WILL GET YOU.

A newspaper photo of a dead black girl filled the screen. It seemed oddly familiar to Ethan. Where had he seen it before? This was replaced by a magazine photo of a murdered bureaucrat. Next was a picture of an electrocuted Oriental astronaut. Some managers at a defense contractor. Then a college girl from the University of Nebraska.

The images changed faster and faster, until they began to blur together in a morbid montage. Ethan's mind registered three or four other familiar photographs.

The montage stopped. A video clip began. It jarred Ethan when he realized what it was. Paramedics wheeled out a stretcher from a middle-class home. A firefighter held a towel to his face. As they lifted the stretcher into the back of the ambulance, the sheet fell back a little, revealing blackened temples.

The screen went blank.

Ethan almost took off his portable VR gear. That was footage from today, outside this very house.

There were too many connections to sort out.

First. The person who had been hacking Ethan's computer knew

< virtually eliminated >

about Ray Feathers's electrocution. The clip he had just pulled from Bullwinkle's horns was of the Feathers's house. This hacker, then, had to be considered a suspect for Feathers's killer.

Second. The person who hacked Ethan's computer knew about the other electrocutions as well. The montage.

Ethan's mind struggled against the complexity of the knot. He'd never been very good at logic puzzles. That was Kaye's realm.

Third and last. The person who knew about Ray Feathers's electrocution, who also knew about the other electrocutions, was the person who was trying to break into Ethan's computer. Full circle.

Ethan felt as though he was falling into a pit. He reached to pull his headset off. A familiar image appeared on the screen, halting him. It was Ethan's author photo from the flap of his new book. A woman's voice — only faintly artificial-sounding — began to recite.

"Ethan John Hamilton. Age — thirty-five. Chief systems analyst, Digital Environment Specialists. Married fourteen years. Spouse —" Kaye's driver's license photo flashed on the screen. It was an unfortunate photo, even in Ethan's opinion. "—Kaye Simms Hamilton. Age — thirty-four. Housewife. Daughter — Katherine Elizabeth Hamilton —"

Katie's little face filled the screen. It appeared to be a detail of the family picture in their most recent on-line church directory.

It was an eerie presentation. *This Is Your Life* planned and executed by a stranger. Who was it who knew so much about him and his family?

"Age — eighteen months. Delivered in distress. Hyperbilirubinemia. Cholecystitis."

Another photo of Katie, newly born, appeared. An IV stuck in her head because they couldn't find a vein. Yellow skin. Blue lights. In a clear plastic box — the incubator — that helped her heal, but held Ethan away from his baby girl.

Ethan's vision blurred. Who could've gotten this photo? Any of these photos, for that matter.

Didn't this pit have a bottom?

Ethan became aware of a new sound. It was a soft buzz, like a

< jefferson scott >

swarm of killer bees approaching from a distance.

The screen went blank.

Suddenly the dark theater was full of what looked like sparks from a bonfire. Orange and yellow points of light swirled around Ethan and Bullwinkle like a flock of birds moving together by some secret communication.

The buzzing sound tugged at Ethan's mind. There was meaning in it, whispered words, from a thousand babbling voices. As he listened, the voices coalesced into a raspy chant.

"Don't you have a son?"

The sparks vanished with a *whish.* A single prick of yellow light flicked on briefly as it crossed the theater. The way the light blinked on and off struck Ethan as odd. It didn't look like a spark, after all, its flight was too regular. It looked more like a glow-in-the-dark bee. Almost like a firefly.

"Don't you have a son?"

Ethan hit bottom.

He tore his headset off and looked at his watch — 3:35. Jordan's ride usually got him home just before four. Ethan was in Dallas, in rush hour — forty-five minutes away, at least, from their Fort Worth home.

Why hadn't he listened to his son? Jordan said he was meeting someone in cyberspace today just as soon as he got home from school. He said he was going to hurry home so he could get on-line.

So he could play the firefly guy.

Jordan Hamilton's day began, as far as he was concerned, when he got home from school and ended when he had to turn the computer off at night. His bookbag lay on the game room floor beside his chair. Exactly ninety-six seconds had elapsed between the moment he had unlocked the front door and the moment he had entered cyberspace.

He'd been thinking about this all day. This man in black, this firefly guy, had scared him last night. But not now. Now he knew how he

< virtually eliminated >

wanted to square off against him and how he was going to triumph.

He shuttled all incoming phone calls to the answering software, just like his dad had taught him, and initiated the Venue Texas link. He hoped his opponent would allow him to choose the game and battlefield, because he had it all planned out.

He booted *Starfield Warriors,* his favorite VR game, and chose the surface of Mars for his battlefield. For himself he chose the guise of a Sand Sniper, a fast-running, quick-firing character. Jordan's entire strategy was based on speed.

The orange Martian desert stretched out before him. Olympus Mons, on the horizon, blotted out almost half of Phobos. Jordan walked over to a windswept sand dune and sat down, staring up at the stars. Up to now he'd been hoping the firefly guy would delay, to allow him to get set up. But now that he was finished he wished the guy would hurry up already.

"Ah, the bringer of war."

Jordan sprang to his feet. Where had the voice come from? Then above him he saw his opponent floating down to the Martian surface like a vulture descending on a carcass.

Okay, Jordan thought. Showtime.

"You're going to get us killed, Hamilton!" Special Agent Mike Gillette lunged for his seatbelt after Ethan ran a definitely red light. "What's gotten into you?"

Everything was moving too slowly. Why didn't they get out of his way? "Move! Move!" Ethan shouted at the traffic ahead of him. He swerved his minivan through a gas station, pulled across two lanes of traffic, made a U-turn, crossed two more lanes, then turned right on red to get onto the access road for I-35.

"Hoo-dawg!" Gillette shouted, laughing. "Hamilton's got himself a Batmobile!"

Ethan punched the air-conditioner off to accelerate faster. Still his

< jefferson scott >

family car knocked, gaining speed only reluctantly. He threw his cellular phone into Gillette's lap. "Call this number, 817/2 —"

"I'm not calling diddly till you tell me what's going on."

"Call the number, Mike." Ethan looked at him. Gillette saw his entire body was clenched. "Please, Mike. My boy…"

"Okay, okay. You just — look out!"

Ethan swerved, passing the rush hour queue by pulling onto the shoulder.

Gillette swore. "Watch what you're doing!"

"Dial the number!"

Ethan gave Gillette his home number, and Gillette dialed. "Nobody home, Hamilton. Answering machine picked it up."

Someone else thought of the shoulder trick and pulled out in front of the minivan. Ethan slammed on his brakes. "How could I be so stupid to teach him that?"

"I've seen plenty of people drive on the shoulder, Hamilton."

"Not that! I taught Jordan how to send calls to the answering machine so his games wouldn't be interrupted."

"Jordan's your son?"

"He's home all right. And he's on-line. Try it again. Can't you get the operator to break in on calls? You're the FBI."

"Why you want to cut in on your kid's game? I don't get it, Hamilton."

The car in front of them was going dangerously fast now, almost 50 mph on a narrow shoulder. But it wasn't nearly fast enough for Ethan. "Get out of the way!"

Other drivers, themselves frustrated by the traffic jam and the hot Texas afternoon, honked and shot crude gestures at them as they passed. I-35 was close, but looked packed, even from here.

"There *is* a Mr. Computer Psycho out there," Ethan said.

"That's your theory."

"He killed that boy at the house back there."

"Why do you say that?"

< virtually eliminated >

"He also did the Chinese astronaut, the defense contractor managers, and all the rest."

"You getting enough air, boy? Turn that AC back on."

Ethan whacked the steering wheel, accidentally honking the horn. "I was right, Gillette. I've been right the whole time. There's a guy out there and he's killing people. And now he's after me."

"Watch that truck!"

"Only I guess my security was too good for him at work. Made him mad. So he's going for Jordan."

"That was *him*? You're telling me the guy that tried to break into your work computer just now is the guy we're trying to find? The guy who did poor boy Feathers? Give it a rest, Hamilton. Why would he be looking for you?"

"What I can't figure out is why he didn't take a shot at Jordan last night."

"Wait a minute." Gillette braced himself against the dashboard. "If what you're saying is true, and this guy's a legit threat... You say he's after your son? He's trying to fry your kid — he's on the phone with him right now!"

"What do you think I've been trying to tell you?"

Gillette's face turned grim. "What's your problem, Hamilton — you're going too slow. Step on it!"

Gillette rolled down his window and stuck his head out. "Get out of the way, you heifers! Get out of the way!" He sat back down and dialed into the phone. "Let's get us some forces mobilized here." He turned to Ethan.

"Don't worry, Ethan, buddy. We're going to pop this guy."

< jefferson scott >

chapter. 14

"YOU SURE YOU DON'T WANT to pick somebody?" Jordan asked.

His opponent wanted to play in his black robes. That spooked Jordan. He'd already seen the guy fly in those robes. His strategy hadn't accounted for someone more mobile than he.

"There's this great Battlemech called Samson. I wouldn't stand a chance against you if you used that." That wasn't precisely true. The Samson Battlemech had firepower out the ears, but it was slower than a Pentium. As a Sand Sniper, Jordan could beat any slow opponent.

"No," the firefly guy said. He stood atop an orange boulder, his black robes billowing in the Martian wind. He wore a hood over his face. He looked like a warlock on some dumb Halloween picture.

"Okay," Jordan allowed. "What about weapons?"

A black-gloved hand emerged from hidden sleeves, holding a wicked-looking rifle of some kind. Jordan thought he saw a golden sight on the end of the barrel. "The truth is often a terrible weapon of aggression," he said. "It is possible to lie, and even to murder, for the truth."

"Whatever." Maybe this wasn't going to be as easy a victory as Jordan had been hoping for. "Okay," he said, "you know the rules?"

< virtually eliminated >

"I think I have this, of all games, figured out, Jordan."

"It's not fair you know my name but I don't know yours. You want me to keep calling you the firefly guy?"

The firefly guy didn't answer for a moment. "Why call me that?"

Jordan was sorry he'd asked. This was taking too long. His mom would be home any minute, and she'd want him to turn off the game to do homework. "Because that little yellow light of yours looked like a firefly the first time I saw you. Can we play now?"

The black hood dipped slightly. "As you wish. Commence at your discretion."

Jordan dive-rolled over the nearest sand dune. His rival's voice crackled in on his speakers. He sounded far away and weak.

"I suppose I might tell you my name before we begin. I would like someone to know me. I did not know how lonely the path I have chosen would be. 'If a man could mount to heaven and survey the mighty universe,' Cicero wrote, 'his admiration of its beauties would be much diminished unless he had someone to share in his pleasure.'"

Jordan giggled. He knew this trick. Try to keep your opponent talking; mess with his mind while you move in for the kill. Jordan wasn't going to fall for it. Maybe he could even turn it on his adversary. "That's dumb."

"Perhaps. Cicero also said 'There is nothing so absurd but some philosopher has said it.'"

"Cicero said this, Cicero said that. Don't you ever say anything nobody's ever said before?"

The man in black didn't answer. Jordan thought he might have spotted his flanking action and was moving to intercept. But a peek over a dune showed his foe hadn't budged.

When he finally spoke, he sounded almost sad. "You are too young, Jordan, to understand. Sometimes a man can find himself in the lives and words of others. The sayings I utter belong to other men and women, it is true; but their amalgamation is wholly mine."

"Whatever."

< jefferson scott >

"That was an astute question, young man. I shall have to compliment you to your father when next I see him. In the meantime, I have promised to divulge my name to you, Jordan, and that I will do. I am called Patriot."

"What kind of name is that?"

"A good name, I think. A respectable name."

Jordan had flanked his enemy and was almost in position. He loved the Sand Sniper's speed. "Patriot? That's not a real name. Why don't you call me 'Bowl of Cereal'?"

"You want my *real* name? Hmm. I suppose I could, since you are not likely to be in the position to tell anyone. No one has ever asked me before."

Jordan was directly behind Patriot now. He activated his heat-seeking missile array and targeted it. He wasn't really listening. "Uh-huh."

"My real name, Jordan John Hamilton, is Louis Parks. Louis David Parks."

Jordan locked in his targeting solution and smiled. "Eat plutonium, Louis." He fired.

Patriot's body disappeared in a cloud of fire, smoke, and Martian sand.

Jordan didn't stay to watch. He didn't know what kind of armor or shielding his foe might have. He left his missile array, still firing, behind him, and darted to his next defensive position.

Patriot watched him, seeing effortlessly through the smoke, the fire, even the planet itself. He liked this boy, this Jordan Hamilton.

Such a pity.

Kaye longed for the day when Katie could keep up when they walked. Just getting into the mall was an ordeal. There was the stroller, the diaper bag, her purse, and, of course, Katie. She was loaded down before they ever went shopping, and heaven help them all if Kaye ever bought anything.

< virtually eliminated >

Kaye had bought something.

Katie was walking well enough, but her little legs were no match for her mother's. Especially when they were in a hurry.

Kaye's Sunday school class was having a fellowship this weekend and, as usual, she somehow found herself in charge of it all. She'd had to pick up some gift certificates and other paraphernalia here at the mall to be given away as door prizes.

But now she wanted to get home to start dinner. In this day of microwave meals and prefab desserts, Kaye still cooked her family's dinner in the oven. Besides, she knew Jordan needed to get started on his homework.

"Chuck!"

Kaye held her hand over her eyes, searching for their car. "We're not in a truck, honey. Daddy took the van. We're in the blue car."

Katie pointed at the nearby highway. She was insistent. "Chuck!"

"Oh, I see them now." An ambulance screamed by on the highway, soon followed by two police cars. Somehow, Katie had come to associate sirens and flashing lights with the word *chuck*. "That's good, honey. Ambulance."

"Chuck!"

Kaye spotted their car. Up on the highway, a fire engine roared by. "Somebody must be hurt. We can pray for them, Katie."

Katie put her hands together and prayed.

Ethan prayed, too.

Father, help me get there in time. Please, Lord, protect Jordan. He's in Your hands now. You're the only one who can protect him. Please, Lord Jesus.

"….their way."

Ethan looked at Gillette. "I'm sorry. What?"

"I said I've got the police, the fire department, and an ambulance on their way to your house. In just about two minutes, your neighborhood's in for it big time." Gillette looked at the clock on the minivan's

< jefferson scott >

dashboard. "It's just four now. Maybe he's not even home yet."

Ethan left Airport Freeway six exits before the one nearest his home, hoping to bypass the rush hour stack by staying on the access road. They had made it to I-35 all right, and the transition to 635. Now they were in Fort Worth, leaving 121 at Central.

They pulled to the red light at Central. The access road before them — across one simple intersection — was clear. Ethan judged he could reach 80 mph before he would have to slow down. He might just make it home in time, after all. He started to pull through the light.

And was halted as two motorcycle policemen sped by with their headlights on. A line of cars stretched back under the overpass as far as Ethan could see. All with their lights on.

Jordan was having the time of his life. He circled Patriot, showering him with automatic weapons fire, rockets, plasma, wooden arrows, rocks. Patriot endured it silently, like a black statue left by some long-extinct Martian civilization.

"Boy, are you bad!" Jordan said. "I've never beat anybody this bad. Not even when Gramma played me last Thanksgiving. I've racked up so many points you'll never catch up. I thought you were going to be tough."

Jordan's first barrage of missiles had left Patriot unscathed. Jordan had then launched his second attack, this one with anti-matter mortars. Also to no effect.

Not even the effect of rousing his opponent to action.

He'd gradually gotten bolder and bolder, staying extra long in the open, running dangerously close to shoot, standing directly in front of his foe, taunting him. It became clear that this guy, this Louis Parks, was not going to play right. That was fine with Jordan, Sand Sniper extraordinaire. Direct hits scored the same whether they did damage or not. He couldn't wait to tell his dad he'd topped the one million mark in *Starfield Warriors*. Talk about your bragging rights.

< virtually eliminated >

The black figure came to life.

Jordan shrieked and scampered for cover. Maybe his enemy was finally going to do something. If this Patriot's weapon was as good as his armor and shielding, Jordan had better find a very good hiding place.

Patriot was finally ready. It had taken longer than expected to call together the requisite power for the surge. The program he had initiated to generate it had failed to access a credit card number when it had needed one. Apparently, someone had erased the huge data safe house he had set up on a KKK man's service provider. He would have to punish the offender. With extreme prejudice.

He poured his frustration over the lost data files into his anger toward Ethan Hamilton. Patriot was uncharacteristically troubled by the decision to eliminate Jordan, so he used every means at his disposal to harden his resolve. Ethan had defeated him twice now, first with a lizard and second with a moose. Humiliating defeats. He must be punished.

Besides, now Jordan knew Patriot's real name. Ray Feathers had died for far less than that.

The power surge, coming this time from Portugal, lay beneath the trigger of his rifle. He knew, further, from the police frequencies he monitored, that it would behoove him to complete his task with alacrity.

"I believe," he said casually, "that it is now my turn." He raised his rifle.

Jordan heard something strange from beneath his helmet. He felt Wysiwyg, who had crawled into his lap, penetrate his thigh with her claws and dive off. "Wait a minute. Ouch! What's that noise?"

"The sound, perhaps, of Death's chariot?"

"No, I think there's something going on here, at my house."

Patriot saw — peering straight through an artificial Martian boulder — the Sand Sniper's hands go to his head. "Wait, Jordan! Don't jack out!"

"But I think there's siren —"

"Jordan."

< jefferson scott >

"Yes, sir?"

"Do you wish to forfeit our game?"

"No."

"Then let us continue."

"But —"

"Jordan."

"Okay."

The hands came back down.

"Pay, pay, pay, Mommy!" Katie was wild, thrashing in her car seat as if she was drowning.

"What is wrong with you, child?" Kaye risked a look over her shoulder into the back seat. "We can pray when we get home, Katie. We're almost there."

"Pay, pay, pay!"

Kaye turned onto their street. "What's all this?" A fire truck stood in the street near their house. Firemen in tan coats ran about, pulling out hoses, racing to the door with axes.

To their door.

Kaye sat at the corner, transfixed. This wasn't happening to her house, was it? She didn't see any smoke.

A van careened around the corner, missing their car by inches. The driver gunned the engine, driving over the neighbors' yard, up to their own front door.

"Daddy, Daddy."

"It *is* him," Kaye gasped. "Oh, no, Jordan!"

Ethan dove out of the minivan. One of the firemen with an ax turned to intercept him. "Wait," Ethan said, "I've got the key!"

Gillette slammed the van door and ran around, flashing his badge.

Ethan fumbled with his keys. His fingers felt like clubs.

< virtually eliminated >

A car screeched to a stop at the curb. Kaye kicked the car door open. "Ethan!"

Ethan dropped his keys into the flowers beside the porch. He saw the paramedics open the ambulance doors. He had a sudden vision of Jordan being rolled out on a stretcher, claws for hands, blackened forehead.

"Break it! Break it!"

"Ethan! O Father, please!" Kaye cried. "O Father."

Katie shrieked, still shackled to her car seat.

"Jordan," Ethan shouted at the second story window. "Get off the computer!"

"Do it!" Gillette yelled.

The firemen hewed at the door.

Jordan was radically exposed. Everything inside him screamed, "Run, RUN, RUN!"

He ran.

He dropped his weapons. Took off scrambling over orange dunes. In a line directly away from Patriot.

He felt Patriot's gun pointed at his back.

The Sand Sniper bobbed above the gold sight on the end of Patriot's rifle.

"Wait for me across that river, Jordan. I will be joining you there soon."

He pulled the trigger.

The surge sprang after Jordan at the speed of light.

Jordan felt it coming.

Dove for cover.

And was thrown back hard against the floor.

Tearing at his ears, scalp, temples.

A flash of light.

Thunderclap.

< j e f f e r s o n   s c o t t >

Smoke everywhere. Something burning. Heat.
Nothing.

It hit like a bomb. The explosion demolished every piece of electronics in the room. Set the wall on fire.

Everyone shouted at once. Gillette kicked pieces of debris away from where Ethan covered his son's body. Firemen pushed through, blowing clouds of white smoke at the electrical fire. In the hallway, a smoke alarm screamed its faithful warning.

Kaye shoved her way up the stairs into the game room. She saw her husband and son on the floor. "O dear Lord, no." She fell at their side, sobbing.

Ethan lifted his son's inert body from the charred carpet and carried him into his bedroom.

"Medic!" Gillette shouted down the stairs.

Ethan lay Jordan on his bed, the boy's head cradled in Kaye's lap. "Jordan?" He shook his son.

Kaye looked up sharply. "Katie! I've left Katie in the car!"

"We'll take care of it, ma'am," Gillette said. He nodded to a police officer, who headed down the stairs. The fire was out now.

"Jordan? Jordan!" Ethan's face was fierce. "Wake up, son."

Wysiwyg, her tail puffed out from all the noise, jumped up from her hiding place and licked Jordan on the forehead.

Jordan moaned and stirred.

Kaye sobbed.

Paramedics came in. Ethan got up to let them work. The cat bolted under the bed.

Ethan walked out to the devastated game room, staring at the foam-drenched wreckage. So similar to Ray Featherss's room. Gillette said something, but he didn't hear.

Ethan picked up an ax, stepped out into the hallway, and with a single swing silenced the smoke alarm.

< virtually eliminated >

He advanced on Gillette, still hefting the ax. Gillette backed up.

"You give me what I tell you" — Ethan snarled the words —"and I will *STOP* the man who did this!"

< Part II >

Anger is a brief madness.

HORACE, EPISTLES

■

< virtually eliminated >

chapter.15

LINDA HAHN — SHE WENT BY HER MAIDEN NAME now — wanted to go to Jamaica. She hadn't gone anywhere in the twelve years since the divorce. No vacations, no weekends out, not even day trips. Her friends told her she needed to get away from it all, and she knew they were right. Now that she'd met Todd it seemed the perfect time to go.

But how could she? How could she leave her baby all alone in that sickbed of his? Wasn't switching back to her maiden name after all these years enough of a sign of independence?

That, however, was not what stood in her way now. Yes, she felt terrible about leaving him. And, no, it wasn't fair that she could go jaunting off to the Caribbean and he couldn't. What held her back now was that she would have to ask her son, her baby, lying in the bed to which he was eternally confined, for the money for the trip.

He handled all their money. Had done so, in fact, since soon after returning from the clinic. What was that, thirteen years ago now? She'd had other worries at the time.

Like a disintegrating marriage. She deserved it, that voice kept hissing, after what she had done.

< jefferson scott >

Another voice had risen in her consciousness quite recently. A voice that said she'd been punished amply. A voice that said she wasn't over the hill yet — she still had almost five more years before the half century mark, that she was still attractive, still desirable. A voice that said she'd been shackled to that blasted sickbed, blaming herself, long enough. When Todd — young, beautiful Todd — mentioned Jamaica, that voice had all but roared.

Even the place names had rhythm. Montego Bay. Maroon Town. Port Maria. Just saying them made her feel she might actually be able to sing Reggae. She couldn't remember the last time she'd sung at all.

Yes, she could. It was in that white-white hospital room with the yellow curtains. Blue-green fluorescent lights. Bandages. Beeping instruments. Sucking tubes. Bars over the bed like a cage. She had sung to her little boy then. His favorite lullaby. He was as helpless then as when he had been a baby, though he was nine.

There was nothing more the doctors could do. Even with all her husband's money. They had done the best they could. It wasn't their fault, really.

It was her fault.

No one said it, of course. No one had to. She had been driving, hadn't she? She had run the light, hadn't she? She and no one else had moved her son's broken body from the wreckage. Only now they told her that move was what had made the injuries permanent. Her heroic, tearful act.

"Keep him comfortable," was the best the experts could offer.

Yes, that was the last time she had ever sung.

She stared at her boy now. Twenty-five years old. His whole life ahead of him. Some life, she thought.

He was on the computer, of course, so he didn't know she was in the room. It wasn't like any computer she'd ever seen, though that wasn't saying much. There was no TV screen. Just some white boxes on the floor against the wall. They looked like part of his medical equipment. In fact, she wasn't sure where the medical machines in this bedroom stopped and the computer began.

< virtually eliminated >

Where was that idiot William, anyway? Late, as usual. She wondered if even he, their full-time medical technician, could tell her what was what. *He'd rather read his disgusting paperbacks than watch my son, anyway.*

Instead of the traditional computer monitor, her son used some kind of device that went over his eyes like a blind person's black glasses. Why not add blindness to the list, too? They were virtual reality glasses, he had explained once. Whatever that meant.

They'd gotten him into computers at the clinic. Somehow they could hook his brain to the computers so he could control things. He'd ridden around the room in a wheelchair once, using their implants. It seemed to make him happy. When he came home, they set him up with a system of his own.

That was about the time her husband took his leave from the family. She couldn't blame him. Who wanted to be stuck with a hag and a cripple? What had she ever seen in that lout, anyway, besides his money? Thirteen years of her life — her best years — wasted.

Christmas that year was grim. Her family helped a little. She remembered reading up on those poor, incapacitated souls who painted with their toes and their mouths. Surely her son could achieve what those kids could. She bought him art supplies for Christmas.

But he didn't want art supplies. He wanted computer supplies. A more powerful computer, some specific software, and a special phone line. She refused. She didn't want to spend their precious reserves on expensive computers for an invalid. In her heart of hearts, she didn't think he'd ever amount to much now.

He told her not to worry about the price. Apparently, he'd gotten some kind of job on that Global Net thing. Money wasn't going to be a problem now, he had assured her.

Boxes had started to arrive almost immediately. Men came and installed it all, though she'd never so much as placed a phone call. Other people came, again appearing out of the blue, to do special modifications. She hadn't remembered actually giving her son permission to order any of it.

< jefferson scott >

Thinking back on it, Linda realized that was probably the first sign that their relationship was forever altered.

She never did see a bill for it all. Whatever job he had was certainly lucrative. For some reason she couldn't identify, she was reluctant to ask him what it was he did. Never mind. Perhaps computers just weren't as expensive as she thought.

It wasn't long after that before he asked to take over the book-keeping. He said money was electronic anyway, so why not let him pay all the bills electronically? Once he proved he was quite capable, Linda was happy to let him have it. She wasn't very good at it.

The problem with it all was that now she had to ask her child for the money to go to Jamaica to copulate with a man half her age. Maybe she wouldn't ask him, after all. Why should she, anyway? She was a grown woman — his *mother*, for crying out loud.

Maybe she wouldn't even tell him she was going.

"Whoa, mighty Nerfblatt!" Ethan shouted over the wind. "Not so fast, girl."

Soaring high over a primeval forest astride a fire-breathing dragon was, for most people, pure fantasy — something out of a movie or a dream. But for a sorcerer adept in the black art of virtual reality, it was a commonplace thing.

Why he had named his ferocious, green-scaled monster *Nerfblatt* was a matter beyond even his own discerning. Something about not taking himself too seriously.

Ethan banked his winged mount for another pass over the approach to Falcon's Grove Castle. It had to appear normal from all angles. He didn't know how his adversary would come upon it — if he came at all.

Ethan was fairly convinced he would. Surely he knew by now that his electric spike had missed Jordan. He had access to the local news and obituaries, in which Jordan's name had not appeared. His foe had

< virtually eliminated >

been so careful thus far, so thorough, that Ethan believed he would seek to tie off this loose end.

Especially since he'd told Jordan his name. What kind of patriot goes around killing people? Killing children?

It didn't surprise Ethan that he could find no sign of the username Patriot on GlobeNet.

His real name, Louis David Parks (if Jordan's memory could be trusted) wasn't much help, either. There were five possibilities in Fort Worth alone. What were the odds this international serial killer lived in the same nation, much less same city? Gillette was checking out those five, just the same.

The name sounded Western enough. But did that mean he was from America, England, Canada, Australia, South Africa? Even if his nation of origin could be determined, what cause was there to believe he lived there now? Assuming that was even his — or her, or their!— real name. There was simply too much they didn't know.

But that was Gillette's headache. Let the FBI track this punk down in reality, if they could. Ethan would get him in VR.

He glided over his castle in a careful arc. It looked beautiful. A grey stone set like a gem in a verdant expanse. Even from this height Ethan could see the azure pennants on the parapets snapping in the simulated breeze. His eye picked out the catapults and ballistae on the towers. Automated men-at-arms paced the wall-walks.

It was a concentric castle, which meant there were two sets of protective, or curtain, walls, one within the other. Each set of curtain walls had its own gatehouse. Each gatehouse — a miniature fortress, really — had its own drawbridge. Both drawbridges were down.

Ever since the attack on Jordan, Ethan had felt remarkably free of the battle he'd been waging over the line between real and virtual worlds. Perhaps he was cured. Perhaps, and this was more likely, one side or the other had just won. Judging by the amount of time he was spending in Falcon's Grove these days, Ethan thought he could tell which side had prevailed.

< jefferson scott >

He didn't feel over the edge, though, he didn't feel addicted. He felt wonderful — so long as he stayed in VR. He managed to do that almost every waking hour these days. In this he was justified, after all. He had been right about Mr. Computer Psycho, and now he had to prepare to confront him. There was no time for anything besides that. Kaye would come to see it his way eventually.

Ethan saw something he needed to change — none of the guards in his castle had detected him flying overhead. What if this Patriot flew in, too? They couldn't be much of an early warning system if they didn't even look up. He urged his dragon downward.

The ancient warmaster Sun Tzu advised generals to pick, as much as they could, the site of an upcoming battle. That way friendly forces could build defenses, while the enemy would have none. Friendly troops would be rested, while the enemy would be travel-weary. The advantages of terrain, morale, and intelligence would belong to the friendly side. For this battle Ethan had picked Falcon's Grove. His ambush was almost set. He'd spent the better part of the last three weeks since the attack working on it.

It was true he hardly came home at all now, except to eat dinner and go to sleep. He'd even skipped those on occasion, or made do with Payday bars and a stretch of carpet. Kaye was not adjusting well to this new schedule. But she would. Ethan had a purpose now, a purpose for which it seemed he had been born. He was not about to betray that just because one woman couldn't understand why he was spending so much time there.

"There" was the Dallas headquarters of ImTech International. Shortly after the attack, Ethan and Gillette had approached Ron Dontwell, ImTech's CEO, with a request. They wanted to use Dontwell's revolutionary new M7 Reality Engine to go after Patriot.

Dontwell had eventually agreed, on the condition that Ethan write a favorable review of Dontwell's forthcoming book. It was only fair, he said, after his kind words about Ethan's.

Ethan was amazed at the M7's fluidity and grace. The illusion of

< virtually eliminated >

actual presence in the virtual world was astounding — a true evolutionary leap above the industry standard. Dontwell showed him everything, including the weaknesses in the system. Ethan had had a few ideas about how to correct those, and Dontwell had gotten people right on it. One day Dontwell, only partially joking, had offered Ethan a high position at ImTech. Ethan had just laughed.

The glass-walled office Ethan had been provided with was a thing of beauty. Of envy. He had his computer from DES there now, with its now-legendary security system, side by side with his mini-network from home. These five computers, along with a new SuperStor tower, were coupled most intimately with the blessed M7.

The office became a shrine, of sorts. A place of pilgrimage for the ImTech programming staff. It wouldn't be long before someone claimed a miraculous healing. To Ethan it just felt like a fishbowl.

He lifted his visor and looked at his watch — 5:15. Plenty of time. Kaye said something about a special dinner at seven. Why did she have to plan it on a Saturday night? He lowered his visor to work again on his castle.

If it wasn't one thing with Kaye, these days, it was another. It seemed like every time he talked to her now she pestered him about when he was coming home, why he spent so much time at ImTech, and when was he going to take her out. She was just getting selfish. Maybe turning thirty-five was finally getting to her.

Where was the appreciation? Where were the thanks for spending countless hours up here trying to bring this maniac to justice? He was working for the FBI, wasn't he? It wasn't as if this was his own pet project. Why couldn't that woman understand how important this was? The man had tried to kill her own son, for crying out loud. You'd think she would give him a word of encouragement now and then, instead of nagging him all the time. She hadn't always been like this.

Maybe, he thought wearily, surprising himself with the thought, they were just growing apart.

< jefferson scott >

The translation was precise, if not elegant.

One would think that in the ten years since language translation software began to come out, the process would have been perfected. But no such program, no matter how sophisticated, could yet interpret the style and tone of a given document, much less the subtleties of humor or satire. The best the user could hope for was a literal, word-for-word transliteration, with the word order adjusted somewhat for English readers.

Thus Patriot read a slightly questionable version of Chairman Yasunari's speech. It was a work-in-progress, actually, since it didn't need to be ready until after the negotiations were complete. But the thrust of the thing was clear enough.

Patriot was in a vulnerable position, he knew. He was deep inside the computer system of the world's most powerful conglomerate, Matsuichi, Inc, scanning the chief executive officer's personal files. One wrong move could prove disastrous. Not to his own life or safety — he wasn't much concerned about that — but to the Plan. He had needed a certain electronic address, however, and this was the only computer on which it was recorded. While he was there, he could not resist a peek at the man's speech.

It read like a declaration of war.

No, like a declaration of victory.

And why not? Patriot wondered as he made his way out. Why not, indeed?

< virtually eliminated >

chapter.16

KAYE HAMILTON OPENED THE OVEN and inhaled. A wave of heat swept across her face, blowing her bangs. The fragrance of lemon and chicken blended delicately with Old English cheese. Almost done. She called this dish Engagement Chicken, since Ethan had prepared it for her the night he proposed.

The first and last time he ever cooked for me, she thought. She sighed, then, and asked God for forgiveness. She didn't want tonight to go that way. Tonight was the fifteenth anniversary of the night he proposed to her.

Not many people understood why she and Ethan celebrated that night — or how they could even remember it. They also celebrated the anniversary of their first date, the day they conceived their first child, and the day Ethan got hired at DES. From the beginning their relationship had been so good, so special, that each important event bore remembering.

Was all of that crumbling now?

She tried not to think about it, burying such thoughts with preparations. She put her best white lace tablecloth on the dining table

< jefferson scott >

and got out the matching napkins.

Ever since that terrible attack on Jordan, her husband had been different. She still remembered the look in his eyes that day. The eyes of a stranger. The way he'd slammed that axe into the smoke alarm. It made her shiver now, three weeks later. What else was he capable of?

In the days since, Kaye had seen Ethan less and less often. He was working with some company in Dallas — InTech, she thought it was. They had this super-duper computer that was supposed to help them catch that Patriot wacko. If it was such a great computer, so fast and advanced, shouldn't that allow him to be home earlier?

Kaye had to admit that Ethan had been right about Mr. Computer Psycho. She admired her husband, of course. God had given her a mate who was everything she wanted: man of God, bread-winner, compassionate, funny. The way he had saved his son had been truly heroic. She had encouraged him, at first, to do what he could to stop whoever had attacked Jordan.

But she didn't want him to do that anymore. Ethan was different now. 'Obsessed' seemed too weak a word to describe him. 'Controlled' might be better.

Her worst fears had come to pass. Ethan had found a killer on GlobeNet, as she knew he would. The killer had come into her own home and her son had almost been killed. Their game room was burned out and their front door chopped up. And now, instead of steering clear of the dangers, Ethan had plunged into the computers even more, perhaps never again to surface.

And no wonder he preferred his computers to her now. The computer never refused him, never made demands. It always had time for him, always wanted to do whatever he wanted to do. It was the perfect mistress.

But he had a wife who had more right to him. Ethan's family needed him now. Needed his leadership, his protection, his presence. Kaye was determined to get those things in short order. Or else take steps.

This was all Ethan's fault. Because he had gotten involved when she

< virtually eliminated >

didn't want him to. Because he had a stupid theory. Because he had thought it might be fun to play cops and robbers.

Kaye went to the cupboard for their finest china, trying to contain the anger.

Jordan and Katie were spending the night with some friends from church. When dinner was ready, Kaye was going to put on the gown she'd worn on their wedding night. It wasn't what she'd worn fifteen years ago on their engagement night, of course, but she thought the need was dire enough to bend the rules a little.

After dinner, she had an evening of passion planned the likes of which he would not soon forget. *Just let him try to ignore me tonight.*

Computer mistresses, she was learning, were difficult rivals.

The main gatehouse was where he would make his gamble. As in a real castle, if an enemy army breached the drawbridge, it would then have to move through the deadly gatehouse.

In an authentic gatehouse, the enemy would be trapped in the little hallway by a portcullis and oak door on one side and the press of his own army on the other. Those enemy soldiers unlucky enough to be at the front of the army would be assaulted from three sides: the left, the right, and from above. Archers in protected alcoves fired at them from the sides, and men in a chamber above poured hot sand or boiling oil down through little slots called murder holes. An attack through the gatehouse was rarely successful.

Ethan didn't have access to a massive power spike, as did Patriot. His attack would therefore have to consist of combined arms. Ethan's "warriors" were his synthetic helpers, his infobots. Most had been created in the last three weeks. Each had a specific purpose. The castle itself had some new modifications, too. Ethan hoped the cumulative effect of his small arms would be sufficient for his task.

Though part of him would like it — a very loud, angry part — he was not out to kill Patriot. That would make him just like the thing he

< jefferson scott >

hated. His mission here was to capture Patriot electronically. If Ethan could hold him on-line long enough, Gillette's people could attempt a phone trace. If things went very well and Ethan could lure Patriot into the gatehouse, perhaps the little ambush he'd prepared would even put his enemy temporarily out of business.

"Away, mighty Nerfblatt!" Ethan commanded his dragon. "Await on yon peak for thy master's bidding."

The green-skinned serpent leapt into the air with a shriek. It circled once, its beautifully rendered wings catching the artificial sunlight. Ethan wondered if the tactical virus embedded in the dragon's belly would make any difference when the time came. For that matter, would any of his men-at-arms — all designed with some kind of electronic weapon — have any effect? Ethan shrugged. Time would tell.

Only one thing left to do, Ethan thought. He needed to go out into GlobeNet and bait the trap.

He looked at his watch — 7:10. Uh-oh. He shut down the computers and headed for the door. On the way out he grabbed his notebook computer.

Kaye had said seven o'clock. He was still in Dallas at ten after. This was not going to be good.

It was good, after all. In fact, it was delicious. Both the meal and what came after. Kaye looked beautiful in that white gown, amid candles and Chopin. She hadn't seemed to mind that he was an hour late. During dinner it had actually been possible to forget — just for a moment — the name Patriot. To leave behind the murky waters of assassination and mystery and guile.

Ethan longed for the day when he could leave those waters behind, returning again to the *terra firma* of family and work. But for now he sailed the capricious sea, searching, like Ahab, for the great white. He loved his family too much to give up the hunt now, all unresolved.

At least that's what he told himself. He was doing this for them,

< virtually eliminated >

wasn't he? For Jordan. For Kaye. For little Katie. For the FBI — the American people. The world at large.

A thought came to him softly yet insistently, like a mosquito diving into his ear. GET HELP. Ethan smirked. The thought was absurd. He felt better now than he had in years. YOUR WIFE NEEDS YOU. No, what my wife needs is an attitude adjustment. YOUR CHILDREN NEED YOU. I'm helping my children — what do you think I'm doing?

Ethan's mind was invaded by an image of himself as if seen through someone else's eyes. He looked pale and withered, like a cocaine addict. Desperation made him frantic. In the image he lunged for a VR headset and pulled it over his face. His mouth melted into ecstasy. He tore his mind from the image in disgust. He was not that person. He was not an addict. He could stop using the computer if and when he ever felt the need to.

I MISS MY TIME WITH YOU. Now that was a low blow. It was supposed to be God's voice, of course. But it wasn't. Ethan was spending every spare moment in the pursuit of the purpose God had created him for — if that wasn't spending time with God, Ethan didn't know what was.

He left these thoughts, and his sleeping bride, behind and snuck downstairs to his study. He powered up the notebook computer, put on his VR gear, and entered GlobeNet. He still had one more thing to do.

Kaye was not asleep.

Despite all her feminine charms, her husband had left her bed to go after his mistress, his concubine. He was down there now, fondling her. *Fine, he's made his choice. I've made mine, too.*

Her friends would bring Jordan and Katie to church in the morning. After she collected them, Kaye would need time to throw some things together. She didn't have to wonder if Ethan would be distracted with something else as she did so. If all went as expected, she should be able to pull off her design by mid-afternoon.

< jefferson scott >

The notebook computer couldn't provide the same fluidity as the M7, but for Ethan's purposes it was adequate. He arrived at Patriot's defensive perimeter a little after midnight, Fort Worth time. He didn't know what he had been expecting, but it certainly wasn't this. A white picket fence surrounding a woodframe house, bathed in artificial sunlight. It looked like someone's idea of the dream house.

Ethan approached carefully, knowing the idyllic scene concealed awesome anti-intruder firepower. Both Thumper and Meely had met with violence here. Perhaps Patriot's picket fence was electrified.

He didn't have to find out. All he needed to do was bait his trap. Ethan spoke a command, and one of his new helpers appeared. It could have been a dog if it hadn't had wings. Ethan scrutinized it a moment, then led it to its post.

"Stay, Phideaux." He scratched it behind its hound ears. "You know what to do. When he gets here, you bring him home with you, got it?"

Phideaux licked Ethan's face.

"Okay. Now, I'm going to put this on you." Ethan brought out a collar with a little antennae concealed in the buckle. He put it on his helper. "This'll just let me know when you two meet."

Phideaux whined a little when Ethan moved away. Then he sat down and scratched at an imaginary flea.

Ethan shut the computer down.

When he got up he noticed his trusty leather-bound Bible on the corner of his desk. How long had it been since he'd had a quiet time? Three weeks at least. Not good. But, honestly, he didn't really feel like having one now. It's just this Patriot business, he assured himself. When it was over he would get back into the daily habit.

Ethan slipped into bed beside his wife only forty-five minutes after he'd left. As far as he could tell, she hadn't even stirred. He closed his eyes and drifted into dreams of flying hound dogs.

< virtually eliminated >

Edgar Ramirez unfolded his map on his pool table. He held the corners down with balls. Colored lines and symbols covered the United States map like a highway system gone mad. Edgar's trained eyes made perfect sense of it all.

The black squares were central switching stations. Green triangles, repeaters. Satellite ground stations were red octagons. Blue dots representing cellular transmitters speckled the map like population points — heavily concentrated in the East, moderate in the South, sparse in the Southwest and great plains, heavy again on the West Coast. Fiber optic cable arrays streaked across the country like multicolored varicose veins.

Edgar lit a cigarette.

The assignment was simple enough: cut off all long distance service going into Oregon from the continental U.S. this Tuesday at 5:20 P.M., Texas time. He saw clearly the line he would sever. He even knew the perfect spot for the deed, less than five miles north of his hometown, Paris, Texas.

The issue wasn't if he could do it, but if he should. He'd done some contract work for Burst when they'd laid their new coax cable, and now and again he'd been hired to fix a downed line. But he hadn't exactly worked for a phone company since Southwestern Bell went under, back in '98. Intentionally cutting a long distance line — especially one of the expensive fiber optic lines — was a federal offense, punishable by fine and mandatory prison.

Edgar Ramirez could afford neither. Four kids in school, house payments, his wife's parents now living with them. If he got caught doing this job, it would be disastrous.

On the other hand, this job offered him a way out of the quicksand he'd found himself trapped in: get the debts paid off, get little Hector's eyes fixed. Maybe buy that new Jeep Aztec — drive it right down the main drag.

He would have to be careful. What was the word? *Discreet*. Like

< jefferson scott >

whoever it was who wanted this thing done. Edgar didn't even know who he would be working for.

The man at the Sizzlin' seemed to know Edgar well enough, though. Said Pete Davis told him to look Edgar up. That was possible; Pete had been known to open his mouth too wide when someone else was buying the drinks. But even the Sizzlin' guy said the job was for someone else entirely.

Edgar didn't really care. One hundred thousand dollars wasn't as much as it was a few years ago, but it still sounded mighty good to him. He folded the map back.

He would be discreet.

< virtually eliminated >

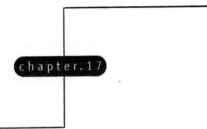

chapter.17

"PERHAPS I'M SPEAKING TO SOMEONE here this morning. Perhaps someone within the sound of my voice is saying, 'Leave off, Preacher! You hit too close to home. I'm a grown man, or a grown woman. Let me have my little habits if I want them. Don't I have the right to choose?' And I say to you, dear man or dear woman, 'No, you don't have the right to choose to sin in the eyes of the most holy God!'"

Someone in the congregation said, "Amen."

"You take your very soul in your hands — and for what? The passing pleasures of sin? The deceitfulness of riches? Wine when it sparkles in the cup? The poisoned honey of another man's wife or another woman's husband?

"I don't know your sin, that secret room in your heart that is off-limits even to God. Perhaps it's drunkenness. Perhaps it's gluttony. Are you lazy? Do you steal from work? From your parents? Your children? Men, do you indulge in pornography? Is there a secret closet or hide-away where you keep that magazine? And how many women do I know who have been led into sin through daytime soaps or talk shows? Do you treat your body — the temple of the Holy Spirit — with contempt?

< jefferson scott >

Poisoning it with alcohol or drugs or nicotine?"

Ethan glanced over at Special Agent Gillette and tried to subdue a smile. The FBI agent sat very still. He looked shrunken somehow, as if driven deeper into the pew by every word the preacher said. Brother Dan was definitely on one of his soapboxes this morning.

Kaye and Jordan sat on Ethan's other side. Katie was in the nursery. Ethan put his arm around his wife. She didn't snuggle into him like she usually did, however. She had been acting strange all morning. When he had made the innocent statement that he was going to skip church so he could get started with Gillette, she had almost hit the roof. So here he sat, virtually chained to the pew but trying to make the best of it. If he had to come, though, Ethan made sure Gillette was going to suffer with him.

Suffer? What was he thinking? He used to love church. He used to teach a Sunday school class and sing in the choir. He used to have his family up here whenever the lights were on and the doors were open. Now everything seemed false and garish. The whole thing tasted sour in his mouth. All he wanted to do was get away from it. What was wrong with him? He tried to make himself like it again.

He admired how Brother Dan could find everyday applications for the most archaic-sounding passages of the Bible. He could find the principle behind the Scriptures, even when the words themselves were tied to a culture hopelessly foreign to the average American.

His sermon this morning was on idolatry. Not about worshipping little figurines, but about worshipping gods of the twenty-first century. Money was always one candidate for modern worship. Technology was another. Hobbies or habits, especially sinful ones, were always popular choices. Almost anything or anyone could become the object of someone's reverence. Even for the Christian.

"I know you say to yourself, 'I can stop whenever I want to.' But you cannot. That is a lie of the devil, designed to keep you from trying."

"Amen," Ethan said, as much to show off his godliness to Kaye and Gillette as anything else. But he also knew how blind people could be

< virtually eliminated >

to their own problems. It was a shame about those people.

"An idol," Brother Dan said, "is anything you sacrifice to besides God. Sacrifices of time, money, energy, creativity, devotion."

Something stirred in the back of Ethan's awareness. An imprecise hiss, like someone whispering across a room. Was it about the sermon? About Kaye? About Gillette or Patriot? Maybe. The answer was sure to come. He had had these feelings before. Something important had occurred in his mind, but the results of it weren't clear yet. Like the white puff from a distant cannon seen whole seconds before the boom arrives. Before the bombshell arrives.

It was almost here.

Ethan's phone rang, a siren in the hushed auditorium. He snatched it off his belt, muting the ring. He read the caller identifier, LASSIE COME HOME. Patriot had taken the bait.

He nudged Gillette. "Let's go."

"Don't have to tell me twice." The special agent was already on his feet, headed for the aisle.

Ethan felt Kaye's eyes on his face. He suddenly felt bad for leaving. But she had known this might happen. He had told her about the trap. Still, it seemed impossibly wrong to go now, as if this was a far more important moment than it obviously was. Her eyes held him in place, just for an instant. Why was her neck flushed?

"I'm sorry," he whispered. "I've got to go. This is our chance to get Patriot." She didn't react. They really should turn the air conditioning up in here, he thought. "Pray for me?" Was that a nod or a shudder?

Ethan kissed his wife on the cheek and followed Gillette out the back of the church.

Men-at-arms paced the walls in twos, spears at their sides. Lookouts strained their gifted eyes to the corners of the digital domain. An unseen sun bathed the castle with heatless light. Across the forest, on one snow-capped peak, a dragon awaited a call from its master.

< jefferson scott >

Ethan stood atop the easternmost of the two drum towers that made up the gatehouse. From here he could see inside the castle walls as well as outside. But he didn't see anything at the moment. He stared, unfocused, out across his demesne, thinking about his pastor's sermon. At a tap on the shoulder he spun around, ready to command his troops into battle. But no one was there.

The tapping was still there, though. Ethan pushed up his NASA Ames VR helmet.

"Everything's set up," Gillette said, standing over Ethan's chair. The special agent leaned back against the glass wall of the fishbowl office. "Phone tracing ain't as easy as it used to be. You've got your cellular phones, your radio phones, your satellite phones, your Internet phones." He swore. "Of course every one's different. You've got to trace them all differently. But we've got good people on them all."

"Good." Ethan wanted to go back to Falcon's Grove.

"Ethan, buddy," Gillette said, sounding a little strange. "You sure you know what you're doing?" For once he met Ethan's eyes without a smirk.

Ethan smiled back, touched. "Let me show you something, Mike." He put the helmet in the chair and stood up. He picked up the cable connected to his helmet. "This cable goes from my helmet to the back of this over here." They both walked around the back of the computer array.

The floor behind the computers looked as if it had been designed by H.R. Giger — cables of every color and size snaked away like tentacles. Ethan expertly followed the cable to its destination. "All the computers and peripherals come together into this box right here."

He indicated a pale blue box that might have been a refrigerator lying on its side. No fewer than six fans spun in high-pitched frenzy to keep the beast's temper down. "This," Ethan said reverently, "is the M7 Reality Engine. The finest virtual reality computer on the planet." He shrugged. "For now, anyway. By this time next year, there will be a new champion, and you'll be able to buy the M7 in a desktop unit or maybe on a wristwatch."

< virtually eliminated >

"You have a point, Hamilton?"

"As I was *just* about to say, everything comes together into the M7. And the M7 goes into this." He patted a black metal cylinder roughly the size and shape of a scuba tank. One heavy duty power cable ran from the M7 to the cylinder, and another ran from the cylinder to the wall socket. A little green light shone near one end. "This is the Terminator III, GE's top-of-the-line surge suppresser/spike deflector, capable of defeating an electrical current three times more powerful than a lightning bolt. Clamping time, .0001 seconds."

"Is that good?" Gillette asked.

"The best. I asked for it and your people in D.C. sent it down. Your taxpayers' money at work. If Patriot tries to get me this way, this baby will save my hide. Giving its meager life in the process, of course."

"Make sense, boy. How else could he get to you? Electric shocks use electricity, right? Or is this New Physics, like New Math?"

"Remember Ray Feathers?" Ethan leaned against the glass and crossed his ankles. "Did you look at the electrical outlet in his room?"

"Fried."

"Wrong, Mr. FBI agent. The outlet was the only thing in the room that wasn't fried. And the cable from that outlet to the back of the computer was the only cable that didn't explode."

Gillette waited. "So?"

"So the spike that killed Ray Feathers didn't come in that way." He emphasized his words, "It didn't come in through the electrical socket."

"Don't tell me. God got him, right? Like your preacher said. He musta had some girly magazine in his underwear drawer, right? Spontaneous combustion."

Ethan moved to the other kind of outlet leading into the office. "It came in through the phone line, Special Agent Gillette. Through the telephone line.

"Think about it, Mike, how else could he direct a power spike to a specific location? If he just released it through the electrical system, it would blow out the transformer nearest its origin and that would be the

< jefferson scott >

end of it. At best it would just scatter out to a thousand or so homes and businesses. The worst result would be about a hundred blinking clocks. Pinpoint accuracy like he needs requires a *point-to-point* connection. Something to channel all the energy straight to the target. Something like a phone line."

Ethan knelt and patted another scuba tank. "That's why I asked your good people in D.C. to send me this, the modem/fax/phone version of the Terminator III. Same deal, only for phones." He straightened up. "I'm totally safe. To hurt me, he'd have to come over himself and hit me on the head. But you'd be here to stop him, wouldn't you, Mr. Gillette? You and your six-shooter."

"Maybe I'll just let him come do you in, podner," he said, the familiar smirk back on his face. "Maybe I'll do it myself."

Ethan sat in his chair and lifted the helmet. "Anyway, thanks for asking."

Gillette nodded. "Betcha. We'll get this outlaw."

Anything I sacrifice to. The words resounded in Ethan's mind as clearly as if Falcon's Grove Castle itself had shouted them. *An idol is anything I sacrifice to.*

Ethan paced the grey walls of his artificial castle. All was quiet. The light source was as high in the blue sky as it had been before. As before, the synthetic defenders maintained their patient vigil. Ethan had inspected the siege weapons on every tower: catapults, ballistae, boiling oil, quivers of arrows. But now he just circled the parapets restlessly, passing his infobot warriors without returning their salutes.

YOUR COMPUTERS.

There was that annoying voice again. *What about my computers? Do you think they're pretty? Why don't you just shut up, whoever you are?*

GET HELP.

If I keep talking to myself, maybe I should.

Then it struck him. The connection that had been made at church.

< virtually eliminated >

The thought had been there since then, there in the corner, waving its arms at him. But it was simply too ridiculous to merit serious consideration. Wasn't it?

I can stop using computers whenever I want to.

"I know you say to yourself, 'I can stop whenever I want to.' But you cannot. That is a lie of the devil, designed to keep you from trying."

That's for those other people, not me.

He did love his computers, true. But that didn't make them his idols. If simply loving something made it an idol, then his wife and children were idols, too, along with his favorite movies and Payday bars.

On the other hand, he was big enough to admit that there were times when he would rather work on his computer than take out the trash or mow the grass or take Jordan to soccer. What was the crime in that? Surely Kaye would rather talk on the phone than do laundry. Was talking on the phone Kaye's false god?

Computers — especially VR apps — were his hobby. Where in the Bible did God prohibit hobbies? Another voice came to him, then, of a lady at church who had lectured him on the evils of virtual reality.

"Our enemy's favorite tool," she had informed him piously, "is deception. That is precisely what this virtual reality is. Pure escapist deception. 'Do not exchange the truth of God for a lie,'" she had quoted, "'lest the enemy devour you.' When was the last time you wondered at *God's* creation instead of your own? The majesty of the stars, the multicolored beauty of the undersea world, the magnificence of the human body. 'See then that ye walk circumspectly, not as fools, but as wise, redeeming the time, because the days are evil.'"

Funny, but that particular lecture — and the attitude behind it — had not settled with Ethan very well. Nor did its memory. He was willing to bet that that woman had some hobbies of her own — gardening or music or something — to which she devoted enormous amounts of her resources. Who was she to judge?

The issue wasn't whether or not Ethan loved his computers, but whether or not he loved them more than he loved God. It was a question

< jefferson scott >

of priorities. Was his VR more dear to him than his Savior? Would he rather spend time on the computer than on his knees, in Falcon's Grove than in the Garden of Gethsemane?

That hurt. He thought of his old Bible sitting at home on his desk, collecting dust, while he sat at ImTech hooked up to the M7. How long had it been since he'd spent any decent time with his Lord Jesus? A month? No wonder he felt so unbalanced. And now he'd walked right out of church, skulking out the back door like a defiant teenager.

Ethan pulled his helmet off and set it in his lap. Gillette was snoozing in an office chair. Ethan felt a little drowsy himself. Outside the glass fishbowl walls, ImTech was dark and empty.

His computer array surrounded him. Computers, monitors, input devices, surge protectors, keyboards, cables, 6DOF devices, wristpads, speakers... All in support of the blessed M7. He did look like an idolater, after all, even to himself. Ethan Hamilton, High Priest of the Most Cybernetic Silicon God.

He shut his eyes. Immediately an image came to his mind.

He saw himself in a black hooded robe, standing before a flaming maw — the devil's own acolyte. The blaze crackled and popped. Tongues of fire reached dangerously close to his hood. Underneath, the throaty roar of the god. *More!* it demanded, insinuated, *More!* And always Ethan returned to his master bearing an offering.

First it was a small bag of gold, enough to purchase a juicy computer game. He took it to the foot of the dais and tossed it into the mouth from there. *More!* He paced off into the darkness and returned, as surely as if he was chained to the altar, with another offering. This time a larger bag of gold. Enough for all the computer power he could afford. *More!*

Next came offerings of time, of creative energy, of devotion. *More!* He vowed to read up in all the best computer magazines. He pledged to the beast that he would shop for new equipment and new software and new peripherals whenever he could. He offered up his free time for voluntary sacrifices.

< virtually eliminated >

Still his silicon calf was dissatisfied.

The hooded figure walked out of the firelight. When he returned, he carried an awkward bundle. Arms and legs struggled weakly against his grip. He laid the adult body before the furnace. It bellowed in anticipation. Flame surged outward, consuming the wooden articles of worship, melting the golden lampstands. There was something familiar about the body laid prone before the god. The sacrifice turned its head toward Ethan.

It was Kaye.

She looked not at the hooded figure but straight at Ethan, watching. He saw the betrayal register in his wife's eyes. She looked at him as at a rapist. She struggled against the acolyte as he inched her toward the inferno.

How could he betray his wife? His beautiful, faithful wife! How could he feed her to this insatiable god?

All right! he wanted to cry, all right! I exchanged the truth of God for a lie! I worship the created thing over the Creator! I serve a false god!

But he didn't cry out. He only watched in horror as his dark self prepared to deliver his wife to oblivion. His eyes swept over her and he saw, already bound and ready for human sacrifice, Jordan and little Katie. They watched as their father pushed their mother past the stone teeth into the blazing throat.

"No!" Ethan jumped out of his chair; the helmet crashed to the wooden floor.

Gillette sprang up, striking his knee on the desk. "Ow! What happened?"

"Never mind, it's okay," Ethan said, more to himself than to Gillette. "It was just a dream. A dream." He laughed. "Just a dream."

"What is wrong with you, boy? You're going to pay for my orthoscopic surgery."

"Sorry." He picked the helmet off the floor and sat down.

He stared into space, stunned. *So I'm an idolater.* He felt terribly small and ugly. The familiar arguments came to his defense — I can quit

< jefferson scott >

whenever I want to, I'm working for the FBI, I'm helping the general public, I'm working to ensure that what almost happened to Jordan never happens to anyone else — but this time they carried no persuasion. For every protest he raised, three counterarguments rose to shoot it down. Idolater, addict, junkie, Judas.

He had to get away from it. He had to dry out somewhere, to begin a twelve-step program. There was so much damage he needed to repair. He might need to swear off computers completely for awhile. Maybe he was too weak to ever work on them again. He should leave right now, while God had broken open the prison cell he'd locked himself in.

He looked at Gillette and the computers around him. He'd started this whole thing. He was the one who had called the FBI in the first place. And here Ethan sat, in ImTech headquarters, with temporary access to the world's most powerful virtual reality computer...and Patriot still on the loose. As far as Ethan knew, no one else in the world was even onto this guy. He couldn't back out now.

But as soon as this was over — in just a few hours, if all went well — he would leave his graven image behind to go make things right both with God and with his family.

He put his helmet back on.

And stared right into Patriot's eyes.

< virtually eliminated >

chapter.18

"JORDAN, GO GET KATIE PLEASE."

Kaye Hamilton watched her son run out to the McDonald's Playland. She picked up the rest of her trash from lunch and took it to the trashcan, then put her face in her hands.

Was she doing the right thing? She felt so guilty for abandoning her husband like this. So petty. She should turn around and go back. Give him another chance. She believed in what Ethan was doing, didn't she? Wasn't he protecting his family in the best way he knew how?

But when he'd walked out on her in church, that was the last straw. She'd had to almost force him go to church at all. They'd been so concerned that Jordan would one day go through a phase when he didn't want to go to church, but that phase hadn't come yet. It was here in living color in Ethan, though. At least for now he was over the edge.

If she couldn't rely on him to take care of his family, then she would just have to do it herself. But she wasn't going to do it in that house. That house had been violated; she didn't feel safe there anymore.

Jordan and Katie raced up, elbowing and arguing.

"Please, kids, not right now." She herded them toward the door.

< jefferson scott >

"How come Dad doesn't have to go see Gramma?" Jordan asked peevishly.

A tear shot down Kaye's cheek. Her tears were close to the surface today. "Your daddy — your daddy's too busy, honey."

Kaye got back out onto the Interstate at 75 mph. She wanted to reach her destination before too late.

She didn't notice the car that pulled in behind her.

They'd done their best to warn him. All Ethan's castle defenders stood around the intruder, brandishing their weapons, waiting for orders. But, of course, Ethan hadn't been on headset, so he'd missed all the ruckus.

For a moment he thought he was back inside his vision, looking at his dark alter-ego. The trespasser simply stood there, hooded and patient, on the parapet of Falcon's Grove Castle. His black robes fluttered east to west, though the wind through the castle blew south. In his right hand he held a mighty staff, topped by a golden orb. He looked like Merlin and Moses rolled into one.

"Ethan Hamilton, I presume?"

Ethan licked his lips. What was his great plan again? "Patriot, I presume?"

"Your cybernetic retriever was most amusing," Patriot said. "Though I had to laugh at its crudeness. Like your other creations, it was farcical and sophomoric."

Ethan was pretty sure he'd just been insulted. "It got you here, didn't it?" He was beginning to remember his plan.

"Functionality I grant you. The sad part is you believe you have created something marvelous. Within your imbecilic little circle, I suppose you have." Patriot lifted his staff, and Ethan's infobots cowered down. "In the immortal words of Horace, 'The mountains will be in labor, and a ridiculous mouse will be born.'" He lowered his staff. The castle defenders closed in again, feigning valor. It looked like a samurai movie. "Do you read much Horace, Ethan Hamilton? No, I guess not."

< virtually eliminated >

With his toe, Ethan pressed a button under his desk, activating an external monitor so Gillette could see and hear what was going on in Falcon's Grove. He knew Gillette would already have people attempting to trace the call.

The game was afoot.

"Take these minions of yours," Patriot was saying. He swung his staff in a wide arc. Ethan's helpers stumbled over themselves trying to get out of its way. "Take this pitiful fort and environs. I imagine you've spent months building it all, even years. Am I correct?"

"I've been working on it, off and on, for about a year, I guess." He began backing toward the nearest tower. The M7 was so smooth, so natural. Ethan felt himself sinking into the murky waters of his old addiction. He'd better get out of this quickly, while he still wanted to.

Patriot followed him, the pack of men-at-arms right with him. He looked like a celebrity wading through reporters. "An entire year of your life, down the legendary drain."

Ethan reached the tower and its spiral staircase. "Don't sell these little guys short. They're my pets, my friends, even."

"Ah, the company of peers."

"Watch this. I'll go down and call them all to me. They'll leave you alone." He bounded down the stairs. When he emerged onto the grassy ward and looked up, Patriot wasn't on the wall-walk anymore. He was hovering like Mary Poppins over the slate roof of the great hall.

"Careful what you do, Ethan Hamilton." The golden orb seemed a little brighter, but that was probably an illusion. "Remember with whom you are dealing."

"I just wanted to show you a trick they can do." Ethan turned to his helpers, who were crouched on the ledge, like curios, tracking Patriot's flight. Ethan aired his crudest wolf whistle. His helpers didn't move. On a distant mountain peak, however, a fire-breathing serpent took to the air.

Patriot laughed. "Spectacular. Conclusive. But don't be too hard on them, Ethan Hamilton. 'Beyond his strength no man can fight, although

< jefferson scott >

he be eager.' Fortunately for you, you have me. And, in the words of Conrad, 'You shall judge of a man by his foes as well as by his friends.'"

Keep him talking, Curly. Reel him in.

"Are we foes, then?"

"You have to ask?" Patriot descended to only a few feet above the grass. "For what purpose have you called me here, if not for your attempt at vengeance?"

Ethan ambled in the direction of the massive gatehouse. Patriot floated along beside him. "Revenge? Oh, I guess you mean about Jordan? Yes, I was a little miffed about that, I suppose. But I'm a Christian, you know. Jesus tells us to do good to those who persecute us. Turn the other cheek. You know. It's supposed to heap burning coals on your head. Has that happened?"

"Terribly sorry to disappoint. It wouldn't be the first time that sort of thing had no effect on me, though. I seem to be immune to the devices of the Christian God. Something about his past dealings with me, I suppose. I prefer Sartre's god — 'Things are entirely what they appear to be and behind them, there is nothing.'"

"Why did you attack my son?"

"Ah. Leave it to a Christian to be concerned about the death of a son. He didn't die, by the way, did he?"

"No."

"Ah, well. 'Sometimes even excellent Homer nods.'"

"But you're not Homer, are you? You're Louis Parks."

Patriot laughed. An energetic laugh, tinged perhaps with something else: malice? hysteria? His perfect vertical stance relaxed a little. He began a slow roll. "So the little tyke remembered that, did he? Well, no matter. I notice you haven't found me yet. You and your FBI pals — brotherhood of vipers that they are. Not as good a lead as you thought, was it?"

They reached the mouth of the gatehouse. Ethan peered through the dark passage. Flagstones on the floor reflected the artificial sunlight and bathed the walls with a silver luminescence. All the portcullises

< virtually eliminated >

were up, all the doors were open, the drawbridge was down. Ethan's architect's eye traced out the murder holes in the ceiling. He was vaguely aware that his helpers had taken their positions in the gatehouse. Somehow he had to get Patriot to go in there. His dragon should be here within five minutes.

"Who says we haven't found you yet? Who says we don't know where you are right now?"

"Please, don't embarrass yourself." Patriot was almost horizontal. His necromancer's robes still 'blew from right to left — which now meant from down to up. "Perhaps you refer to the beatnik boys in our nation's Capitol attempting to trace this call. I assure you, Ethan Hamilton, I am quite safe from their prying. By the by, you should refrain from trusting your Department of Justice comrades too fully. They're not actually on your side, you realize." Patriot rotated away, turning his back toward Ethan. "If only you had seen what I have seen."

"You haven't answered my question," Ethan said. "Why did you attack Jordan?"

Patriot sighed. He righted himself slowly and touched down, facing Ethan. "'Sweet and glorious it is to die for one's country.'"

"Come again."

"Every war has casualties, Ethan Hamilton. Surely you won't disagree. Without casualties you don't have a war, you have only posturing."

"Here's a news flash for you, Patriot — we're not at war with anyone. America hasn't gone to war since Latvia, and you can't really count that. The United States is at peace."

"'A bad peace is even worse than war.'"

Ethan caught a green flash through the open gatehouse, but still minutes away. "Okay, I'll bite. Who are we at war with?"

"With whom are we at war," Patriot corrected. "Our old enemies, of course: the Japanese and the Germans. Most especially the Japanese." He stamped his staff on the ground. "Who built your car, Ethan Hamilton?"

"Ha! Dodge. That's an American company."

"In 1998, Torito Shiho purchased a controlling interest in Chrysler Corporation, of which Dodge is a subsidiary." He stamped the ground again. "Who built the computer you are using?"

"Built by ImTech, headquartered in Dallas, Texas."

"Made up of components made by Teac, Sony, and Matsuichi — all Japanese companies." Stamp. "Who owns the land your house is built on?"

"I do. I'm buying it from the bank."

"Bank of Northeast Texas; part of the Continental Finance Consortium, owned by German interests. Your bank, in turn, purchased the land from Toho Properties, which owns 42 percent of the land in Fort Worth and Dallas." He stamped the ground again. "Need I go on?"

"That doesn't mean we're at war with them."

"Doesn't it? Haven't you read your Sun Tzu? 'To fight and conquer in all our battles is not supreme excellence; supreme excellence consists in breaking the enemy's resistance without fighting.' Nothing of real value in America is owned by Americans anymore," Patriot said. "Or didn't you know that 82 percent of America's crucial industries, technologies, and communications corporations are owned by the Japanese, with the rest gobbled up by the Germans, the Pakistanis, and the Koreans? Except one. And that one not for long. We are at war, Hamilton! Only no one realizes it. We've been ambushed more completely, more expertly, by far than we were at Pearl Harbor. We've almost lost a war we didn't know we were in.

"However, the Japanese will not defeat my nation without paying dearly for the victory. The United States will go down — that much is cast in iron — but it will not go down undefended."

What troubled Ethan most was that Patriot's words made sense. The racism was unacceptable, of course. But his words carried the ring of truth. This was supposed to be a madman, a lunatic who killed for the sheer thrill. Not an articulate, refined intellectual with a passion for

< virtually eliminated >

the country Ethan himself loved. He wondered how Gillette was taking it, watching and listening on the monitor.

Ethan understood why Patriot had selected that particular name. He really did see himself as a patriot, the final flag-waver standing alone against an insidious threat. Ethan's mind filled with images: purchases he had made, movies he had watched, clothes he wore, advertisements and news — all of them reinforcing Patriot's words, "Nothing of real value in America is owned by Americans anymore."

"But what about all those innocent people you murdered? What did they do against America?"

"Innocent? 'The innocent and the beautiful have no enemy but time.' None was innocent, oaf. Each one had compromised U.S. sovereignty in some way or another. Some by commission; others by omission. Others just by getting in the way of the war effort."

"Getting in your way, you mean." Ethan stepped into the gatehouse passage.

Patriot's golden orb seemed to pulsate softly now. What eyes Ethan could detect beneath Patriot's deep hood glinted hard as well. "'The only excuse for war is that we may live in peace unharmed.'"

"What about my son? He got in the way of your little war, I guess. He found out your name. That could hurt you, couldn't it? He could turn you in to the government you're trying so hard to protect. And they —"

"I'm *not* protecting the government! Cabinet of fools. Bureaucrats and grandstanders, whose only concern is to stay in office for another term. 'Where the State begins, individual liberty ceases.' Mikail Bukanin. 'That government is best which governs not at all.' Henry David Thoreau."

Patriot stalked under the arch of the gatehouse. His black form blotted out the light. He looked like Death personified, advancing on Ethan.

"Yes, your son got in my way. He had to be eliminated."

"He's just a boy!" Ethan felt his self-control deserting him, that old

< jefferson scott >

fury bubbling over. "He's only nine."

"You are to blame for your son's danger! You were the one who attacked me. If you'd stayed put, you would be dead and your son would be out of danger. If you hadn't been so tiresome with your computer security, I never would have investigated."

"That's brilliant, professor! I'm un-American because I protected my company's computer. I nearly got my son killed because I didn't let you look at my stupid files. I'll give you the files. I'll give you the passwords, the directories, everything. They're worthless to you. Just go away! Leave us alone."

They were in the center of the gatehouse now. Hidden infobots pointed electronic weapons at them both, awaiting Ethan's order.

"You know I can't do that, Ethan Hamilton. My biggest coup is only forty hours away. My death is at hand. My plan is at fruition. I cannot allow you to interfere."

Ethan heard the *woof* of his dragon's wings. Just a few more seconds. He maneuvered around so that Patriot's back faced the dragon's approach. "What is this plan? What's your biggest coup? Tell me — maybe I'll help you." Patriot wasn't buying it. "No, I'm serious. What you say makes sense to me. Can't I help you?"

"I'll show you how you can help me most." Patriot held his staff high. The golden orb shone brightly, fully illuminating the gatehouse passage with yellow light. "'The tree of liberty must be refreshed from time to time with the blood of patriots and tyrants.' I am Patriot." He tilted his staff at Ethan. "The tree of liberty will have my blood." The globe flared.

Ethan dove backward, shouting, "Attack!"

< virtually eliminated >

chapter.19

THE GATEHOUSE ERUPTED INTO BATTLE. Men-at-arms dropped boiling oil — mild electric feedback — onto Patriot's head. From slits in the wall archers fired flaming arrows — data trackers — into his cloak. Portcullises — signal harnesses — slammed down. The drawbridge and doors — power dampeners — began to close. Ethan's green dragon swept over the drawbridge and under the portcullis with a shriek, careening into Patriot just as he released his electrocution spike.

Ethan tore off his helmet and threw himself away from the desk, overturning his chair — surge protectors or not.

"Incoming!" Gillette shouted, hitting the deck.

Thkk. It was an ominous sound. It prolonged itself, echoing off the glass walls as if reluctant to die.

But there was no explosion. The lights didn't dim; the monitors didn't flicker. Nothing even smoked.

Gillette uncovered his head. "Was that it?"

"That was it."

Ethan crawled around the desk to inspect the Terminator IIIs. The one assigned to the electrical line was fine, but the one on the phone line

< jefferson scott >

was dead. The little green light was off.

Gillette crawled up to stare, wide-eyed, at the monitor. Something like a Roman candle shot out of the gatehouse. "Whoa." Gillette's phone rang, and he answered. After listening a moment, his body seemed to slump. He mumbled something and hung up. He didn't face Ethan.

Ethan didn't notice. He righted his chair and scooted back up to the M7. He retrieved his helmet and put it on. The roar inside the gatehouse had receded. Ethan ached to see what had happened. First, though, he equipped himself with a sword — a mild logic bomb — and a shield — an energy mirror. He scrambled to the drawbridge mechanism. The battle din was gone now. Cracking pennants made the only sounds. Ethan made himself count to five, then hit the switch.

Chains clanked, wood creaked. Smoke issued out, finding an outlet at last. Ethan hopped down to the front of the gatehouse, shield and sword ready. There was no movement in the dark passage. The gatehouse walls, floor, and ceiling were caked with soot, the murder holes plugged by the bodies of his helpers. Everything smoked. It looked like a Dachau furnace.

An indistinct lump lay on the flagstones. Blackened. Fleshy. Ethan poked at it with the tip of his sword. Kicked it. A green head lopped over — his dragon. Ethan poked through the rest of the pile for signs of Patriot, but found only decomposing serpent.

Before he'd met Patriot, Ethan had never suffered the loss of one of his artificial friends. That they were synthetic didn't ease his grief. Thumper, Meely, Nerfblatt the dragon, all his men-at-arms. He still hadn't seen Phideaux. Perhaps it was appropriate that cybernetic innocents should be casualties of a war in cyberspace.

But there were human casualties, as well. The war had exceeded its borders — if it had ever been contained at all. Death surrounded Patriot like an aura. If one entered his nimbus, bereavement was sure to follow. Ethan had managed to cheat it twice now. Who said there were no more miracles?

Back in the inner ward of Falcon's Grove Castle, Ethan stretched to

< virtually eliminated >

the cloudless, cerulean sky, and smiled. His devices had done the trick. He hadn't killed Patriot, that wasn't the plan. But he had put him out of commission for a while. Plus he had enough data tracking units in him to pick up his trail with a flashlight and a Sherlock Holmes magnifying glass if the FBI came up empty.

Speaking of that... He removed his helmet and put it on the desk. Gillette was on the phone.

"Well, why not? I thought you guys were supposed to be good!" Gillette noticed Ethan. He put a hand over the speaker. "You okay?" Ethan nodded. "Get someone else? Like who? Ma Bell? How much you pulling down a year, Maynard? Yeah? Well it's too much." He punched the off button and swore.

"Who was that?"

"Just the local head of FBI communications. What's the FBI coming to if they can't even tap a phone?"

"You didn't get him, then?"

"We got butkus. Something about a cellular repeater site messing up the trail."

"It's okay. I can trace him myself."

Gillette leaned forward. "Now? Didn't you just take him out?"

"No, he's alive. He's fine. Though I'd like to think I stung him a little. If so, he's probably running home right now. We'd better move while he's still on-line."

"So, you can trace him but federal surveillance agents can't?"

"Look, do you want my help or not?"

"Do it."

Ethan pulled a keyboard forward. "You know those flaming arrows my little castle guys shot into him?"

"Yeah," Gillette pointed at the screen, which at that moment displayed Ethan's smoking gatehouse. "I watched it all here. Sorry about your fort, cowboy."

"It's all right. Only took me a year to build it. Anyway, those arrows weren't just pretty decorations. They were data trackers — little signal

< jefferson scott >

transmitters. I use them for debugging. They tell me where they are in a program. They also happen to work in GlobeNet."

"What, you mean like tagging a bear?"

"Exactly. They go wherever the bear goes. And right now they're with Patriot. We find those trackers and we find him. A firm electronic address — traceable even by the FBI."

Ethan pounced at the keys. On the monitor, Falcon's Grove Castle faded to black. A few more intricate hand movements and a new image appeared on the screen.

"What is that?"

"It's a tree."

"I know that, smartmouth. I mean, what's it for?"

Ethan shrugged. "I don't know. I just like it. It's my home page, so I get to design it any way I want. I like how it looks. It does something for me. Just let me work, please."

Gillette pulled his chair up to the monitor. For a full thirty seconds he didn't say anything. It might have been a record. He watched Ethan navigate through his home page. "What's that?" He pointed at a yellow flare sputtering at the base of Ethan's tree.

Ethan didn't take his eyes off the monitor. "It's one of the trackers. It must've come loose when he went on into GlobeNet. That's strange…"

"What?" Gillette watched Ethan's thumb go to his teeth. "What's strange?"

"It shouldn't be here."

"What's the big deal? So one fell out, so what?"

Ethan did look away then. "The bear-tagging thing was just a metaphor, all right? Data trackers attach themselves directly to the address string of the host. They become part of it. Like cheese to a chip. They don't just fall out."

"Maybe you hurt him worse than you thought. Maybe pieces of him are just falling out all over."

"Mike, if you really want to help me, get on that phone and tell your

< virtually eliminated >

people we may be onto something after all. Tell them to be ready to move when I get them an e-mail address they can trace."

"Right." Gillette pulled out his phone.

Ethan donned his NASA Ames HMD. The instant he was immersed he regretted it. His addiction clamped its tentacles around him, draining his desire to ever forsake it. With effort he managed to pull the helmet off one eye. "Mike, could you call my wife at home? Tell her…tell her I'm sorry. That it might be another hour or so before I can leave here." The helmet dropped back down before he heard Gillette's response.

It was nearly impossible to retrace Patriot's steps. Ethan had to tap every resource of computer savvy at his disposal to go from one sputtering flare to the next. He didn't tell Gillette how many times he was dipping into the wells of intuition, luck, and Eenie Meenie Miney Moe.

But something about it felt easy.

The important thing was they were still on the trail. Carrying his sword and shield, Ethan felt like a fantasy warrior tracking a wounded orc.

Still, something about it all bothered him. His data trackers shouldn't be strewn around GlobeNet like so many breadcrumbs. Every one he found brought him renewed elation and dread. Elation that his Net skills had once again prevailed. Dread that he was being led along as surely as Phideaux had led Patriot.

Ethan was amazed at how crisp GlobeNet seemed when seen through the eyes of the M7. He could move at any speed without the images before him suffering or the animation becoming choppy. He had already come to love the M7. From now on, he would be dissatisfied with anything less.

Ethan saw the flaming computer maw again, loud and hot. He saw himself in his robes. Jordan and Katie tied up. The look in his wife's eyes.

He glided to a stop near the entrance to the famous virtual library.

< jefferson scott >

He was getting close to Patriot; he could taste it.

As much as Ethan wanted to scoff at Gillette's idea that these were pieces of Patriot's digital persona dripping out like blood, he couldn't argue with what his gut was telling him. There did seem to be something odd about how and where the data trackers were distributed. As if they were dropped out by someone in distress.

Ethan could almost imagine Patriot staggering through GlobeNet, colliding with barriers and obstacles, spilling out data trackers with every impact. He imagined himself in a dark, wet alley, rounding a corner to find Patriot slumped down against a dumpster, gasping his final breath.

The virtual library originated on the old Internet as a nexus of on-line information resources: anything from aboriginal studies to Zoroastrianism. When the Internet gave way to GlobeNet, the virtual library went 3D.

Ethan stood at the purely ornamental circulation desk looking back into the stacks. His Bozo Filter screened away the thousands of patrons, making the open air library appear deserted. Mahogany tables tiled the center of the bottom floor. Bookshelves surrounded the tables on three sides, with the circulation desk on the fourth. There were three more floors ringing the central reading area and looking down upon it. Stained-glass windows in the outer walls tinged the repository with yellow, blue, and red light.

Ethan could see his next data tracker. It was on the second floor, stuck, it seemed, to the corner of a bookshelf. Perhaps it scraped off as Patriot staggered by, trying to hide. Maybe Patriot had a secret passage from here to his home page. Ethan gripped his shield and hefted his sword.

Only one way to find out.

Colonial American Studies. Of course.

Ethan leaned with his back against the bookshelf — in the best Hollywood tradition — ready to come around the corner swinging. He

< virtually eliminated >

bobbed his head to look between the shelves and bobbed it back fast, half expecting someone to take a shot at him.

Nobody took a shot. He looked again.

Patriot was there, just as Ethan had imagined. Huddled against the wall beneath a yellow and green stained-glass window, all but buried by his black robe. Not moving. One of Ethan's data tracking arrows still smoldered on top of the pile. The robe was tattered and frayed, like a thirteen-star American flag Ethan had seen once.

"He's dead!" Gillette's voice penetrated Ethan's headset. Ethan felt his shoulder slapped.

Of course Patriot wasn't dead. But this might be even better. If Patriot's on-screen persona had been badly damaged enough, it was conceivable that his system might just drop him from GlobeNet, leaving his synthetic body where it stood. With that, Ethan could essentially read Patriot's diary. He would know much more than simply where his signal originated from, though he would know that. He might also be able to discern how Patriot floated around the Net, what computer system he used, and even how he summoned his spikes.

Though everything in him urged him to rush to the body and begin dissecting it on the spot, Ethan made himself advance slowly.

Ethan stepped into the aisle between two shelving units full of books on American art and architecture. He felt silly with his medieval weapons. Soothing music settled around him, and the stained-glass window bathed the whole scene in golden light.

The moment he touched Patriot's cloak, he knew he'd been tricked. It wasn't Patriot's on-screen persona. It was a carefully designed decoy, created to do exactly what it had done. Draw him in.

Ethan sensed the bookshelf falling before he saw it. He dove back the way he came, but he was too late. One bookshelf clipped another, causing it to fall, creating a deafening contagion and pinning Ethan down.

Patriot must have changed the benign library graphics into weapons of malicious logic. Nothing in the virtual library should be able

< jefferson scott >

to fall at all, much less pin anyone.

Ethan shoved aside the books that had buried him. He pulled himself to the edge of the bookshelf on top of him, but could not pull free. Somewhere under all the rubble were his sword and shield.

A shadow fell across the pile. Ethan turned to the stained-glass window in time to see it explode. A black-hooded figure stepped through the fragments, crunching them into dust.

Patriot. He didn't look injured at all. In fact, he looked quite potent. He held a fistful of golden javelins in his left hand. He put one leg on top of the rubble as if claiming it for his sovereign. He spotted Ethan and laughed. There was no mirth in the sound.

Behind Patriot, Ethan could see a portal. The passage to Patriot's home page, he was willing to bet. If only he could get to it.

"Ah, Hamilton," Patriot said. "I see you are in agreement with Francis Bacon's words, 'Some books are to be tasted, others to be swallowed, and some few to be chewed and digested.' Forgive me for interrupting your repast."

Patriot leaned the javelins against the wall and selected one. He licked his finger and touched it to the point. He climbed onto the shifting pile — which pinned Ethan even tighter — and walked up to Ethan's head. He shook his elbows out, checking his robes for constriction.

"You know, Ethan Hamilton," he said, holding the javelin in throwing position, "what you did to me back in your citadel was most un-American. One might even say un-Christian."

Ethan's first thought was simply to bail out. Pull off the helmet, turn off the computer, and be done with it. Especially since he was performing, as it were, without a net. If Patriot sent another electrical spike through the phone lines — which was likely what each of those javelins was — Ethan had no protection.

Two things prevented him from jacking out: his belief that the M7 was a better machine than whatever Patriot might be using and his desire to find Patriot's home page. If he could just get free, he was sure

< v i r t u a l l y   e l i m i n a t e d >

he could dive through the portal and at least get an electronic address before Patriot caught up with him.

There was a third reason, as well. It just might be that this show of strength from Patriot was a ploy to disguise how badly wounded he really was. It's what Sun Tzu would do.

But right now Ethan was trapped. There must have been some kind of arrestor in the code of these bookshelves. He thought he might have to jack out, after all. Then his PowerGlove found something familiar under him in the rubble.

The javelin point rotated in a tiny circle over Ethan's temple. "As a gentleman and an American," Patriot said grandly, "I offer you the opportunity to make a final statement. Prithee, bestow upon us the legacy of thy final words."

"How about, 'It ain't over till the fat lady sings'?"

Ethan had to keep reminding himself that this wasn't a game. Every other "death" he'd experienced in VR could be erased with the press of a button. If his plan didn't work, he would be dead, as in no longer alive. The only resurrect spell that could be cast then was in the hands of the Almighty.

If it did work, however, and he did stop Patriot, maybe he could save Patriot's future targets. Like his family. His wonderful, irreplaceable family.

Someone was tugging on his shoulder. Gillette's voice came to him as if from a distance. "Pull out, Hamilton, pull out!" Ethan shrugged him off.

Patriot smirked at Ethan's last words. "As you wish. But allow me to add my own benediction. You have been a meritorious antagonist, Ethan Hamilton. I wish you to know I have never been injured as you have injured me today. I shall always remember you and your nefarious moose security program."

The golden spear pulled back. "But you should never have interfered with national defense. 'Show me a hero,' wrote F. Scott Fitzgerald, 'and I will write you a tragedy.' But take heart, for I am about to set you

< jefferson scott >

free from your meaningless life. In the words of Seneca the Younger, 'Anyone can stop a man's life, but no one his death; a thousand doors open on to it.' Farewell, Ethan Hamilton."

Patriot plunged his javelin.

Ethan pulled his shield from under the rubble and brought it over his face.

The spear struck the mirrored surface and lit, for a split-second, the entire library with Transfiguration-bright light.

In that flash, Ethan's mind registered a remarkable thing. Phosphorescent fingers reached far into the folds of Patriot's hood. Ethan saw, as if burned into his eyes, the face of a young, white male, with dark hair. The cheeks were sunken under high cheekbones. The nose rounded into a ball.

There was no guarantee that this was Louis Parks's actual face. If it was, however, Ethan knew he would be able to pick it out of any line-up or mug book. He would remember this face forever. It dropped like a stone to the center of his psyche. He could already tell it would become a regular in his dreams.

If he lived to ever dream again, that is.

The electricity from the javelin reflected off Ethan's shield and ignited a bookshelf on the fourth floor, initiating another domino effect. The shield burst into powder.

Though Ethan felt none of the pain intended for him, he was nonetheless knocked down into the rubble — a movement which unpinned his body. A quick glance at Patriot showed him on the floor by the balcony railing, knocked sprawling from his own weapon's recoil. Ethan swept a final time with his hand, but failed to find his sword. He pushed himself out of the wreckage and sped for the hole where the stained-glass window had been.

Ethan stopped at the threshold.

The javelins.

Patriot's other lightning bolts were just sitting there, propped against the library wall.

Should he take them? Wouldn't that make him just like Patriot? If he did take them, maybe he could hide them or discharge them. It would be enough just to prevent Patriot from using them on anyone — especially from using them on Ethan. Besides, he didn't have any other weapon.

Over by the balcony's edge, Patriot stood up. Ethan watched him scan the rubble for something. His eyes snapped onto Ethan's. He growled like a wolf and charged.

No time for ethical debate. Ethan grabbed at the javelins but knocked them over instead.

One fell against the corner of a bookshelf and snapped. Streaks of blue lightning zigzagged outward, sizzling. A light bulb exploded in the ceiling, showering the darkening alcove with simulated sparks.

It was a scene from a dream or a movie. Ethan saw it as in slow motion. Patriot rushed at him, roaring. Sparks alighted in his cloak, igniting into pinpricks of yellow flame. Pieces of the ruined stacks tumbled from his feet in landslides. Arms reached forward, unseen hands only inches from Ethan's throat.

Ethan dove into the portal.

< jefferson scott >

ETHAN EMERGED ON THE WHITE STEPS OF THE PARTHENON.

Actually, Ethan didn't know it was the Parthenon. To him it was just one of those old Greek buildings with lots of columns. It looked like the back of a penny, only white. The pillars bounded a smaller inner building on four sides. A single door at the near end broke the white purity of the temple proper. Birds sang sweetly in surrounding shrubs.

The Parthenon's significance might be lost on Ethan, but his programmer's eyes could admire it well enough. The modeling and light sourcing were first rate. Long, clean lines. Exquisite coloring. The textures on the floor, the columns, the walls, the sky, were beautiful.

He sprinted for the shelter of the columns. He'd taken his second step when he heard the chime indicating someone had teleported in behind him. He didn't have to look to know who it was.

Ethan ran down the length of the building, weaving between columns with a fluidity impossible with a lesser machine or a lesser operator. At the corner, he glanced back.

Patriot flew at him down the corridor, strobed with alternating light and shadow as he passed between columns. He flew at an odd angle, as

< virtually eliminated >

if gravity were sideways for him. As if he would prefer to bound off each column like a lion from boulder to boulder. With both hands he clutched to his chest a cluster of golden shafts.

Ethan leapt around the corner. This was the narrow end. If he could round the second corner, maybe he could hide behind a column, double back, buy himself some time.

Was this Patriot's home page? He certainly liked Horace or whoever enough to design a home base like this. All he had to do to find out for sure was —

Ethan perked an ear. He had shot off enough bottle rockets in his day to know that sound. He passed the second corner then bellied up to the wall and snuck a peek back. What he saw turned his insides to tap water.

A rocket-propelled javelin, in and of itself, would be bad enough. A surface-to-surface anti-personnel missile. But when the rocket reached the end of the building, opposite Ethan, it did the most disheartening thing.

It turned toward him.

Ethan sprang away from the corner but collided with a column. The impact halted him, held him in place for precious milliseconds as the rocket's *ssshhhh* grew louder. Panic launched itself from his gut out through the top of his head. He abandoned the idea that Patriot might be feigning strength to hide his injuries.

He ran in blind terror, no longer bothering to weave or double back or do anything besides escape.

The door.

Every GlobeNet site had an exit mechanism. Ethan gambled that the exit from this site must be the door into the Parthenon itself.

He bet his last seconds on that gamble. The missile behind him was faster even than the M7 could make him run. He reached the end of the side portico and rounded the corner to the front of the building.

And came face to face with Patriot, javelins poised to throw.

"Boo."

Patriot began to laugh.

The door leading into the temple was shut. The way was blocked

< jefferson scott >

by Patriot's body. Ethan's shield was gone; he had no trick up his sleeve to deflect the javelins pointed at him now. The missile behind him was seconds away.

In that suspended moment Patriot's laughter seemed to create a reality of its own — a hard, cruel place where rockets homed in for murder and electrocutions occurred like clockwork. Ethan imagined Patriot out here with a garden hose, washing blood off these white steps, while artificial birds sang in ridiculous gaiety.

In virtual reality Ethan ran with his back to the masterpiece of Greek architecture.

In actual reality Ethan tore off his helmet and gloves and sprang around the computer desk. He hit the floor against the wall and — knowing it was probably his last living act — grasped the phone line and yanked.

It was late when Kaye and the kids arrived at her parents' house in Tulsa. Mr. and Mrs. Simms came out to the driveway to greet them.

"Bampa, Bampa, Bampa!" Katie wiggled in her car seat.

"Hello, Jordan!" Mrs. Simms said, giving him a hug. "My, you've grown another foot."

"No I haven't, Gramma. See," he showed his shoes, "only two."

"Oh, you joker," Mrs. Simms said.

Kaye's father gave her a hug. "How was the drive?"

"Oh, it was good." She hugged her mother. "Katie slept most of the way, so we may be in for some trouble tonight."

"No, she won't be any trouble, will you, Katie?"

"Bampa, Bampa."

Mr. Simms got her out of the car seat and gave her a hug. "How's my little granddaughter?"

Kaye picked up the diaper bag. "And Jordan watched a couple movies."

"You did?" Mr. Simms said, over Katie's shoulder. "What did you watch?"

< virtually eliminated >

"*Toontown I* and *II.*"

"Sounds...interesting."

Mrs. Simms herded Jordan and Katie toward the house. "Would you children believe I've got chocolate chip cookies in the oven?"

"All right!"

"Let's go check on them, then."

"Wait." Jordan ran back into the minivan and pulled Wysiwyg out of her carrier. "Can't forget Wizzy."

"Kaye," Mr. Simms said when the others had gone inside, "what is this you have done?"

"What do you mean, Daddy?" She crossed her arms against the cool breeze.

"You call us from your car and say you're coming for a visit and that you're only ten minutes from our house. Then you pull up here with no husband." He took her chin and checked both sides of her face. "Did he hit you?"

"No, Daddy."

Now that she was here, Kaye was even less sure she had done the right thing. It seemed so serious seeing it through her father's eyes. Did this mean she and Ethan were "separated?"

"Is there another woman?"

She almost laughed. "No, Daddy, not really."

"Then what?"

"Like I told Mom on the phone. Ethan's tied up with work right now. The kids and I just got the urge to see grandparents." She started unloading suitcases. "What's so strange about that?"

"You got the urge to see us on a Sunday? On a school night? I don't think so."

The tears were near. Who was she kidding? She might be able to put her mom off for awhile, but she had never been able to keep anything from her daddy. She would tell him everything sooner or later.

"Can't we just get inside for now, Dad? I've been driving a long time."

"Sure, honey."

< jefferson scott >

In a car parked six houses down, two men watched Kaye and her father go inside. They sat back in their seats.

And settled in to wait it out.

Special Agent Mike Gillette pulled to a stop in front of the Hamilton home. He shifted his pickup into park and lowered his eyes.

"What's the matter, Mike? You look like somebody died."

"That's not funny."

"Sorry."

Gillette looked at his passenger but could hold eye contact only for a moment.

Ethan smiled. "I didn't die, Mike. It's okay."

"Nah. That's not it."

"Thought I was going to, though. That time I thought I was going to for sure. I'm no FBI agent, you know. Dodging death two or three times a day isn't exactly what I went to school for."

Gillette nodded. He looked up at Ethan's darkened house.

Ethan looked, too. "Kaye must've taken the kids to dinner. Did she say anything about going out when you called her?"

"Mmm-mm." Gillette shook his head and lowered his eyes again.

"Well, I hope they get back soon. Have I got some things to clear up with Kaye." He gazed at the dashboard until his vision began to blur. "I can't go back on-line, Mike. I can't. The computers...the immersion... it's too much for me. It drags me down, steals my soul."

"What are you talking about?"

"I just can't. You'll have to do this without me, Mike."

"Without you?"

"Or we'll have to look for him another way—no computers. It's... it's just too much for me, Mike. Too strong. It sucks me in." Ethan shook his head as if waking from a daydream.

< virtually eliminated >

"You okay, Hamilton?"

"Yeah, sorry about that."

Gillette didn't say anything.

"Mike."

"What?"

"What's the matter with you tonight? You act like you were the one who almost got deleted, not me. Cheer up."

Gillette nodded unenthusiastically and shifted back into drive.

Ethan got out and shut the door. He leaned back in the open window. "Go get you some pancakes at Old South, why don't you?"

Gillette started to pull away but stopped when Ethan called. He lowered the window on the driver's side. "What?"

"Call me tomorrow about trying to track Patriot on the outside? No computers."

"Hamilton, you are our computer expert, remember? Supposed to work on the computer. If you start playing junior spy guy, you're just going to get yourself killed."

"As opposed to how safe I am on the computer. Look, Mike, I can't help you anymore on the computer. Didn't you see? Weren't you there when he kicked my tail? I've never been so scared in my entire life. It was like a bad horror movie."

Ethan turned aside a little, as if replaying the scene in the air just to the left of Gillette's face. "I was outclassed, outgunned, outrun, and outmatched. He beat me in his territory. He beat me in neutral territory. He even came to my place and beat me in my territory. How do you expect me to fight that?"

Gillette didn't answer.

"Besides…I can't explain it to you, Mike. I just have to stay off of computers for a while. It's a lordship thing. But we can do it another way, can't we? We've got the guy's name, for crying out loud. Let's work on that. I've seen the guy's face. Show me some mug books. He talked about his big plan happening forty hours from then. Let's find out what's going on in the world Tuesday."

< jefferson scott >

Gillette just shook his head.

"Come on, Mike. I know a little about him now — maybe I can predict what he'll do next. Besides," Ethan stepped back from the truck, "I think you owe me this."

"I don't owe you squat, Hamilton."

"Okay, okay. But haven't I shown I know a few things even your experts don't. What do you say, Mike? Let me have a chance."

Gillette looked past Ethan to the house behind. Then he sighed. "Maybe I do owe you, after all. Or will. All right, Hamilton. I'll give you a call."

"Thanks, Mike."

But he'd already rolled the window up and pulled away.

His house was empty.

The minivan wasn't in the garage. No surprise — that was Kaye's vehicle of choice. Only Ethan deigned to drive the old Dodge Intrepid. Nor were there any lights on in the house. Nothing to be learned from that; Kaye wasn't especially good at remembering details like that. He walked to the Master Control wall pad and instituted a house-wide lighting selection.

"Wysiwyg?"

The fact that there was no note alarmed him. His mind was instantly full of grotesque images of his family strewn about the highway. Those images brought another, even stronger, image back into his mind. Jordan and Katie tied up. A gigantic fireplace that was his god. Kaye's eyes looking at him in horror.

That was the other reason he didn't want to fight Patriot on the computer anymore. The rest of what he'd told Gillette was true; he had been outmatched and he did want to pursue other means of catching him. But Ethan knew he needed to swear off computers for a while. Maybe forever.

Surely his family was all right. His first priority while he awaited

< virtually eliminated >

them was to put Jesus back in charge of his life. He remembered the
story he'd told Jordan to explain Christianity. He had Jordan imagine
himself as a bus driver who sees Jesus waiting at a stop. He stops and
opens the door, and Jesus climbs aboard. But Jesus hasn't come for a
ride — he wants to be the new driver. Jordan has to decide whether to
keep on driving, with Jesus taking a back seat somewhere, or to get up
and let Jesus drive. You became a Christian when you let Jesus in and
let him be in charge.

It didn't end there, of course. That was only Ethan's rendering of
conversion. The whole Christian life, then, was a series of crossroads at
which Jordan had to decide whether he was going to trust Jesus to make
the right turns or if he was going to seize control himself. Everyone
doubted and so took over from time to time, but the Christian was the
one who consistently repented and replaced Jesus behind the wheel.

Ethan had kicked Jesus out of the driver's seat in a big way. Now he
needed to get up, ask forgiveness, and let the Master drive.

Further, he needed a concrete grasp on the difference between virtual and actual reality. That line, if he'd ever known it, was gone for him.
Only time spent with the real thing would help him identify and expose
the counterfeit.

For both of those reasons, he needed to stay away from his computers. For awhile he just needed to stay away from his former slave-
master. He had to treat it like any other addiction. It might seem silly to
avoid a check-writing program or a telephone messaging system
because of problems with virtual reality, but Ethan knew himself.

"Here, kitty."

Ethan took a shower and changed clothes. He cozied up on the living room couch with a glass of Sprite and his faithful leather Bible. He
looked at his watch — 10:17 P.M. He would work on priority one until
numbers two and three got back from dinner or a movie or wherever it
was they were.

Where was that cat?

< jefferson scott >

chapter.21

"WHERE IS SHE, MIKE?"

This time it was Gillette's turn to be on the wrong side of a wake-up call. He looked pale in the vidphone monitor, despite the low light and almost twenty-four hours worth of beard stubble. He opened and closed his mouth dryly, rubbed his face. "Who is this?"

"It's me," Ethan said. "Where —"

"Huh?" Gillette obviously didn't excel at mornings either. "What time is it?"

"It's after 2:30. Sorry to —"

"Hamilton? That you? What's wrong?" He looked off screen. "It's after 2:30 in the A-M, boy. What do you want?"

Ethan leaned into the camera mounted on his own monitor. "Mike, tell me where my wife and children are."

"How should I know?"

"Mike."

"What?"

Ethan sighed. He didn't want to play this game. He prayed for help.

When he spoke again, he was calmer, more controlled. "The cat is gone."

Gillette responded to the change. "Is that like 'the rabbit died'?"

"Mike, what have I done? I'm a monster. What have I done?"

"Take it easy, cowboy."

"Mike, I have to talk to her. I know you know where they are."

The FBI agent didn't answer.

"Where are they, Mike?"

"They're okay, Ethan. Just relax."

"I am relaxed, Mike. Where are they?"

"They're up in Oklahoma. Tulsa. Your —"

"Her parents, of course."

"—wife's parents' house."

Ethan accessed his phone directory in another window on the monitor. "Thanks, Mike."

"Wait, don't hang up yet."

Ethan paused, his finger resting on the disconnect key. "What?"

"We didn't take them. To Tulsa, I mean."

"I didn't say you did."

"We only followed her. I mean, it's not like we kidnapped them or anything."

"Kidnapped? Mike, it's all right. I'm actually glad you had some-body watching them." Ethan looked at his watch again. "Is 2:30 too late to call?"

"I just want you to remember that we didn't make them go to Oklahoma. You know, if anything else happens."

"What are you trying to tell me, Mike?"

Now that Ethan was paying attention, Gillette looked like he wanted to run away. "I didn't say I knew anything. Now don't go putting words in my mouth, Hamilton. I only said 'if.' If doesn't mean a thing's neces-sarily so."

"Mike, are you going to tell me what you know or not? Because if not, I'm going to bed. I've got to get up early to call my wife."

< jefferson scott >

Gillette swiped a hand across his cheek. "Look, I'm only trying to warn you. Okay? Because I like you, you little chump. You just need to know that y — What I'm trying to say is that sometimes in my line of work I have to — Sometimes in the pursuit of justice the federal government has to...take steps. And all I'm saying is that I don't always like it. Because I don't. But I don't have to like it. They didn't say, 'Mike, do this or that if you'd like to.' They just said, 'Do it.' So I do it. And so does everybody else in my line of work."

Gillette looked better and worse at the same time, as if he'd just done something he shouldn't have but was glad he had. Or maybe he was relieved he'd gotten that off his chest but was afraid of the consequences.

Either way, it was all lost on Ethan. He couldn't figure out what his friend was trying to convey. Maybe it was enough to realize that something, very possibly unsavory, was going on, that it somehow concerned Ethan, and that Gillette knew but wasn't very happy about it. Whatever it was would, Ethan surmised, eventually become quite clear.

"All right, Mike. I'll remember that. I know you guys didn't make Kaye go off to her parents' house — I did that one all on my own. And I like you, too, Mike. I'll keep what you've said in mind."

"Okay, cowboy. You take care, hear? Why don't you give me a ring when you've got everything patched up with your sweet thing."

Patriot strolled down the beautiful fairway, taking in a quick eighteen holes before breakfast. He had to admire the negotiators' choice of boardrooms. Saint Andrews' Royal and Annuitied Old Course handsomely excelled another conference room he'd once visited.

Patriot had never had the chance to try golf before the accident. From what he'd seen on this course and others, it was a diversion he would have enjoyed. Correction, it was a diversion that other Louis Parks would have enjoyed. The Louis Parks who ceased to exist one rainy day in March. That person, had he endured, would have been

< virtually eliminated >

happy and good-natured, benign, quintessentially dull with middle class success. The wife. The kids. The dog. The house. The job. And the golf clubs.

Patriot didn't like that Louis Parks very much. He was glad he had died. Glad he had surpassed his genetic inheritance, exceeded his programming. The person he was now had substance: talents, intelligence, power. Freedoms. A purpose.

Why, then, if he was so gratified at that old Louis Parks's demise, did Patriot become furious at the mere thought of Ethan Hamilton?

It became clear at once. Hamilton was the embodiment of what the old Louis Parks would have become, had he survived. But Hamilton probably saw himself as superior to everyone who didn't believe as he did. He and his weepy, forgiving God.

Patriot could program circles around Ethan Hamilton. He'd already bested him in cyberspace on every side — though somehow both Ethan and his son remained alive. Patriot had the knowledge, the mechanisms, and the motivation to accomplish his plan with his characteristic panache. But he knew—and he chafed at the thought — that he would forever envy Ethan Hamilton and what he had.

It could have been his.

Thwack! The simulated golf ball shot away from the tee. It had not yet reached its apex when it passed over the green. Patriot lost sight of it when it went behind a stand of larch trees.

He decided against finishing the round. He'd seen enough. There were several good ambush points: blind curves, bridges, narrow forest pathways. Any one of those would do nicely. He always had the option of striking in the open, too. He was even toying with the idea of letting the targets decide the site of their deaths themselves. Wherever the deal was about to be struck, there Patriot would attack.

He shoved his bag into a nearby waterhole and flew up through the sky-ceiling. The realization about Hamilton had disturbed him. When Patriot was disturbed, people and computers stood in increased risk of death or dismemberment.

< jefferson scott >

Kaye and Ethan stared at each other in the vidphone monitor.

Kaye shut her eyes.

"I'm so sorry, Ethan."

"It's all right, honey. I know why you did it. I would have done the same thing." He looked away briefly. "Kaye, you…you were right about me. From the beginning, you were right. I was…addicted to computers. Still am. I have to tell you about this vision God gave me that finally cut through all the layers of junk I'd built up to keep me from seeing the truth.

"I'll tell you the whole thing later, but the long and the short of it was that my computers were becoming a kind of false god to me, and I was its high priest. I sacrificed more and more to it—time, money, energy—you and the kids. It owned me, Kaye. It possessed me. I was its slave. It was like I had blinders on my eyes and plugs in my ears. You were trying to get through to me — I see that now — but then I couldn't hear you or understand what you were trying to tell me.

"But when I saw myself about to sacrifice our children to the fire — and when I saw your eyes, Kaye, looking at me in real terror — I knew then I was out of control, that I needed help. O Kaye, I'm so sorry. Can you forgive me for choosing a machine over you, for trying to hurry up time with you and the kids so I could have more time on the computers?"

"Yes, Ethan, I can forgive you. Can you forgive me?"

"For what?"

"For being jealous of your computers. For taking your son and daughter and running off to my daddy? For abandoning you in a burned out house without even a cat for company? And for being petty?"

"Kaye, stop it. I brought every one of those things on myself."

"No. I didn't have to run off like this. I guess I just wanted to get your attention or hurt you back for how you'd hurt me. Will you forgive me?"

< virtually eliminated >

"Of course, honey." Ethan touched the vidphone screen. "I love you."

"I love you. Well, your family will be home by dinner."

"Do you think your parents would mind letting you stay there for awhile?"

"Here? For how long?"

"I don't know. Maybe a week or two. Until this whole thing blows over."

"But I want to see you."

"I want to see you, too. I just don't feel safe with you here anymore. I may have to leave you alone, and I'd rather you were with somebody who could take care of you."

"Well, I guess."

"I was even thinking—and I don't know how you're going to take this—about moving. How does that sound?"

"Moving? Could we build a new house?"

"Are you sure you really want to, after all the work we did designing this one?"

"Yes! There's so much I would do differently on the next one."

"Okay, then, it's a deal. Do you think your parents will mind having you all there for awhile?"

"Are you kidding? They're loving it. They're taking us out to the Port of Catoosa today and to dinner after that. I think they've got something planned for us every night for weeks."

"Good. But, hey, they don't get to keep you for good."

Kaye smiled. "Don't worry. Tulsa doesn't have enough going on to offer something new every night for very long."

"I'm also swearing off computers, Kaye."

"Say that again?"

"I have to get away from them for awhile."

"For how long?"

"I don't know. Maybe for good."

"Are you still working for the FBI?"

"Yes."

< jefferson scott >

"What are you going to do for them if you're not using a computer?"

"Well, for one thing, I'm going to try to find out where this Patriot lives. He's got to have a physical body somewhere, and I want to find it."

"I know you can do it."

"Thanks, Kaye." Ethan sighed. "It feels so good to be, you know, *back* with you again."

"Wonderful."

Ethan sat in his study at home, writing on a clipboard. He'd had to drive to the nearest convenience store just for a tablet of paper. He usually did this kind of brainstorming on a blank computer screen. But he was going cold turkey. Besides, it wouldn't hurt him to take up pen and paper for a change.

Ethan thought about enlisting the aid of the Internet cult hero Tsutomu Shimomura. Shimomura had achieved fame in the mid '90s for counter-hacking one of the most infamous hackers in Internet history, Kevin Mitnick. Before the adventure was over, Shimomura had worked with the FBI, Sprint, and GTE and had even driven the streets of Raleigh, N.C., holding a portable cellular antenna. Mitnick went to jail. Shimomura became permanently enthroned as an Internet deity.

But something kept Ethan from calling on the legend for help. Probably pride. He wrote the idea on his clipboard anyway.

He lifted his glass of Sprite to his lips, careful to set it down on the cork coaster Kaye had placed on his desk.

Louis David Parks. How many of those could there be, really, in America? A couple hundred. That was way too broad, but it was a good starting place. He would ask Gillette if census records might help at all.

It didn't even occur to Ethan anymore that Patriot might not be from the United States. America was Patriot's country. Hadn't he even made some comments about "our nation's capital" and "as a gentleman and an American"?

Ethan wondered if Gillette could hook him up with a police sketch

< virtually eliminated >

artist. He still saw Patriot's face; it was seared in his mind as permanently as the image in the Shroud of Turin. Patriot didn't seem the type to have spent time in the local slammer, so Ethan's hopes of finding him in a mug book weren't terribly high. But maybe a good rendering, posted on GlobeNet, would generate a few leads.

Ethan leaned back and put his feet on his desk. He cast a guilty look at the door to his study, even though he knew Kaye was in another state. He unfolded the newspaper he'd purchased at the convenience store. It whispered and crackled. Its mix of crispness and linen-like softness felt sublime in his hands. Whoever said that print was dead just needed to get his hands on a Monday morning edition.

Ethan scanned the newsprint for big stories. Issues of national security interested him most, though he did pay close attention to the business section. He was looking for something big set to occur or culminate tomorrow. The front section held the usual fare: unrest in the Middle East, civil war in former Communist countries, and the embattled president defending his EDAP (Emergency Deficit Action Plan).

He noticed that the Cowboys had lost to Jacksonville. Things must be desperate for him to miss a Dallas game on TV. Twenty-eight to ten. Not good.

Back to business. The only thing he saw in the front section that was scheduled to take place tomorrow was another summit between Israel and the PLO. It was just possible that this was Patriot's target. It was certainly big enough. Though Israel was like a favorite nephew to the U.S., from time to time ugly rumors surfaced about that country's true character.

The clincher was that the summit was slated to take place in cyberspace. A decade of controversy between the two factions over neutral meeting sites had finally been settled when a junior aide in the PLO leadership suggested they meet in GlobeNet.

The idea met with instant success and had been used in negotiations of all types around the world. It was perfect for just this kind of brinkmanship. No one had to leave home. No one had to compromise.

< jefferson scott >

No one had to fly through debatably safe airspace. On this issue at least, no one had to trust anyone else.

Ethan cut out the article. He wondered what Gillette's people could do if Patriot made a strike there. He turned to the business page to avoid the answer to that question.

The business section didn't offer much, either. Another of the communications-information giants that had merged in the late '90s had now bowed out of the fight. The comeback the U.S. dollar had been making against the yen was showing itself to be transitory. Fuji was ready to introduce their new HUD (Heads Up Display) system for their '06 model cars. There were the usual notes about fired CEOs, failed takeover bids, and upcoming products.

Ethan folded the paper away in frustration. He dropped his legs and rocked forward in the leather chair. He looked at his clipboard.

1. Shimomura, Mitnick. Call? Drive the streets?
2. Census.
3. Post sketch on-line.
4. Israel/PLO summit Tuesday.

All questions and no answers. Doing it this way, on the outside, the task seemed impossible. Everything was too far away. Inaccessible. Israel. Japan. Even Tulsa seemed a world away.

He wasn't ready to call Gillette yet, not with this paltry list. It was just past 9:00 A.M. If he hadn't come up with anything by 9:30, he would go ahead and call.

He replayed his experience with Patriot. Maybe he could shake something loose.

He'd never met someone so adept in cyberspace. Like a fish in water. As if he'd been born there. Ethan thought of those monkeys NASA had bred on the space station. The chimps had adapted to weightlessness with astonishing ease. Millions of years of terrestrial gravity fell away in a single generation.

He felt the stirring in the back of his mind. The old tickling that told

< virtually eliminated >

him when he was onto something. But it was buried beneath too much reason. He needed to get free of his rational shackles. He prayed to the Father of Creativity and took out a new sheet of paper.

He wrote down the word *unconfined* in the center of the page and circled it. From there he branched off with other words or images as they came into his mind. *Free, cut loose, like a bird, like a fish, no gravity.*

This was a method he'd learned in college for opening the floodgates of his subconscious. One word followed another, each in its own bubble, until that line of thought petered out. Then he'd return to the original word and begin a new string of pearls. He would work like this, sometimes using two or three pages, sometimes starting over with a new central word, until the thought he'd been trying to reach at last dawned on his consciousness.

Unfettered, unrestrained, no limits, no boundaries. He felt his brain go fuzzy, the sign he was in his free associative zone. He kept replaying the image of Patriot floating over Falcon's Grove, cartwheeling slowly.

He made a new branch from the original word. *Drifting, floating, flying, free from GlobeNet's gravity, free from GlobeNet's normal passageways.*

These were close, but not exactly right. He thought again of the weightless monkeys. A new branch. *As if born there, natural, adept, normal for him, natural habitat, as if he lives there.*

He was getting warmer.

It was as if Patriot lived in cyberspace. Only artificial intelligences actually had their sole existence in a computer. Patriot was no artificial intelligence. And it wasn't just that he seemed to spend all his time in GlobeNet — there were plenty of high-school dropouts who did that. No, Patriot seemed at home in VR.

At home in virtual reality. As if he lived there. Ethan read back over his sheet. As if he was born there. Natural. As if it was normal for him. As if it was his natural habitat.

What kind of person spent that kind of time hooked up to VR? Not even Ethan or any VR programmer he knew of spent enough time "under" to be as fluid as Patriot.

< jefferson scott >

He pounded his forehead with the heel of his hand. He was so close. Why couldn't he think?

What kind of person spent all day every day hooked up to VR? Why would anyone spend —

And then, there it was.

< virtually eliminated >

chapter.22

WHAT WAS IT HE HAD SAID? "The tree of liberty must be refreshed from time to time with the blood of patriots and tyrants."

The tree of liberty. Willy liked that. He underlined it in his journal. Maybe he could use it in his paper due Thursday.

He'd better snatch up all the good stuff he could while he was still here. This job had been a source of all kinds of riches. But he'd had a better offer. Someplace that actually paid closer to what he deserved. He didn't know how he was going to tell the old lady he was quitting — even though he'd been fantasizing about it for months.

He thought about just leaving while she was gone, letting her find his note when she got back home. But he didn't know how long she was going to be away. Somebody had to ride the meters on this stiff. And change the bedpan and refill the IV. If the old witch got home and found her "baby" dead as a doornail, she'd probably track him down and yank his heart out.

So Willy Stanton contented himself with jotting down any good lines that drooled from the patient's mouth. Maybe he'd hear something he could use on the hag when she got back in town.

< jefferson scott >

"Yes, we do that sort of thing. Wheelchairs and robot arms, though, mostly."

It was a small window on a small-to-medium monitor, but Ethan thought the scientist talking to him looked a lot like Elmer Fudd. Big, round head, narrow shoulders, receding hairline. He kept waiting for the man to end one of his sentences with, "Be vewy, vewy quiet."

But of course he never did. He was a serious man with a serious job. Dr. Roger Owens was deputy chief of staff at the Oregon Research Institute, a leading facility in the use of virtual reality for the severely handicapped.

Ethan stifled the urge to ask when wabbit season opened. "What do you do for the worst cases? You know, the ones who are 100 percent paralyzed or whatever."

"For 100 percent paralysis there's really not much we can do. For success in our program, patients must have at least one viable appendage, be that a finger or toe or elbow. We concentrate on mobilizing our patients into their world. Our motto here is, 'Normalize for Normal Lives.'"

"Cute." *I am Elmer J. Fudd, millionaire. I own a mansion and a yacht.*

"We give them the tools and the training to fully enjoy their life. We're working on an exciting system right now that will allow a patient up to 90 percent paralyzed to drive a modified car."

"Amazing." Ethan wasn't sure he wanted a 90 percent paralyzed driver on the road with him.

"Yes, it is a major breakthrough."

"If I'm hearing you right, Dr. Owens, you concentrate more on allowing people to function in the real world. Is that right?"

"That's correct, Mr. Hamilton. Our patients report an almost unbelievable improvement when they return to their homes. Some say their lives didn't begin until they came to ORI."

"But you do use VR, don't you?" Ethan felt his theory melting away.

< virtually eliminated >

He'd been so sure he was on the right track. The faculty at UT Arlington said this place in Eugene was the one to call. But this was all wrong. He didn't want to know about how well a paralyzed person could relate to the real world. He wanted to know how well such a person could move around in the virtual world.

"The virtual reality we use," Owens explained, "is designed to heighten the patient's perception of the real world. In our car driving system, for instance, the driver wears a helmet equipped with machinery right out of army attack helicopters. He has a better field of view, in fact, than you or I could have with a hundred rear view mirrors.

"Other VR applications include telepresence for the virtual arm robotic arm and tactile feedback devices for controlling wheelchairs." Dr. Owens squinted out at Ethan. "That's what we do here, Mr. Hamilton. Now," he leaned forward, "is there someone you know who might be interested in our program?"

"Actually, I'm just doing research."

"I see."

"What I'm really interested in is using VR so handicapped people can move around freely in artificial worlds. Like on GlobeNet, for instance."

Dr. Owens leaned back in his chair. "Oh. No, I'm sorry, Mr. Hamilton. You see, we don't believe that sort of thing has any real merit. How is escaping your life supposed to help you live it to the full?"

Ethan didn't like the man's tone. "I don't know. Some people might want to escape into GlobeNet so they could have a life at all. Maybe their bodies are like anchors to them. Maybe they like the feeling of freedom they can have on-line. When you're on-line you can do any —"

"But that's just the sort of thing we strive to avoid. Those bodies you spoke of, like anchors, are challenges. We all have obstacles to overcome in our lives, don't we, Mr. Hamilton? But if we run away from them, if we hide in some world of make-believe, we are just as ignorant as the ostrich who sticks his head in the sand."

"All right, Dr. Owens. I'm afraid this isn't going the way I meant it

< jefferson scott >

to. Thank you for your time."

"Very well, Mr. Hamilton. Pleasure talking with you."

Ethan reached for the "terminate call" key.

"Oh, there is something you should know," Dr. Owens said.

Ethan sighed. "Yes."

"If you really want to pursue that method of treatment, there is someone you should call. I would be entirely remiss if I didn't, in all fairness, help you find what you're searching for."

Spit it out, Doc.

"Call Dr. Lois Hosokawa at Loma Linda University Labs, in California. Loma Linda's really been the leader in the kind of research you're interested in. And Dr. Hosokawa's top flight."

"All right, Dr. Owens, I'll definitely give her a call. Thanks."

Dr. Hosokawa wasn't in yet. It wasn't even 8:00 A.M. in California. Ethan left a message on the machine. Then he called Gillette. The special agent gave Ethan a GlobeNet address where he could review every U.S. census from 1790 to 2000.

"Oh, yeah, I forgot," Gillette said. "You're not doing the computer thing, are you?" He grinned devilishly from his window on Ethan's monitor. "Aren't you taking this Jesus thing just a tad too seriously? Besides, you got to get with the times, Ethan, old boy. Everything's on computer now, didn't you know? If you can't use a computer, you're like an airplane without wings. The world's left you behind, you sorry sod."

"Ha ha. You haven't heard a few of those comments aimed at you, now have you, Special Agent Gillette?"

"A few."

"And, yes, I am taking the Jesus thing very seriously. I have to follow Him all the way or not at all."

Gillette looked at him like Ethan had just thrown up on himself. "If you say so."

"Just send me paper copies, okay?"

"Of what?"

"The censuses."

"'Cen-sus-es...es.' Is that a word?"

"It is now."

"How far back do you want them?"

"Better give me from 1940 on."

"Gotcha." Gillette wrote it down. "By the way, the CIA thanks you for the tip. They're helping the Arabs step up their security for the summit."

"Wow. The CIA thanks me?" Ethan grinned like a mule.

Gillette looked at a legal pad. "Having trouble getting one of our sketch artists out this way. Maybe you could contact your local PD. Tell them it's for us. Have them call me if they don't believe you."

"What do you think about driving the streets with a hand-held antenna?"

"Say again."

"Remember that story... Never mind. When your phone tapping people tried to trace —"

"Nobody tapped the phone!" Gillette crouched down and looked off screen. When he spoke again his voice was hushed. "Didn't mean to say it that loud. We're all just a little sensitive about that right now."

"Okay, so, when your information surveillance technicians—"

"Thank you."

"— attempted to trace Patriot's call, did they get anything we could use? A relay station; a long distance carrier; cellular, wireless, or coaxial? Anything?"

Gillette was writing. "Have to get back with you on that." He set his pen down. "All I remember at the time was them saying they lost him when he 'hit the bird.' They lost me after that."

"A bird's a satellite. Just let me know, okay? Maybe we can use Mr. Shimomura's tactics, after all."

"Shimomura? Ain't that the lady in California who's calling you back?"

"No, that's Dr. Hosokawa."

< jefferson scott >

"Hosokawa, Shimomura, Yamaha, sushi." Gillette shook his head. "I'm beginning to think Patriot's right about Japan owning this man's country. All right, Ethan, buddy, I'll get moving on this right away."

"Remember those paper censuses."

"Censuseses, right. Sayonara, cowboy." He hesitated before hanging up. "Say, what's up with this place in California, anyway? You think you're on to something, hot shot?"

"I think maybe, Mike. I was almost positive when I made my first call, but they didn't —"

"You think Patriot's some kind of scientist or something?"

"No. I think he might be handicapped, though."

"No way! Lame? Hamilton, don't you remember running for your life yesterday? Does he have one of those turbo wheelchairs? Is he going to run you down with it?"

"Just because he can run in VR doesn't mean he can run in real life. You've seen me when I go under. How much running do I do, Mr. Computer Expert?"

"So who's this Hokomoko?"

"Dr. *Hosokawa* runs the VR research labs at Loma Linda University. I found an article in one of my old magazines. They do lots of cool VR stuff. But one thing they do is help paralyzed people use VR to do things in cyberspace."

"Like what, play games?"

"No, like study and travel and talk with people. The full GlobeNet experience."

"W-w-well, excuse me. The full *NerdNet* experience."

"They've got this system where a guy straps in to one of those gyro-things and actually flies an airplane from the lab."

"No fooling?"

"The military wants their system, of course. Think about it — no more pilot losses. Just send up a robot plane, shoot down the bad guys, and fly the thing home. Like a radio-controlled model."

"I used to fly those."

< virtually eliminated >

"Loma Linda's been helping invalids use VR for decades. Back in the '90s one of their people flew a flight simulator with just EEG monitors stuck to his head."

Gillette didn't react.

"They piloted an airplane without using their hands, Mike."

"No hands?"

"No hands, no feet, nothing. Just electrodes stuck to a guy's head. Maybe some voice commands."

"Oh, I get it now." Ethan thought he actually saw a light bulb go on over Gillette's head. "You think Patriot's using this EEG thing to fly around in vir-tu-al re-al-i-ty."

"Congratulations, detective."

"But wait a minute. What makes you think he's crippled? Like you said, just because he swims like a fish on that World Net doesn't mean he can't walk."

"True. I don't know, Mike. It's just a hunch. You get those, don't you? Something about the way he moves or the way he doesn't move — I don't know."

Ethan wasn't talking to Gillette anymore. He was trying to figure this one out for himself. It was just as well, since Gillette's eyes had begun to glaze over.

"Remember how he turned flat out at my castle, Mike? And the way he chased me at that Greek building. He turns sideways all the time."

"Like he's laying down and that's what he's used to?"

"Maybe," Ethan allowed. "Or maybe he's just not interested in an up and down world. Maybe he's been free-floating in GlobeNet for so long — and not walking around in the real world for so long — that up and down don't mean much to him anymore."

"Isn't that what I just said?"

"Yes, that's what you just said. Anyway, that's why I'm waiting for a call from Dr. Hosokawa. I want to ask her if they've treated anybody named Louis David Parks."

"Tell you what, Ethan, buddy. I'll do you one better."

< jefferson scott >

"What?"

"Why don't you go out there yourself?"

"Why? Mike, she's just in a meeting. She'll call me back in a minute." Ethan felt something going into motion. He wasn't sure he would like it.

"Nope, you're going. And I'm going with you." He typed at his keyboard. "Even though it means reneging on what was going to be a sweet date with Liz. But it's important. Because I just remembered something else the phone tap guys told me yesterday."

"What?"

"They said that for less than one second they got a clean look with one of their special spy probes. They couldn't pin it down, but they said Patriot's call probably originated from somewhere on the Pacific Coast."

Louis Parks didn't remember ever knowing the technician's name. He was just that brown face bobbing over the instrument panel or exercising Louis's legs. Louis had never spoken more than twenty words to the young man, even though he'd probably been his med-tech for three or four years.

Louis watched the young black man now, through his goggles. The goggles worked like tinting on car windows — they allowed Louis to look at whoever he wanted without the target knowing. The med-tech was sitting beside the bed reading a paperback. There was a clipboard beside the chair.

How much, over the months, had he heard? Would he need to be eliminated? Probably not. It will all be over before he could cause much trouble.

He graced the servant with a rare direct address. "Get my mother." The tech looked up. "Uh, sorry, Mr. Parks, but, uh…she ain't here." "When is she due?"

The tech just nodded his head and rubbed his chin. Louis would get Mother to replace this fool immediately.

< virtually eliminated >

"She…" the tech laughed nervously. "She didn't say."

"Where is she?"

He laughed again. "Nah. No, see, I ain't allowed to say. I'm not *supposed* to say, is what the lady told me."

"What is your name?"

"Willy Stanton. William Trimble Stanton. The First."

"William, do you value your employment here?"

"Well, now that you mention it…"

"Because if you wish to maintain said employment, you will tell me post-haste the location, itinerary, and expected arrival time of my mother."

"As much as you may want to fire me, mister, and as much as I may want to quit, it would probably be better for us both if you didn't. You know what I mean?"

"I'm afraid I do not. Are you, William, or are you not going to tell me where my mother is?"

"See, the thing is, if I don't tell you, you're going to fire me. And if I do tell you, you're probably going to fire me anyway. So what should I do? You tell me."

"Very well, William, I will tell you what you should do. Since you are intent upon resigning, my suggestion is that you tell me where she is, then leave. That done, we shall both have what we want. Agreed?"

"How you gonna live with nobody to change your bags and work your legs?"

"I'll have someone else in here before the day is out. Don't worry about me."

"Okay, man, but you are not going to like it. No calls to my school about this, right?"

"Guaranteed. I don't even know from which institution you hail."

"And I get to put you down as a reference for my next job. Deal?"

"Agreed. Where is she?"

Willy stood up and moved toward the door. There he paused dramatically. He turned back toward the bed and crooned in fine Reggae

< jefferson scott >

style, "Yo momma, she fly to Jamaica to limbo with dat young mon."

He opened the door.

"Later, mon."

< virtually eliminated >

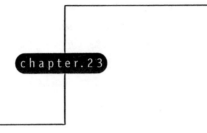

chapter.23

"GOODNESS, MR. HAMILTON. You take unreturned telephone calls quite seriously, don't you?"

Ethan wiped the honey mustard from his mouth with a napkin. "That's right, Doctor. If I don't get a call back within ten minutes, I'm on a plane to find out why."

Dr. Hosokawa was quite blonde. Quite Caucasian. It was her husband, also a doctor, a thoracic surgeon at Loma Linda's famous hospital, who gave her her Oriental name. Ethan and Gillette had met her as she was going out to lunch. She had agreed to accompany them to a local restaurant.

Gillette was gaping beneath the top bun of the sandwich the waitress had brought him. Apparently he had never seen guacamole on a BLT before.

"I was going to return your call, honest. Although it might not have been today. So it's a good thing you did come out here. We're at an exciting phase of one of my projects. Sometimes I just lose track of time."

"It's quite all right." Ethan could hardly tell his hamburger was really

< jefferson scott >

a turkey burger. He did ask the waitress for more honey mustard, though. "It seems we needed to come out here anyway."

"When we get back, I'll show you what we're doing. As a VR programmer you are especially qualified to appreciate it, I think." She looked at Gillette. "You should enjoy it, too, Mr. Gillette."

"Mrrph-uss," he said around a bite.

"That would be great," Ethan said. "So long as we get to look at your records, too."

"Of course."

According to their records, Loma Linda University Laboratories had never treated anyone named Louis Parks. Lots of challenged people: paraplegics, quadriplegics, epileptics, Parkinson's disease patients. Just none named Louis David Parks.

Ethan drove the receptionist almost to distraction by helping her look it up on the computer. He even breached the sacred barrier between server and served by rounding the counter to look over the poor woman's shoulder.

Nothing.

No Louis Parks, no Louis David Parks, no L. Parks, no L. D. Parks. Not even a Lou. They looked under research, physical therapy, experimental care. Nothing on the main hospital register. They even checked the student and faculty rosters of both Loma Linda and her sister school for undergrads, La Sierra University. All to no avail.

Gillette didn't seem worried. He sat in a plush swivel chair out in the lobby, watching the in-house video promotional over and over.

When Ethan finally relented, it was almost three o'clock. Five, Texas time. He was frustrated, Gillette was bored, and the poor receptionist just wanted to get back to her work.

Ethan led Gillette back toward the faculty building where Dr. Hosokawa maintained her office. The Loma Linda University campus was beautiful. It was on a hill overlooking Loma Linda proper. Palm trees lined the brick buildings in luxurious rows. California sunshine bathed the whole scene.

A student grader in Hosokawa's office directed them back to the lab, where the doctor was conducting her research. The lab looked like a television sound stage Ethan had once visited: heavy double doors, sleek concrete floor, a gridwork of pipes on the ceiling to support lights and other equipment. There were about ten white-coated people, mostly young, in the room, clustered around what looked like an MRI machine.

Dr. Hosokawa stood at a console at the foot of the machine, next to the young man operating the controls. She acknowledged Ethan's and Gillette's presence with a clipped wave before turning back to the console. "How's his pulse?"

A plump girl by an array of medical instruments shook back a lock of bleached-blonde hair. "Elevated but steady, Doctor."

"All right." Hosokawa lifted a microphone to her lips. "How you doing, Kev?"

"Just fine."

The voice startled Ethan. It seemed to come from all around them. Gillette pointed out speakers in the gridwork of pipes. They moved to a spot behind Dr. Hosokawa. They could see Kev's legs on the brightly lit platform, but the rest of his body was under the massive cowling.

"We're going to send some things at you now, okay?"

"Bring them on. You've got to give this baby a spin, Doc."

The young man operating the controls pulled the microphone from Hosokawa. "Only if you promise not to throw up again, buddy boy."

There was enough laughter in the room to tell Ethan this was a distinct possibility.

A collective *Whoa!* came from the students standing on the far side of the machine. Ethan saw the telltale blueness on their faces. "Come on, Mike. Let's go watch it on TV."

The image on the screen was so distorted Ethan almost threw up, too. There was a circle of clarity at the center of the screen, surrounded

< jefferson scott >

on all sides by a surrealistic tunnel effect. Images of trees, mountains, and clouds stretched like rubber when they reached the edge of the focused spot, then plummeted backward past the edge of vision.

"It takes some getting used to."

Ethan found Dr. Hosokawa standing between him and Gillette. "I'll say."

"It doesn't look like this to him. He sees the clear spot wherever he looks. The rest is supposed to simulate peripheral vision. When he turns to look at something he sees out of the corner of his eye, he sees it in the clear spot."

Gillette stuck his hands in his pockets but didn't say anything. Come to think of it, Ethan couldn't remember when his partner had last said more than a couple of words. Maybe the guacamole was getting the better of him.

Ethan crossed his arms. He could hear the fans cooling the big machine. "So, are you trying to help a paralyzed person fly a plane?"

"No, no," she said. "But I imagine we could use it for that. No, we're looking for a more ergonomic way to navigate inside a simulation, be it a flight simulator like this one or one my husband might use for micro-surgery.

"All this," she indicated the whole room, "is just an extension of what we've done for disabled patients. It just so happens that the things we've learned helping handicapped people have taught us quite a lot about healthy ones."

"This isn't an MRI machine?" Gillette asked.

"No, Mr. Gillette. Not anymore, anyway. The university was phasing these out and one of my students thought it would be a great way to house this experiment. She was right. There's not much left of the original machine besides the conveyor table and motor. My students and I designed and built the rest."

"I'm impressed," Gillette said.

"The operator inside the bell doesn't move at all. That's a holdover from our work with paraplegics. He just moves his eyes, and the com-

< virtually eliminated >

puter adjusts his vision. It uses laser gyroscope technology — very similar to some top secret guided missiles we're not at liberty to discuss."

As she continued, Ethan was thinking about having another crack at the university computer records. He was so sure this was the right place.

He realized Dr. Hosokawa had asked him something. "I'm sorry?"

She was pointing to the table where, Ethan now saw, Kev was getting unstrapped and uncabled. "Would you like to give it a go?" she asked again.

Yes, are you kidding! "I don't think so, Doctor. Not this time, thanks." She looked a little taken aback. "It's a long story. I'm sort of swearing off computers for a while."

"My, you are an enigma, aren't you, Mr. Hamilton? The computer programmer who's sworn off computers."

Ethan took a step toward the door. "Well, I, uh, guess we better be going. Thanks for the demo, Dr. Hosokawa. Come on, Mike. Don't we need to be getting checked into a hotel?"

Gillette didn't move. "I thought I might take that thing for a spin."

"Why, sure, Mr. Gillette," Hosokawa said.

"Mike, don't you remember your stomach? Somebody's already thrown up in there. You sure you can handle that?"

"I guess you're right. Maybe I'll take a rain check on that one, Doctor."

Ethan tugged at the fifteen-foot door, but Dr. Hosokawa wasn't finished with them yet. She called to them to wait. She gave her assistants some instructions, then came to them at the door. "I'll walk you out, at least."

On the walk, Dr. Hosokawa and Agent Gillette fell into a discussion of football. She was a diehard Chargers fan, it seemed. Gillette, of course, was a Cowboys fan. They reached the lobby before they reached the end of their argument. Gillette was still sore over the officiating in the '03 Super Bowl. He kept saying, "They never should've replaced the line judges with cameras!"

Ethan sat in the same overstuffed swivel chairs Gillette had occupied before. He noticed, belatedly, that the receptionist wasn't at her desk. *Probably went home with a migraine.* He stared blankly at the screen showing the university's self-promotional video.

At length Gillette slapped the back of Ethan's chair. "Let's go, buddy. Seems I am never going to talk sense into this woman."

Ethan lifted himself from the chair. And froze.

"Look!" Ethan didn't take his eyes off the video screen. It showed a non-mobile patient driving a wheelchair with some kind of head-mount apparatus. Two therapists appeared in the shot when the wheelchair skirted one edge of the room.

"Yes, I'm afraid it's a rather old promotional," Dr. Hosokawa said. "We really should make a new one. I've been talking to Dr. Roosevelt about using the RVT — what you saw today — in the next promo."

The video had moved on to another section. "Play this back," Ethan said. "How can we play this back?"

Hosokawa turned to the receptionist's desk. "Now where did she go? It's the school-wide system. It just runs automatically. I could try to call tech support." She walked over to the vacant desk and picked up a phone.

Ethan knelt in front of the screen. Gillette sat in a chair beside him.

"What's so interesting, Cowpoke? I've seen that video a hundred times. It's the same thing over and over."

"Mike, I think —" Just then the video started scanning in reverse. "Here we go. All right. Wait," he turned to Hosokawa at the receptionist's desk. "That's far enough."

She spoke into the phone then hung up.

The segment began playing forward. The narrator said something about Loma Linda University Labs' great advances in helping the severely handicapped. The image faded from black to show the rolling wheels of a wheelchair. The camera tilted up slowly, revealing more specialized equipment. Just as the wheelchair turned forward, the camera reached the boy's face.

< virtually eliminated >

"Ha!" Ethan shouted.

"What?" Gillette shouted back. People strolling through the lobby turned toward the noise.

Ethan ran to the screen. "That's him! That's him!"

"That's who?" Gillette said, standing. "Who?"

The boy, about ten years old, steered the wheelchair past the two physical therapists as the narrator bragged on about why people should donate money to the school.

Ethan would always recognize that face.

"Louis David Parks."

< jefferson scott >

chapter.24

OF THE TWO PHYSICAL THERAPISTS shown in the video, one had been killed in a traffic accident. The other was still with the university.

Burt Wikowski had been fifty-eight in 1990 when that video was taken. Even then he was showing his age. That made him seventy-three now. He was a stalwart fellow, tall and solid.

Burt hadn't adapted well to the new way of doing physical therapy. People a quarter his age were coming out of school with master's degrees in vocational rehabilitation and sports medicine, while he still just wanted to help people get back on their feet again. But Burt Wikowski had something that made him valuable in any era. He cared about his patients.

Ethan, Gillette, and Dr. Hosokawa took Burt aside in the orthopedic wing of the university hospital. What little hair he had left clung to the side and back of his scalp like lichen. His white, loose-fitting clothes made him look more prepared for bedtime than therapy. But his mind was sharp as a pin.

"Sure, I remember the Parks boy," he said, sitting in a chair in an unoccupied patient room. "Poor kid."

< virtually eliminated >

Ethan successfully resisted the urge to cast an "I told you so" look at Dr. Hosokawa.

She couldn't understand how the laboratory records could be wrong. All the way over to the hospital and up to the orthopedic floor she had lectured Ethan on their painstaking record-keeping. She hadn't gone so far as to say Ethan was mistaken, but he could tell she had wanted to.

"That's great, Mr. Wikowski," Gillette almost shouted. "Anything you can remember will help us."

"I'm seventy-two, son, not ninety-two. Hold your voice down."

Gillette hoisted a leg up on the bed and sat down. "No offense."

Ethan offered Dr. Hosokawa a chair, but she refused it, preferring to stand by the door. Ethan sat down facing Burt. "What can you tell us about the Parks boy?"

"Louis Parks? Well, I remember him, for one thing. Louie. Pretty bad, that one. Car wreck, I think it was. Mother tried to help him. Picked him up, moved him out of the street. Probably severed whatever spinal cord he had left in the doing."

There was something soothing about this powerful, gentle man, spinning his tale like an old pirate at the Green Parrot Inn. Ethan leaned forward almost involuntarily.

"When they brought him to me, he was just a kid. Nine or ten. Couldn't even move his head. Couldn't even stick his tongue out at me, though I made him wish he could. Worked with him two years."

"That's impossible," Dr. Hosokawa cut in. "It's not possible for a patient to be here two years and not be on any of our records."

It finally began to dawn on Ethan what must have happened.

Burt went on. "Doctors wanted to try him on all their machines."

"We saw him riding around in a wheelchair," Gillette offered.

"Don't much like those machines," Burt continued. "Keeps a man from doing for himself. But in Louie's case I made the exception. Louie was..." Burt didn't acknowledge the tear that dropped from one eye. "Kids like Louie are why I took this job. Why I'm still doing it. He just wanted to be normal again. He played first base for his baseball team.

< jefferson scott >

So I worked with him. We watched pro games together on TV. I thought if I worked hard and fast enough, there might be some hope."

"What happened?"

"Same thing as happens to most people who come in with his kind of injury. They try for a while. When it doesn't get all better, or when they don't think they're gaining any ground, they cave in. Give up. There's nothing you can do for them. They just sit in their rooms and stare out the window. Won't eat, won't talk. Won't try."

"Is that what happened to Louis — I mean, to Louie?" It made a difference for Ethan to think of Patriot as a kid named Louie.

"He got it bad. Halfway through the second year. Could see it in his eyes."

"He just gave up?"

"There's different kinds of giving up. Some get sad, some get mad. Some, first chance they get, try to stab themselves. Louie just got mean. Got all squinty-eyed when I'd come in the room. Spit on me half the time. Bit me the other."

Burt fell silent, staring into an unoccupied corner. Dr. Hosokawa shifted, knocking her heeled shoe on the tile.

"So what happened?" It was Gillette this time.

"That was it. We worked till the end of the second year, but it was no use. Then his insurance ran out and they had to take him on home. Parents couldn't afford the fancy wheelchair. Breaking up, they were. But Louie's heart dried up a long time before the money did. "Aw, Louie," he said, pronouncing it as a requiem.

"Louie was very lucky to have you, Mr. Wikowski," Ethan said.

Burt didn't look up.

"Mr. Wikowski," Gillette said, "do you think Louis Parks — all grown up — would be capable of murder?"

"Murder? What's he going to do, spit somebody to death? Maybe you haven't been listening too good, son; Louie's paralyzed from the neck down."

Ethan interlaced his fingers. "I think what Special Agent Gillette is

< virtually eliminated >

trying to ask, sir, is if you think Louie could be mad enough to want to kill somebody?"

"Louie?" Burt seemed to shrivel just a little before their eyes. "I don't think so. No. Louie would never do that. He's a good boy deep inside."

Gillette and Ethan traded a look.

"You said he got mean," Ethan said. "He's grown up now — couldn't fifteen or so years stuck in a bed make that meanness grow?"

"I don't want to talk to you anymore." Burt stood up, but didn't leave. "Louie was a good boy! Sure he got mad at me and fought with me a little — who could blame him? The only other time I ever saw him mad at anybody else was when the team he was rooting for lost the Little League World Series. But he wasn't mad enough to kill anybody over it."

"Thank you for your time, Mr. Wikowski," Gillette said, standing.

"Wait a second, Burt," Ethan said. "Do you remember who Louie's team lost to that year?"

"Now how am I supposed to — no wait, yes I do. It was some Oriental team. Japan or China. Korea, Taiwan. One of those."

Gillette raised an eyebrow. "You wouldn't happen to remember where Louis Parks was from, would you?"

"Yes, I remember. He was from St. Louis. But the family moved here to be close. Then his parents broke up. I don't know where his father went after that. Mother stayed with Louie. I went to his house to watch a World Series game once."

Ethan couldn't believe what he was hearing. Were they really only minutes from Louis Parks's house? Could this all be over today, this afternoon? Before dinner? The steps laid themselves out before him in his mind. He would take the evening flight to Tulsa and sleep with his wife that night. The next day they could be in their own home, with all this behind him. It sounded too good to be true.

< j e f f e r s o n   s c o t t >

At the address Burt directed them to, there was now a multi-screen movie theater. The manager of the place recalled that there had been houses on this block before it had been rezoned for business.

"Maybe the old man's memory is going," Gillette said, back in the rental car.

"There used to be houses here, Mike. You heard it yourself. Did he sound like he was losing his memory? Besides…"

"I know, I know. You have a hunch." He steered the car back onto the street.

"It does feel right, Mike. What can I say?"

"Well, Einstein, let's just go over your case here, all right? One, you see a guy on a video who might be, fifteen years earlier, a guy you saw for less than one second in vir-tu-al re-al-i-ty."

"It is him, Mike."

"Two, an old man tells you he remembers 'Louie,' even though some of the greatest scientific minds in our country tell you Louis Parks never set foot on their campus."

"I've got that one figured —"

"And three, you, the great Ethan Hamilton, have a hunch. Well, well, well. The state rests, your honor."

Ethan was laughing now, despite himself.

"Lock this man up, your honor. We've got a guess, a coot, and a hunch. Throw away the key."

"All right, you've made your point. It's not much, I know. But if it's so little, why are you and I out here, huh?"

"I'm watching traffic, Tex. Don't bother me."

"I'll tell you why. Because you've got a hunch, too. And your hunch tells you my hunch is right. Am I right?"

"You lost me, cowboy."

"That's our turn we just passed."

Gillette swore.

< virtually eliminated >

"Besides, I've got number two figured out."

"Move, you sorry beach bums!"

"All their records are on computer, right? And they're connected to GlobeNet, right?"

Gillette made a U-turn. "So they're on NerdNet, so what?"

"So Patriot just erased himself from their records, that's so what."

"You can't do that."

"Oh, really, Professor? And how long have you been programming?"

"You're not supposed to be able to do that."

"Welcome to the twenty-first century, Special Agent. It's not that hard to get into most computers from GlobeNet, especially university computers, since they're typically older systems and the security's not very tight."

"So what's to keep me from going in and erasing you?"

"You could, if you knew every computer I was listed on." It was amazing how something coming out of one's own mouth could propel one to further revelation. "And I've just — whoa, Mike! I think I've just figured out what Patriot's done! I think I know how we can find him!"

"How are you going to do that?"

"Just hurry up and get us to the hotel."

"What do you think I'm doing?"

"I don't get it," Gillette said for the tenth time.

"Just let me get set up. Then I'll have you call out some things to me from your screen."

Gillette adjusted the screen on the laptop computer. He took a sip from the mixed drink he'd ordered from room service and set the glass back down on the hotel table. The remains of their dinner lay on a tray on the brown desk along the wall. "Why do I have to be the one on this thing? You're the computer whiz."

"I know. It seems extremist to you, doesn't it? Look, you wouldn't

< jefferson scott >

offer a reforming alcoholic a drink on his first day in the dry-out clinic, would you?"

"Depends on how much they offer to pay me."

"I know you don't get it, Mike." Ethan tossed the last of the census records onto the tightly made hotel bed. "Just humor me, okay?"

"I'm not going to get zapped, am I?"

"If you do, I'm not cleaning it up."

"You're a real pain in the can when you want to be, you know that?"

"I try." Ethan stacked the huge hotel pillows against the headboard and leaned back.

Somehow Ethan imagined that FBI agents would stay in better places than the Ramada Inn. He knew it was taxpayers' money and all, and he didn't want abuses more than anyone else. But he was a taxpayer, too. He thought it might be about time some of that money went to work in his own life. How much more would the Hilton have been, anyway? He was glad, at least, to have his own room.

"Okay, let's see." The census records were printed on cheap paper, bound with light blue vinyl covers, and held together with long silver brads. They were designated by date in large, government-font letters. Ethan pulled the one marked 1990 into his lap and opened it. "Alaska, Arizona, Colorado. Oops, too far. Here we go, California. You turn to 1990, too. Find California."

In a few moments, both Ethan and Gillette were staring at the same data on two different media.

"Let's start with the theory that Burt Wikowski was right about his address. Search by Loma Linda, then by last name Parks."

"Hold your horses. I'm still trying to get to Loma Linda."

"Then last name Parks."

"Okay. I've got six."

Ethan scanned the printed page in front of him. "Any on Mesa?"

"Well, I'll be."

"You got one?"

"9733 Mesa Drive. Robert and Linda Parks."

< virtually eliminated >

Ethan's task was more difficult than Gillette's. Data on paper didn't rearrange itself according to requested search parameters. He had to compile his own table of findings. He was flipping to his third *See also* when Gillette went on.

"Ah, forget it. Dead end."

"Why?"

"There's no kids here. No Louis David Parks. Old man must have been confused, after all. Senile. Getting our boy Parks mixed up with somebody with the same name. Happens to the best of us."

Ethan wasn't as ready to give up. "Hang on, Mike. Let me check mine." He finally arrived at the right page. He ran his finger down the column, mouthing first names. "Here it is. Robert Parks, 9733 Mesa Drive." He paused, then looked up at Gillette.

"What?"

"I think you'd better have a look at this."

Gillette crossed the room. "Show me."

Ethan tracked the words with his finger. "Occupants: Robert, age 33; Linda, age 30; and…"

"Well I'll be doggone. Louis, age 10."

"I knew it!" Ethan slammed the book shut. "Patriot, in the flesh."

"Well, how come yours says that and mine —" Gillette's mouth actually dropped open. "Naw."

"Has to be."

"No way."

"Yes way."

"So now Parks is messing with U.S. census data? Come on, Hamilton, talk sense."

"Why not? You think he can figure out how to send lightning through the phone lines but he can't change a few records in a database? You're the one who needs to talk sense."

"There's no way."

Ethan stood up. "Come on, Mike. Computers have been in people's houses for twenty-five years. Don't you think the bad guys have them,

< jefferson scott >

too? How long did people have cars before they used them to rob banks?

"Patriot uses his computer as a weapon. And he's good with it. I've never seen anybody so good. He can do whatever he wants with it. He kills people with it, Mike! Deleting himself from your census and from the lab's records, that's nothing to him. And for every guy like Patriot, there's a thousand not quite as good, but just as bad. Computer crime is here, Mike. Stop trying to deny it and get to work trying to stop it."

He sat down at the table, his heart pounding. Where had all that come from?

"Are you finished?"

"No, there's one more thing. For your information, breaking into the Loma Linda computer was probably harder for him than tampering with your precious census. You know, sometimes I can see why Patriot is so mad at the American government. We just give everything away: secrets, property, businesses. At least he's doing something about it."

"So now Patriot's your hero?"

"I didn't say that."

"Did you change your mind about him before or after he tried to kill you?"

"I'm just saying I can kind of understand why he's doing what he's doing. I didn't say it was right."

"Okay, okay. You've convinced me. Let's bag this guy."

"Okay, let's see." Ethan flopped back onto the bed. "What do we know?"

"Louis Parks used to live on Mesa."

"With his dad, whose name is Robert, and his mom..."

"Linda."

Ethan pulled the next census binder toward him. "We'll look under the same name and address in 2000. But since the movie theater manager thought they tore the houses down in '98, we probably won't find anything."

Gillette went back to the laptop. "What'll I do?"

< virtually eliminated >

"You do the same thing. No, tell you what. You look for Linda Parks in 2000."

"Yeah, not the dad. Weren't they breaking up back in '90?"

"Why, Special Agent Gillette, I thought you thought Burt was senile."

Gillette winked. "I'm still a federal investigator, you know. I do know how to listen."

As Ethan had suspected, there was no residence at 9733 Mesa Drive in the year 2000. Nor were there any Linda Parks in all of Loma Linda. He closed the plastic-bound volume. The computer really was the instrument of choice at this moment, though Ethan didn't want to admit it. Unless he had a specific city to search under, the hard copy of the census might as well be a ream of blank paper.

The FBI agent pursed his lips like a toddler working with blocks. "You know, this computer ain't so bad, once you get the hang of it." He looked around the back of the portable computer. "How much one of these little guys cost?"

"More than the big ones, I'm afraid."

"Hmm. Maybe have to get me one, after all."

"Any luck?"

"Bingo," Gillette said, reading the search results as they filled the little screen. "Got her. Well, three of her, anyway. Three Linda Parks. But one's in Atlanta, and the other's in Utah. Only one on the Pacific Coast."

"Isn't that what you said? Patriot's call originated from the Pacific Coast?"

"That's what the man said."

"Tigard, Oregon. Where's that?"

"Don't know."

Gillette read down the screen. "No kids shown here. No husband, either."

Ethan reopened the 2000 census. "Let's see what the print records say."

< jefferson scott >

While Ethan searched the clumsy census book, his mind worked to expand its conception of what Patriot must have done.

It was imaginable that Patriot could have written a simple program to look for his name on all the computers on GlobeNet. If he knew all the places his name was listed, he could then go back and break into every computer, deleting all references to himself. It sounded laborious, but possible.

Why would anyone do such a thing? It might be useful to just disappear off a few choice lists — all his creditors, for instance. But such an act carried with it the possibility of disaster, too. If you delete your name off the electric company's computer, what's to say they don't just shut off power to your house?

Patriot would have thought of that. Ethan felt he knew Patriot well enough by now to know he would have anticipated every detail before making the first move.

So he erased his name from every computer on GlobeNet that had ever recorded his existence. The question remained — why? Not paying bills and taxes certainly had a nice sound to it. But surely someone with Patriot's prowess could generate any amount of capital he might need for any expense. No, saving money wasn't motive enough.

There was the obvious issue of his activities. Wouldn't someone about to go around killing people want as large a measure of anonymity as possible? It had worked, too. Thanks to those efforts, Patriot had managed to remain at large — to impede exactly what Ethan and Gillette were attempting to do — for years.

But Ethan couldn't shake the feeling that there was something more at work. Louis Parks had obliterated every meaningful record of his existence. It was the act of a man either with something to fear or with nothing to live for.

Ethan realized he was staring at the correct spot in the paper census record. Linda Parks, age 44, lived at 11187 NE Valley Court in Tigard, Oregon.

With her son, Louis.

< virtually eliminated >

chapter.25

IN A STATE FAMOUS FOR ITS TREES, how was it that this house had none at all?

Ethan had expected to have to drive through living, surging forests, on roads that slashed through the trees like a saw through timber. He was somewhat disappointed to find the forests well in hand, pushed far back from the roadway.

Such was the case at 11187 NE Valley Court. Many trees had given their all in the construction of the house, though. From their vantage point several houses down, Ethan saw two kinds of light brown wood siding, a medium brown wooden garage door, and dark brown wood-colored shingles. But not a tree on the premises, front or back.

"How long do we sit here?"

Gillette looked up from a magazine he had purchased at the Portland airport. His face bore that roguish grin Ethan had come to beware. "Could be all day."

Ethan checked the low October sun, then his watch — 10:04 A.M., Tuesday morning. They had left their hotel in Loma Linda at five that morning, driven to the Ontario airport, and gotten on a plane for the

< jefferson scott >

Beaver State. Ethan was reminded one more time of how glad he was he didn't travel for a living. When he caught up on his rest, he decided, he might have enough energy for jet lag.

Here they sat, in a generic blue panel van, fifty yards from the squalid house in which Patriot conducted his one-man revolution. In cars nearby, four well-armed special agents waited for Gillette's orders to storm the house.

At least they assumed Patriot was inside. They assumed quite a lot, actually. They assumed Louis Parks was inside this house. They assumed Louis Parks was Patriot. They assumed they had the right Louis Parks. It had sounded much more convincing in the hotel room in Loma Linda.

It must have sounded persuasive to other people, as well. Minutes after Gillette placed his first call last night, things started happening. Now that the operation had moved to the West Coast, Gillette's supervisor, Special Agent Tubbs, handed off control of the case to the regional supervisor. This person, a woman, Special Agent Gerlach, had to be brought up to speed.

The end result was that a large portion of the West Coast FBI was mobilized around Ethan's package of assumptions. Special agents were on-site with every phone carrier in the region. Everything that could be discovered about 11187 NE Valley Court without raising suspicion was investigated. Ethan and Gillette sat out in the high-tech surveillance van watching two FBI specialists watch the house. A special hostage/terrorist team was on maximum alert.

All of them waiting for the word.

Unfortunately, no one knew what the word was going to be, exactly.

It seemed ridiculous to Ethan that they had to wait at all. Why couldn't they just go in right now and arrest Louis Parks? Call it "on suspicion" or something. Gillette had tried to explain it to him, and in some ways he understood. But mostly, it just seemed ridiculous.

Even though they were 95 percent sure they had the right man, and 95 percent sure they had the right house, and 95 percent sure they

< virtually eliminated >

could find something in that house to prove Parks's guilt, it wasn't enough. They needed something else. In Gillette's ever-delicate words, they needed to catch Patriot "with feathers in his grin."

Before this army of law enforcement could move in, they had to be able to prove that the suspect was at home and logged onto his computer when an illegal act was performed on-line.

"That's great," Ethan had complained to Gillette. "You mean you're going to wait until he kills somebody else."

He was watching an infrared scan of Parks's house on a monitor. After thirty minutes of surveillance, the specialists had determined that there was only one person at home. That person was in a back bedroom, lying down. They could also tell from their array of equipment that there were quite a few machines in that bedroom: lots of fan noise, lots of electricity. Could be computers. But it could just as easily be medical equipment or office machines.

The surveillance expert on the headset, a black gentleman named Monroe, elbowed his partner. "Machine kicked in. Sounded like a generator of some kind. If I had to guess, I'd say it was a blood pressure cuff taking a reading."

His partner was a military-type cadet who went by the nickname *Diesel* — flattop, stiff collar, and an upper body that spoke of four hundred pushups a day. Diesel nodded. "Concur. Consistent with previous assessment. Medical equipment." He turned to Gillette. "Sorry to disappoint, gents, but there's no computer in the target's room."

"That can't be right." Ethan was going a little stir crazy in that van. "How can you tell that? Maybe it's just not on."

"Negative," Diesel fairly chopped with his words, "detecting minimal ambient radiation and zero frequency modulated signals."

Monroe pulled his headphones around his neck and turned to Ethan. "What the navy dropout here is trying to say —"

"Marines, sir."

"Marines are part of the navy," Monroe snapped back. "Don't interrupt your elders." He looked again at Ethan. "What the former *marine* here —"

< jefferson scott >

"Once a marine, always a marine! Semper Fi, sir."

Monroe slapped Diesel on the back of the head.

"Hey, cut it out, man."

Monroe smiled indulgently at Ethan. "You'll get used to him. Just have to knock him upside the head once a day."

Ethan laughed politely. He felt as if he was watching some old movie starring Morgan Freeman and central casting's idea of the perfect jughead.

"What he's trying to say," Monroe continued, "is that we don't detect any computer monitors or television screens in the room. Though there is some hint of the right kind of radiation. It might be enough for a small heartbeat monitor."

Gillette knelt down beside Diesel. "What's that yellow there?"

Ethan didn't listen for Diesel's answer. He turned to Monroe. "This guy might not use a monitor. He doesn't need one. See, he'll probably be wearing some kind of headset. Is there any way to look or listen just for the computer itself?"

Monroe listened carefully. "Probably not. Most machines need fans to keep them cool. Sometimes you can tell one kind of fan from another, kind of a fan signature. But usually one fan sounds pretty much like another. I found a Coke machine once that I was positive was a refrigerator keeping some chopped up body parts cool. But that's another story. I've done a few right since then, though. I'll see what I can do."

Gillette's laughter crowded out their conversation. "You mean you didn't make up this program yourself?" They seemed to be talking about something on Diesel's computer. Gillette was suddenly infatuated with computers.

"I wish, sir. No, Uncle Sam sent 75K to Mr. Marty for this baby."

"Who's Mr. Marty?"

"Martin Grant, sir. Founder of Nanotech and Azimuth. Maybe you've heard of him. Richest man in America."

Gillette acted like he knew.

"Even richer now. He's like me — needs a new challenge every few

< virtually eliminated >

years. Took Nanotech from zero to sixty. Now dropping it like a warm beer. Yes, sir," Diesel patted the console like bongos, "definitely like me."

Monroe moved back to his chair. "Hasn't that already happened? I thought it was yesterday. Who's he selling to, anyw—" He held up is hands, interrupting himself. "Hold it. I've got dial tone."

"Confirmed."

"Got a new sound, too." Monroe shut his eyes. "I have systems noise. I have data hiss. Scream. Handshake."

Diesel hooted. "Shake, rattle, and roll."

"What's going on?" Gillette asked.

"Good news, Mr. Hamilton," Monroe said. "Your boy's got a computer in there, all right. A nice one, unless I'm too old for this. He's powered up and he's on-line."

Diesel grabbed a handheld microphone on a spiral cord. "Baker X-Ray, this is Tango Niner, over."

The voice came back from a speaker in the equipment rack built into the side of the van. "Uh-roger, Tango Niner, copy."

"Be advised, suspect is on the horn, over."

"Uh-copy, Tango Niner. We have him on our board. Will advise, over."

"Roger, Baker X-Ray. Over and out."

"Now what?" Gillette asked.

"Now, sir," Diesel said, hanging up the microphone, "we call out for grub." He stood up. "What'll you have, Monroe?"

Monroe didn't take his eyes off his dials. "The usual."

"Right, burrito supreme, hold the onions."

It wasn't the first time Ethan was frustrated with the FBI. "What about him?" he pointed to the monitor. "What if he's going to hunt somebody down? Aren't you going to stop him?"

Monroe did look up then. "There's nothing illegal about making a phone call, Mr. Hamilton. We got to go by the book on this one. Especially after last year." Ethan didn't know what he was referring to.

"Fact of the matter is we have to wait until your man makes his move."

Diesel stood up. "Have to wait for some schmuck to rub the boy's rhubarb. Then we stick it to him like they do downtown." He dug into his pocket. "You gents want some lunch? My treat. Catch is, you have to go get it."

"I don't want to leave," Ethan said.

"I'll go by myself," Gillette said. "I've got to make a call, anyway."

Ethan's stomach couldn't handle much more eating out. Reason #294 against traveling for a living. He squeezed the paper that had kept his tacos greasy and cold into a ball and stuffed it in the bag. The van smelled like...well, Ethan would need some air very soon.

Nothing exciting had transpired in the intervening hour. The special agents working with the GTE technicians thought they had a fairly good fix on where the caller at 11187 NE Valley Court was doing business. It was a financial network in Finland.

They had managed to locate this user's service provider, the Hole. A preliminary call had the Hole rep swearing he didn't have any clients at the given phone number. Ethan had taken the phone then and requested him to investigate all incoming calls. The rep ate his own words for lunch.

So far, though, no one had been able to catch this user — was it Patriot? was it Parks? — doing anything illegal.

Ethan was distracted by a familiar ringing. He pulled his telephone off his belt. "Hello."

"Ethan, they took him!"

"Kaye, is that you? What's wrong, honey?"

"They got him. He just went out to get the mail, and they pulled up and got him."

"Kaye, I need you to tell me what you're talking about. Who got who?"

"You've got to come up here, Ethan. Come now."

"I can't, honey. I'm not in Texas."

< virtually eliminated >

It took a moment for his wife to find a response. "But I called your number…"

"It's a mobile phone, honey. It finds me wherever I am."

"Ethan! Ethan,what am I going to do? They took my baby!"

"Somebody took Katie? Kaye, I don't understand."

"No! Jordan! My baby boy!"

Ethan felt his lunch rise in his throat. "Who took Jordan? Kaye, who took him!"

The two surveillance agents turned to look. Gillette was outside somewhere.

"Two men! Ethan, they took him and I don't know where he is."

Ethan slammed the van door open. "Gillette!"

"Shh!" Gillette hissed. He trotted toward Ethan from a spot not far from the Parks house. The baldheaded man he'd been talking with got into an unmarked car. "Hush up, Hamilton. Why don't you just turn on the siren?"

Ethan grabbed Gillette's shirt in his fists and shoved him against the van. His first words never made it through his teeth. His rage shocked him. He let go of the shirt, but kept Gillette pressed to the sidewall. "Where's my boy? What have you done to Jordan!" He was almost screaming, despite his efforts at control. His whole body shook.

Gillette shut his eyes. "He's okay. He won't be hurt. They just need him for awhile."

Ethan took a step back. "What do you mean they need him? Who needs him? Need him for what?"

Gillette straightened his shirt. "You remember what I told you, that sometimes I have to do things I don't like? But that I have to do them anyway?"

Ethan didn't answer. He didn't want to acknowledge that maybe Gillette had tried to warn him about this moment. The rage was just too insistent right now.

< jefferson scott >

"I'm sorry, Ethan, buddy. You have to know it wasn't my idea."

"What, Mike? What wasn't your idea? What's happening to my son while I'm out here helping the — the FBI." He was stunned by the words his mind kept supplying to his tongue.

"He'll be okay, Ethan. We've got our best people on it." Gillette didn't meet Ethan's gaze. He slid along the side of the van, mopping up months of California dust. "The order came from upstairs, Ethan. Higher than I've ever heard on one of my cases. I think it's the PLO Summit. Maybe you've got them all spooked. I don't know."

Ethan watched Gillette's struggle and felt more of his madness subside. He touched Gillette on the arm.

In retrospect, it was probably the tenderness of that act that finally pushed Mike Gillette across the line. He wasn't supposed to tell Ethan anything. But this Ethan Hamilton had gotten under his skin somehow. It wasn't something he liked to let happen. But it was there, clear as day.

Gillette stood up tall and squared his shoulders toward his friend. "Ethan, federal agents have taken your son to an undisclosed location where they will put him out on GlobeNet as bait for Patriot."

< Part III >

Nothing is too high for the daring of mortals;
We storm heaven itself in our folly.

HORACE, EPISTLES

■

< virtually eliminated >

chapter.26

A HERO, ETHAN HAD ALWAYS MAINTAINED, isn't someone with no fear; rather, he is someone who is afraid but does what's needed anyway.

That was good, since Ethan had a rather large collection of fears at the moment.

For one, his body lay on a cold slab as if entombed inside five hundred pounds of metal. Wires crawled over his face. Canvas straps gripped his head, rendering it immobile. His arms, while free to move about within the cowling, were wrapped in Velcro 6DOF mittens. The beast's stomach groaned ominously with sounds of motors, electricity, and muted voices.

He'd reached Dr. Hosokawa from the phone on the plane. She was staying late anyway and was more than willing to help Ethan in his crisis. Ethan had no doubt the FBI would be able to reclaim the car he had appropriated to drive to the airport. He had parked it in the fifteen-minute lane and for that he did feel slightly guilty. Slightly.

Now he was lying in Dr. Hosokawa's lab being fed to a metallic beast. There was something terrifying about being given over completely to a machine. What if something went wrong? What if the brute threw

< jefferson scott >

off its fetters and decided to plunge him in and out of the dark cave like a piston in a cylinder? The puny mortals on the outside couldn't rescue him.

How appropriate that the man who had symbolically fed his own family to a mechanized idol should now be this machine's main course.

Fear number two was for Jordan. His son, alone, out there somewhere on GlobeNet like a worm on a hook. Absolutely defenseless. What if he couldn't find him in time? What if it was already too late? What if the FBI tried to hinder him, to prevent him from interfering with their trap? He could be in serious trouble.

This was a fear saturated with wrath. The FBI — guardians of truth, justice, and the American Way — had violated his family and intentionally placed his son in the line of fire. Somebody was going to answer for this, no matter what happened next. Someday, somehow, he was going to make his voice be heard.

Ethan had always turned a deaf ear to tales from fringe groups or sensationalist reporters of alleged misconduct by the FBI, CIA, ATF, DEA, and others. Those tales came back to him now, marching by his mind's eye in a macabre parade: Martin Luther King, JFK, Malcolm X, David Koresh. Doubts clung to their memories like cobwebs. There were stories of Americans assassinated by FBI snipers, foreign dictators executed in their own homes by the CIA, a mother shot through the head with a deer rifle while holding her infant.

Add one to the list, Ethan thought. Nine-year-old boy electrocuted to ferret out a killer. Jordan's face floated by, a late participant in the motorcade of death.

In the end, it was this image that vaulted Ethan over his fears and into the ring.

"Turn this thing on!" he shouted.

Dr. Hosokawa's voice came back to him through the spatiated speakers inside the metal cowling. "No need to raise your voice, Ethan. You're on one-hundred-watt speakers out here."

"Sorry. Just need to get moving, please."

< virtually eliminated >

"Initiating imaging array."

For a moment nothing happened. Ethan remained in his tomb, his son's bludgeoned face dancing before his eyes. Then he was falling through spectacular clouds: beautiful, photorealistic cumuli. He had passed through the grey mist and past the lightning-streaked anvil before he realized his was falling up.

"Whoa! How do I stop myself?" He flailed his arms inside his tomb.

Hosokawa's voice thundered around him. "Just relax. Calm down." Ethan felt a hand on his ankle. "Relax your body."

"Okay," he tried to comply.

Fear number three was that Patriot would be too much for him again. He would get there in time, only to watch helplessly as his nemesis eliminated his son. What had Patriot said? "Show me a hero, and I will write you a tragedy."

Fear number four was the most disturbing of all. There was a reason Ethan had forsworn computers. It had to do with an idol.

It was too soon for him to get back on-line, he knew it with a drowning kind of certainty. He was addicted to computers, still, as tautly as to cocaine. His ability to distinguish between actual reality and virtual reality hadn't had time to return. He needed a month at the least to reestablish his grip, not a handful of days.

Words came to his mind, then, like a long-forgotten song. "My grace is sufficient for you, for my power is made perfect in weakness."

It was one of his favorite passages of Scripture. It spoke of God's power, when his own was so quickly depleted. It spoke of God's awareness of Ethan's situation, of his provision for Ethan's needs, and of his advocacy on Ethan's behalf.

If he's strongest when I'm weakest, Ethan thought, then I almost feel sorry for the other guy.

As if that one verse had punctured the cumuli and set loose a cloudburst, it was followed by a torrent of other verses.

"I will not leave you as orphans; I will come to you.… The Lord will perfect that which concerns me.… Your Father knows what you need

< jefferson scott >

before you ask him.... 'Not by might nor by power, but by my Spirit,' says the Lord Almighty.... The Lord will fight for you; you need only to be still.... Surely I am with you always, to the very end of the age.... Now then, stand still and see this great thing the Lord is about to do before your eyes!... 'Vengeance is Mine,' says the Lord, 'I will repay.'"

He didn't know he knew so much Scripture on a single topic. God's voice in his life again! Prince of Peace, Wonderful Counselor! Praise God he had Jesus on board to calm the raging seas. What did non-Christians do when the storm came?

"Be still and know that I am God."

The panic receded; his fears lost their wallop.

These verses, he realized, were the answer to Patriot's arrogant quotations.

Confidence surged through his veins as he soared over the thunderstorm. He bent his mind at stability and his flight leveled off. There was a focus now at the center of his psyche, a calm in the eye of the hurricane.

"Hook me up, Doc."

"You okay in there? Thought we were going to have to pull the plug. Your heart rate went through the roof."

"I'm fine now. Ready for GlobeNet."

"All right. Initiating GlobeNet link."

It hadn't been too difficult reconfiguring Dr. Hosokawa's computer for Net compatibility. Ethan had just scavenged the modem from his portable and copied some software over. What had been difficult was convincing Dr. Hosokawa's superior, Dr. Roosevelt, to let Ethan use the RVT prototype at all. He didn't have any FBI credentials anymore. No badge to flash. From here on in, he was strictly a free agent.

Dr. Hosokawa's contraption was Ethan's only hope against Patriot. He was desperate to use it. He would have offered almost anything. After a short, closed-door conference between Dr. Hosokawa and Dr. Roosevelt, the blonde researcher had come out to Ethan, all smiles. His request had been approved. Ethan got the feeling he owed her one.

< virtually eliminated >

A portal opened up in Ethan's peripheral vision. He turned toward it, and it snapped into magnificent focus. It looked like something out of a cheap sci-fi movie — a black oval drawn right through a white cloud.

But the poor effects didn't diminish Ethan's admiration for Dr. Hosokawa's RVT system. It excelled anything he had ever experienced. The M7, for all its ease of movement, boasted only average range of vision. With the RVT's bug-eyed peripheries — which took some getting used to, admittedly — Ethan could see virtually all the way around himself. If there was a blind spot at all, he could force it into his field of view with only a flick of his eyes.

He controlled his flight through a combination of eye movement and simple urges of thought. EEG monitors and something called PKs interpreted his brain waves into commands. Ethan did a few somersaults and lunges through the clouds to assure himself he could command enough agility for what might lay ahead.

Then Ethan Hamilton entered GlobeNet to try to save his son.

It wasn't as if Jordan was scared senseless.

Sure, it had been scary when the men walked up to the mailbox, flashed their badges, and asked him to come with them. He'd seen it a thousand times on TV. That might not have been so bad if his mother hadn't freaked out over it. She came running out of the house chasing after the car like a crazy woman. Jordan figured then that there might be more going on than he thought. Now that he thought about it, he couldn't remember ever seeing a nine-year-old get arrested by the FBI on television. That's when he started to get scared.

Jordan knew he shouldn't get into a car with strangers, but these guys were FBI agents. Besides, the two agents — Ricky and Paul — seemed nice enough. They said they wanted to take him computer shopping. What could be wrong with that?

And did they ever take him shopping! It was like Christmas, only

< jefferson scott >

he got to pick out all his own presents. They took him to a really nice computer store and told him to pick out the coolest stuff for net surfing. Everything — even a computer! They must've been rich, because they didn't even blink when he picked out the most expensive computer in the store.

They wouldn't let him buy any games, though. What was the use of this great machine if they weren't going to play with it? They said they already had a game. They said their game was out on GlobeNet, and the sooner they got out of there the sooner Jordan could start playing it.

"You mean *I'm* going to use all this stuff?" he had said at the checkout line.

"Sure, kid, what'd you think?"

"I thought maybe we were getting all this for you or your kids."

"No, Jordan," Paul had said, "all this is for you."

"Cool. Oh no, wait!"

"What is it?" Ricky wasn't having quite as much fun at the store as Paul and Jordan were.

"If I'm going to be the one playing, then I'm going to need a few more things."

Jordan only pulled one fast one. One of the control gloves he picked out came bundled with seven cool games. He made the agents look at something else fast before they saw the same glove cheaper, only without any games. They sure didn't know much about computers, those two. But Jordan was just a kid. If these guys wanted to let him buy the best stuff on the planet, he wasn't going to say no.

Lucky for them they were driving in a kind of station wagon. Otherwise all that stuff never would have fit in the car with the three of them.

Jordan didn't know Tulsa very well. He didn't know anywhere very well, truth to tell. They drove around town for about fifteen minutes, then they went into an ugly building that looked to Jordan like an old post office or school or something. Boring.

There was this room where nobody was, so they set up all the stuff

< virtually eliminated >

in there. Paul and Ricky opened the boxes and lifted the equipment, but
Jordan had to do all the cables himself. Ricky had to go out for a multi-
plug thing, since there was only one outlet in the room and they had
five things to plug in.

They sure were in a rush to get him playing that game. Maybe there
was some tournament about to start or something. Jordan didn't care so
long as he got to play. It had been so long — ever since the game room
blew up.

But these guys didn't understand that you couldn't go that fast.
They had bought all the best stuff, but they still had to load it onto the
machine, configure the devices, fix the interrupts, and everything. Even
Jordan didn't know how to do all that. He made Paul read manuals
while he played one of the Oh-wow-I-didn't-know-it-came-with-that
games he'd bought on the sly.

Ricky wasn't very nice about it. He got kind of mean after a while.
Everybody seemed really upset about something. And in a huge hurry.
He kept talking about Special Agent Gerlach and Special Agent Gillette
and Special Agent Tubbs and Special Agent Russell. Jordan thought it
was supposed to be *secret* agent, not special agent. But he was glad that
everybody in the FBI was so special.

They finally got everything up and running. They put the stuff on
Jordan and got him on GlobeNet right away. It took him a minute to figure things out, since his dad had all this part on a macro. But he got on
okay. Then Paul told Jordan where to go.

"Wait, I have to pick a persona."

"A what?"

"You know. How I look on the other guy's screen."

"Okay, just hurry it up. Ricky's about ready to cut a switch, I think."

"How do you cut a switch? You mean a light switch?"

"Just hurry, Jordan."

"Okay." This was serious business, Jordan knew. It required an
appropriately serious persona. "I've got the perfect one."

"Fine. Just go to that address I gave you."

< jefferson scott >

"Halfway there already."

It didn't look like such a cool game. No dragons or tanks or Martians or basketballs. What it really looked like was one of Katie's 3D art pictures: white fence, yellow sun, two-story wooden house, blue sky. It had everything but little *m* characters — supposed to be birds — flying around.

He pushed the expensive helmet back with a gloved hand—the straps didn't go small enough to make it fit snugly. "What am I supposed to do now, Paul?"

Paul reminded Jordan of his friend Dominic's big brother, Michael. He was real tall, with kind of normal colored hair and glasses. "Just hang out, my friend. We're supposed to be meeting someone here."

"When we meet up with this person, then are we going to play this cool game?"

"Yeah, bud." Paul rubbed Jordan's shoulder. "That's when."

Jordan dropped the headset back over his eyes to wait for his opponent. Maybe he'd see if that gate was unlocked.

< virtually eliminated >

PATRIOT WAS NOT AT THE FINNISH financial institute, as the FBI assumed. Had not been there, in fact, for years. Sending the false destination to the phone carrier was not an intentional effort to throw off his Department of Justice pursuers. He had no reason to suspect that this call, above all others, was being monitored. It was simply one of his standard precautions.

If Patriot could be said to "be" anywhere besides where his physical body lay, then he was in Japan, monitoring Chairman Yasunari's online movements. Tee time was only forty-five minutes away. Yasunari was making sure his press conference was on schedule.

Patriot battled the impulse to eliminate the chairman now, instead of according to plan. He could still accomplish his goals: the negotiations would be halted, his message would still be heard, the betrayal would be prevented. More importantly, his apoplexy would have an immediate outlet.

He would not deviate from the Plan. Not now, after so many months of planning. Edgar Ramirez still had his task to accomplish,

< jefferson scott >

after all. Patriot intended to make full use of the freedom the cut phone lines would provide.

He made a mental note to procure the promised $100,000 for Ramirez. The man who had offered the deal to Ramirez — in a Sizzlin' restaurant, he recalled — would have to be eliminated. He made a mental note of that, too.

Jamaica. The betrayal cut to his heart. If she had only asked, he would have sent her on a month-long trip around the world. Now, however, he was not in so charitable a frame of mind.

On his way to Nanotech, Patriot detoured to the Portland airport. Neither his mother's married or maiden name appeared on any of the carriers flying directly into Kingston. Duplicity heaped atop treachery. Very well, she left him no choice.

A short conversation with the Jamaican constabulary computer separated Linda Hahn, alias Linda Parks, from her passport, her visa, and her exemplary legal status. Perhaps a night or two in a Jamaican prison would give her a hint of the misery her desertion had caused him.

What kind of a monster was he, sentencing his own mother to the penitentiary? Next, perhaps, he would have his dog put to sleep.

But of course he had no pets. Mother wouldn't allow it. She didn't want to take care of it, she said. Why couldn't he have had a little puppy or kitten, curled up at his shoulder, licking his face? He would hire somebody to take care of it. He was an adult, wasn't he? Things might have turned out otherwise for him if he'd only been allowed a blasted furry pet.

Now that he thought of it, many things in his life would have turned out differently if it hadn't been for his sainted mother. Maybe a month in jail would be more suitable.

Unfortunate that he had not faced these demons previously. Perhaps he could have had his mother committed long ago. Then he might have lived his last thirteen years on a yacht off Jamaica himself, instead of in this shanty hovering inches above condemnation.

If he had reached these conclusions earlier, even weeks earlier, he was positive he would have had both a puppy and a kitten — maybe

< virtually eliminated >

two or three of each — brought to his bedside. Their comforts, he was sure, would have far surpassed the maternal ice to which he had become accustomed.

It was too late, of course, to get a pet now. In less than two hours it would all be over.

Did they have the death penalty in Jamaica?

Patriot initiated the jump to a certain American computer system to check the progress of the other party to this negotiation. It still was an *American* computer system — for at least another hour.

What an idyllic scene they had choreographed, Yasunari and Grant. Just two business associates sharing a friendly eighteen on a course in Soctland. Never mind that the United States' last vital corporation was being delivered to her most lethal enemy.

He arrived at his destination. This computer, over which Patriot had established sovereignty, was one considered friendly by the Nanotech network. At the moment Mr. Grant was on a virtual driving range, practicing his swing. Perhaps he would rather not lose his golf game as thoroughly as he was about to lose his country.

Patriot recited Conrad's saying that *All a man can betray is his conscience*, but for some reason that sentiment no longer excused any kind of disloyalty. Lincoln's words seemed more appropriate at the moment, both for Grant and a woman going by the name of Hahn: *Those who deny freedom to others deserve it not for themselves*.

He watched Grant drive a ball. It hooked to the right. "Keep your head down, Martin," Patriot said to himself, bemused by the double meaning.

He felt rather full of himself — buoyed, as it were — when once he moved beyond thoughts of his mother. He was less than thirty-five minutes from the culmination of months of planning. Years, truly, if one counted intentions.

He wondered how others in similar circumstances felt just prior to the fruition of their designs: the World Trade Center in 1993, the Oklahoma City federal building in 1995, the English Channel Tunnel Crossing in 2003. If they were men like him, they felt a distilled excitement

< jefferson scott >

heightened by the imminence of the event and the sublimity of fore-knowledge.

Not that Patriot saw himself as a terrorist. Quite the contrary, though he supposed every terrorist was a patriot in his own eyes and every patriot a terrorist in the eyes of others. He simply agreed with Clausewitz that "war is nothing but the continuation of politics with the admixture of other means." Patriot, then, was a diplomat.

He had all but decided to go to the Royal and Annuitied Old Course and wait, relishing his chilled violence, when one of his perimeter alarms went off.

He'd once been ambushed by a ridiculous green lizard because he had to go to his defensive array to check its status. That very day he had altered the array so that it contacted him when something was amiss, instead of the other way around.

He gestured with a black-sleeved arm and his defensive panel appeared in a window. Someone was at his own front door, trying the gate. Most unfortunate for that individual.

Patriot pressed a button on the display, calling up his available "camera" views. He selected view number one and punched it up in the window.

It looked like James Bond was at his picket fence. In a tuxedo, no less. He couldn't tell much from the appearance, of course. Anyone could take any guise on GlobeNet. He of all people knew that to be true. It was when he read the user's identification at the bottom of his window that he took notice.

"Jordan?"

The police weren't going to be any help. Kaye knew it before her father got off the phone. They would never admit it, of course, but she knew the FBI had contacted them and secured their cooperation. That left options two and three.

Kaye had recovered from the kidnapping of her son only with dif-

< virtually eliminated >

ficulty. It didn't help that Katie cried like a banshee all the time now. Kaye couldn't blame her. All she wanted was what Kaye herself wanted — her family back. Kaye's mom did the best she could to comfort Katie, while Kaye and her father went through their alternatives.

"Yeah, thanks for all your protection. So glad I voted for a tax hike to pay for more of you people." Mr. Simms terminated the video call. He smashed his fist onto the table. The napkin tray fell to the floor and shattered.

Kaye had only seen him this mad once before. "They act like it's no big deal," he said. "'Take a number, sir.'"

He rounded the table swiftly, crunching on the broken glass. Kaye instinctively averted her eyes. As humbly as she could, lest his ire flare out at her, Kaye told him what she suspected about the FBI contacting the Tulsa Police Department. A picture frame came off the wall and broke.

It was good, in a way, that he was expressing his anger so vividly, since she didn't really know how to let hers out. She decided to claim the broken picture frame for herself, as if she had done it.

"They can't do this, can they, Daddy?"

Before he retired, Henry Simms had been an electrician, not an expert on the finer points of the law. But he had, as the saying went, been around the block a few times. Besides, he was her daddy. She had always run to him when she skinned her knee. It had only been in the last five years or so that she had fully switched over to Ethan as the be-all-end-all man in her life.

"No, honey, they can't do this. Not without your permission."

"Then let's call a lawyer. Maybe they can draw up some papers or something to get Jordan back."

"No attorney in his right mind would go up against the FBI in the middle of an operation. Maybe when the thing dies down. But we can't wait that long. We've got to do something now." He went into the living room and punched a couch pillow this time. "I hate not being able to do anything."

"Okay, Daddy. I have one other idea."

< jefferson scott >

"Jordan Hamilton, what an unexpected pleasure."

Jordan yanked his helmet off and tore at his gloves. "Unplug it! Unplug it!"

Paul and Ricky rushed to his side. "What's wrong?" Paul said. "What are you doing?"

"It's him! The guy who blew up my computer." He had one glove off and was peeling the other one over his fingers. "Pull the plug or he'll do it again."

"Jordan," Paul began.

The boy pushed him aside on his way around the grey metal desk. He grabbed the multiplug cable and pulled.

A strong hand arrested his movement.

"Ricky! Let go!"

"I can't let you do that, kid."

It occurred to Jordan that he should never have gotten into the car with these two. He hadn't really looked at those badges they flashed. His mom sure didn't think it was all right. Who'd ever heard of the FBI taking a nine-year-old boy computer shopping? He was a milk carton kid now; he knew it.

Jordan yanked his hand away and slumped down against the wall. Paul and Ricky exchanged serious looks.

"Should I tell him?" Paul asked.

Ricky made some kind of face. "Oh, that. Yes. I mean, if you think we should."

"I think we should."

Paul knelt in front of Jordan. "What I'm about to tell you is top secret."

"Yeah, right. This is just another trick, isn't it?"

"Kid," Ricky said, unholstering the pistol Jordan had seen glimpses of, "if you repeat anything of what he tells you, I'll be forced to kill you."

Paul frowned at Ricky, then turned back to Jordan.

< virtually eliminated >

"Jordan," Paul said softly, "the man you saw just now on the computer is a very bad man. He hurts people. Sometimes he even kills them. Did you know that?"

Jordan nodded.

"Well…" Paul sighed. "This guy — they call him Patriot — has done something really bad now, and we need your help to try to stop him before it's too late."

"Did he kill somebody else?"

"Not yet," Ricky said ominously.

Jordan saw Paul bite his lip. He didn't look right at Jordan, and that scared him. Maybe what he had to say was too terrible.

"Jordan," Paul said, staring at the speckled floor tile, "Patriot has kidnapped your little sister."

Jordan's forehead wrinkled. "How?"

"Well…"

"It's a long story," Ricky covered. "He's going to kill her, too."

"Why?" *What could Katie have done to make somebody that mad at her?*

"It doesn't matter, kid. He just is."

Paul nodded. "But there's still a chance to stop him."

Jordan looked at him dully. Who were these guys anyway? Maybe if he pinched himself he would wake up from this crazy dream.

"If you can go back on the computer and trick Patriot into telling you where he's keeping your sister," Paul explained, "then we can send a SWAT team in to rescue her."

A SWAT team sounded cool. "But what if he tries to blow me up again?"

"It's either you or your sister, kid." Ricky had a way of making things black and white. "Which would you rather?"

Jordan put his gear back on.

< jefferson scott >

chapter.28

CONTRARY TO POPULAR BELIEF, the average FBI office was usually as calm or calmer than the average civilian office. People went about their business confidently, often with kindness. Absent, for the most part, was the cutthroat atmosphere prevalent in the corporate world.

At the Tulsa office of the Federal Bureau of Investigation this tranquillity was shattered with the simple opening of an elevator door. Three cameramen with video gear, three reporters with microphones, and one assistant with a tripod poured out of the lift and surged against the receptionist's window.

"Is it true," one reporter shouted over the receptionist's *May I help you?* "that FBI agents from this office have kidnapped a nine-year-old boy and are holding him from his mother?"

"I —"

"On whose authority was this done?"

"What'd the kid do?"

"Who gave the order?"

"Isn't this another Waco?"

"How long will he be held?"

< virtually eliminated >

"The district attorney's office says it has not issued a warrant for the boy's arrest. Would you like to make a statement?"

The receptionist, whose name was Laura, made sure the door was locked and stepped away from her desk.

"Connie," Laura said to an agent passing by. She indicated the lights and cameras at her window. "Maybe you could get Special Agent Holt out here."

Of course it was a trap. Young Jordan, so alone and vulnerable. So inviting. Patriot was not fool enough to fall for it. It surprised him that Ethan Hamilton would stoop so low as to offer his only son like this. He must be taking his *Imitatio Dei* quite seriously.

Jordan's reaction had been famously unrehearsed. Doubly low, to offer your only son without even telling him what was happening. Perhaps this was some kind of Passion play, and this was the scene in which Abraham sacrifices Isaac.

Patriot circled Jordan's tuxedo-clad persona. It remained standing where Jordan had left it. The boy was currently having an out-of-body experience.

Jordan intrigued him almost as much as the child's father did. This whole Hamilton family exerted an almost gravitational force on him. *Jordan has a pet, I'll wager.* How Jordan reminded him of the boy he once was.

Would it make him feel better or worse to end Jordan's little dream life? Patriot could not decide. It was beyond égalité that this boy should have the ideal existence when it was denied other children. When it was denied him. The cretin had no concept of the riches he enjoyed. Just another spoiled American child. Unworthy of rescue. Is this what Patriot was fighting so ardently to protect?

Yet it was Jordan's very naïveté which was so appealing to Patriot. To be so innocent again! Surely that was what he was fighting for, wasn't it?

No.

< jefferson scott >

They weren't in Kansas anymore.

At least that's what his dad would have said. Jordan's only frame of reference for what he saw before him was something at the Chinese food restaurant his family would sometimes go to after church.

There was a huge statue of this big, fat, bald guy sitting Indian-style, kind of up on a rock table. The collar on the guy's shirt was really stretched out — Jordan could see his big gut, the front of his shirt hung down so low.

There were other statues, too. They looked like metal plants with big bird baths or lillypads on top. Jordan stood on the stone floor inside a round enclosure. Beyond the surrounding wall he could see green hills and leafy trees. The place was paved like his playground at school — to which he hadn't been today, he didn't mind remembering — but without the play equipment. The fluffy clouds overhead were kind of pink, like it sometimes was at sunset.

When he'd left GlobeNet a minute ago, Jordan had been outside what he now knew to be Patriot's front gate. So how did he get here? Must've drifted or something. The place looked deserted. He thought he'd better jack out, maybe get Paul to give him that address again.

Not that he wanted to go back there. But if Katie was in trouble, it was worth it. He'd always promised himself that if anybody ever hurt his kid sister, he would hunt them down and beat them up. Though he'd never say it out loud, he cherished the little runt.

He was about to lift his helmet off when he saw somebody coming toward him across the stone floor. It was an Oriental man in an orange bathrobe. He wore it off one shoulder, like Jordan wore his bedsheet back in third grade when they had Toga Day. The guy wasn't old, though. The hair growing back from a skinhead haircut was black, not grey.

The guy in orange came right up to Jordan and bowed. "You are suffering, little one."

"No, I'm not. I feel fine."

< virtually eliminated >

The orange guy laughed. "Come, walk with me." He put his arm on Jordan's shoulder and made him walk. Jordan heard birds singing in the trees. "The Second Noble Truth is that all suffering proceeds from grasping, you see? Clutching after the wrong things. You cannot get what you want, so you suffer. Tell me, what is it your heart desires most?"

"Right now I just want to find my sister."

"Ah, but you cannot find her? You do not know where she is?"

"No. This guy's got her. Paul says if I don't find out where he's got Katie, he's going to kill her."

"And why would this Paul harm your sister?"

"No, not Paul. Patriot! Patriot's going to kill her if I can't find him and trick him into telling me where he's got her. I — hey, what's wrong?"

The orange guy had stopped walking. But he caught back up with Jordan. "So, you are a seeker, little one. You seek your sister, yet you cannot find her. You seek someone named Patriot, yet you cannot find him. You are surrounded by misery and death. You are suffering, little one."

Why did he keep calling him that? Jordan looked down at himself. He still wore the serious adult tuxedo he'd picked at startup. How did this guy know he was little? Maybe it was because Jordan didn't have his voice-augmentation software running.

"I have to go, mister."

"If you leave this place, your suffering will follow you. Stay, and I will lead you on the Noble Eightfold Path. The end of that path is nirvana."

The Noble Eightfold Path, the Second Noble Truth. Was everything noble to this guy? Besides, he'd never even heard of a place called Nirvana; why would he want to go there? The guy was right about one thing, though — Jordan was suffering, but it wasn't because he was "grasping." It was because time was wasting and he needed to be out looking for Patriot and his sister.

That was when the Wheel of Fortune appeared. That's what it looked like. That or a wagon wheel. It had eight spokes, and each spoke

< jefferson scott >

had a word on it. There was a clicker, too, to show what you got when you spun. It stood — floated, really — right in front of the statue of the fat man. The orange guy went over to the wheel and rolled it around a few times. "Come see."

"All right. But only one spin." Jordan went over, keeping a wary eye on the statue's face in case it was watching him. "What are the prizes?"

His Oriental companion laughed again. Jordan saw bald marks where the razor must have gotten too close. "You do not spin the Wheel of Life, little one. The Wheel of Life spins you. Come, I will show you where you are on the samsara cycle."

So this wheel went with some kind of cycle? Must be a big one.

The orange guy rotated the wheel to a certain spoke, then stopped it. "You are here, little one."

Jordan looked at the spoke. He didn't see himself on it. He couldn't read the word written on it, since it looked like Japanese or something. He shrugged. "Okay. Can I go now?"

"So impatient, you are. To 'go,' to reach nirvana, is a Buddhist's life-long journey. One must let go of this world and all its hungers. It takes many lifetimes to escape samsara."

"Mister, are you from Earth?" Jordan lived for the chance to say that and get away with it. It had gotten him licks once when he said it at school.

"You may thank Buddha that I have another path for you, little one." The orange guy left the wheel and put his hand on Jordan's shoulder. "A shorter path."

Jordan looked up quickly. Had there just been a flash in the statue's head? A yellow glint in the fat guy's eye? He noticed that the statue's right hand was up, making one of those famous-painting signs with his fingers. Hadn't that hand been in the statue's lap with the other hand? And where were those birds he'd heard before? This was getting creepy. Jordan tried to step away.

But was held tight.

"Jordan," the guy said.

His own name coming from this guy's mouth hit him like cold

< virtually eliminated >

water. "What? How do you know my name?"

"I'll tell you in just…one…second."

He squirmed under the man's grip. "Let me go!"

"Who is Paul, Jordan?"

"Why should I tell you? Let go."

"Why did he tell you I was holding your sister?"

"Uh, he didn't! I mean, I made that up myself."

"Jordan," the orange-clad Patriot warned.

"Paul? Who's Paul? I meant Mal. Taj Mahal. I meant I read it when I was studying about the Taj Mahal."

"Wrong religion, boy. But full marks for fast thinking."

It didn't even sound like the same guy anymore. Why didn't he just quit playing Halloween and put the black robes back on? "Where's my sister, vomit breath?"

That's when the statue stood up. It was bigger than a three-story house when it was sitting down. A fat, grey hill made out of concrete. But when it stood up — and it looked real cranky when it did — it was taller than the Washington Monument.

It said something in Oriental, which Jordan didn't speak, but the voice made him cold all up and down his back. The voice sounded like metal. Like when they went on the field trip to the museum every year, and all the boys said "Ha" to make their voices echo.

The huge statue raised both hands up. There was definitely something yellow in its eyes now. When it jumped down off the table it had been sitting on, Jordan would swear he felt it land, even in VR. Plant statues fell over and some of the paved floor cracked where the fat statue's foot hit. It wore the biggest pair of sandals Jordan had ever seen.

The thing looked right at Jordan with its yellow, mad eyes. It didn't take too many Saturday morning cartoons to see one where the monster shot stuff out of its eyes. Time to disappear, like the-orange-guy-who-was-really-Patriot had.

Jordan caught a glimpse of something dark in the pink clouds overhead. *Wish I could just fly out of here like that dumb bird.* But it wasn't a

< jefferson scott >

bird. No wings, no beak, no talons. It got bigger and bigger as it dove toward the courtyard and the angry grey titan.

Jordan backed away as the giant arched its back and bellowed. *Godzilla. That's what this thing sounds like.*

The Buddha's eyes were definitely on fire. It stretched out grey fingers for him.

Jordan felt the end coming on him again, just like on Mars. Only this time he wasn't going to make it.

The statue screamed its metallic scream.

A monstrous shadow buried him like a black tidal wave.

The fingertips touched him.

He threw up his hands.

"NO!"

"Look out, kid!"

"What? Did he shoot? Can we bag him?"

"Stand by." Diesel's face hovered inches from the screen. "Monitoring."

Special Agent Mike Gillette shot daggers at Diesel. "What are we waiting for? We've got a boy in big time trouble out there right now, if he's not dead already. Give the word and we'll hit the house."

"Whoa!" Diesel shouted, reacting to something on the screen.

"What?"

Monroe sprang from his chair. "What was that?"

"I lost him!"

"What? Where is he?"

"I don't know. The kid's just gone."

< virtually eliminated >

chapter.29

GWAIHIR THE WIND LORD it was who thrice aided the wizard Gandalf in the War of the Ring. Ever did that great eagle appear at the instant of direst need to pluck a champion of light from tree or traitor's tower.

It wasn't Gwaihir who saved Jordan, but he was snatched out of danger just as surely and just as swiftly borne away into the sky.

He was saved by Rhatok, Barbarian Prince. With a jet pack.

"Whoa, Dad. Am I glad to see you!"

"Wait!"

Gillette had already opened the door and jumped out of the van. "No! I'm nailing this punk." He pulled out his mobile phone. "All agents, prepare to move in."

"Do and it's your badge." Monroe's voice caught him where he stood. "He didn't send the spike, Special Agent Gillette."

"All agents stand by." Gillette vaulted back in. "Are you sure?"

Diesel nodded. "Affirmative, sir. It was a wash. Something must've happened. The buildup was there — it's still there now — but right

< jefferson scott >

when he should have shot it, he stopped."

Gillette leaned forward. "What's that mean? Maybe your computer's messed up. Maybe Patriot's inside your computer, too. Or maybe he shot it but you just can't see it here."

"No," Monroe assured him, "when he launches this baby, we'll be able to watch it in here like the Fourth of July."

"So, I don't get it. Can I bag him now or not?"

"Not yet."

Gillette swore.

"He hasn't done anything illegal yet," Monroe said.

"But it is him, right? We're onto the right punk?"

"Confirmed, sir."

Gillette softened a little. "You said something happened. What's that mean?"

Diesel turned away from the screen. The light from the monitor painted the back of his neck and his angular jawline blue. "Unknown, sir. Possibly something on the target's end. Or—"

"Jordan."

"Sir?"

"The target. He's a nine-year-old kid named Jordan. Good looking boy."

"Yes, sir."

Monroe leaned against the instrument console. "Parks has a more important problem on his hands right now."

"What's that?"

"He's got to unload that voltage somewhere. You don't just call together 100,000 volts of electricity, then say, 'Sorry, my mistake. Everybody go on home.'"

Diesel chuckled.

"So what do you do?" Gillette asked.

"He's got to send it somewhere," Monroe said. "A lightning rod would be best."

"Yeah, right," Diesel said. "But first he's got to find a lightning rod

< virtually eliminated >

that's hooked into GlobeNet. Good luck."

"And when he does discharge this energy, Special Agent Gillette…" Monroe paused for drama.

"What?"

"When he does discharge this energy, we will be watching him."

"If he makes one wrong move with it," Diesel said, "*then* you can bag him."

"What's his dad doing there?" Special Agent Richard "Ricky" Kidner said, coming to stand behind the boy. "I thought he was in the surveillance truck in Oregon."

Paul Groves released the metal blinds and stepped away from the window. "Don't know."

The last television van had finally pulled away. What would the news crews have done had they known the boy was being held in the FBI's own building? Paul thought it ironic that Special Agent Holt, in his official statement, had promised to look into the matter diligently — since they had seized the boy under direct orders from Holt.

"Well, what's he doing? Is he going to mess up our operation?"

"You mean more than it's already been blown? My wife watches the news at five. Wait'll she finds out one of those two 'faceless government hoods' was me."

"She won't find out, will she? You're not stupid enough to break that oath, too, are you?"

Paul shrugged.

"You blow my mind, you know that?" Ricky said. "Like with this kid. First you act like he's your long lost little brother, then you tell him that snow job about his sister about to be mutilated by a lunatic. You are one cold fish, you know that, Groves?"

"Would you shut up?"

"Fine," Ricky said, picking up a phone. "You talk to your little pal. I'm calling Gerlach."

< jefferson scott >

Ethan carried his son over downtown GlobeNet. They glided over the post office, descending. They touched down on one of the entry platforms.

"Are you all right, Jordan?"

"Yeah, Dad. But how'd you learn to fly like this? This is cool!"

"You like it?"

"Yeah! Teach me how to fly, Dad, please."

"I can't, son. It has to do with the computer I'm using now." Ethan sat on the top step of the staircase leading down to GlobeNet ground level. "Sit here a minute."

Had anyone seen them, the two would have made an unlikely couple — James Bond in a tuxedo sitting next to Rhatok, Barbarian Prince.

Ethan tried to imagine his son in a room somewhere hooked up to a computer, maybe at gunpoint. "Jordan, is there someone in the room with you now, someone who can hear you talking to me?"

Jordan sneaked a peek.

Henry Simms activated the vidphone.

"You a reporter?" Parasite, he thought.

Kaye's idea about mobilizing the media had certainly stirred up public support for Jordan's plight. The FBI office had been barraged with angry callers. Stations in Texas, Kansas, and Arkansas had picked up the story. Mrs. Simms had thought she heard someone mention CNN.

What the stratagem had not been able to do was get the boy released. Yet the reporters kept calling. Now Mr. Simms wondered if they had created a monster. If it wasn't going to work, why keep talking to them? He'd never been much for reporters in the first place.

The man on the other end of the video call didn't look like a traditional reporter. He looked like a drugstore cowboy. Five-gallon straw cowboy hat, button-up roper shirt, two-day beard. Cars drove by on a street behind the man.

"No, sir. Not a reporter." Even over the road noise, the Texas accent was unmistakable. "Sir, are you the father of Ethan Hamilton's wife?"

"Who wants to know?"

"Sir, I'd rather not say who I am, since I'm not supposed to be calling you."

Mr. Simms noticed red streaks through the caller's eyes. "Yes, I am Kaye Hamilton's father."

"Sir, would you be so kind as to deliver a message to your daughter?"

Mr. Simms saw Kaye come into the kitchen. He pointed at a chair and she sat down. "What kind of message?"

"Tell her her son is safe for now."

Kaye was on her feet.

Her father's anger leapt to the surface. "You got a lot of nerve calling this house, son."

"I know, sir."

Kaye slid a piece of paper to her father. It read, "Gillette. FBI."

Henry Simms nodded. "Go on, then, speak your piece."

"I know she's a praying woman, sir. Tell her to keep praying for her son."

"We're all praying for him."

"That's good. It's good to see a man's man praying. I never put much stock in it, myself, before now."

Almost before he realized it, Mr. Simms found himself saying, "God is a father, son."

The cowboy paused. Perhaps he hadn't expected that. He smiled. "Yes, sir. Also, tell Mrs. Hamilton that she might want to start praying for her husband, too."

Kaye rushed into the vidphone camera's field of view before her father could stop her. "What's wrong with Ethan, Mr. Gillette?"

Gillette tipped his Stetson. "Ma'am. Seems we had a little falling out

< jefferson scott >

up here. I don't want you to worry, but I do want you to know. You know, so you could start your praying. Your husband's not with me any-more. He took off when he found out our agents had taken your boy. I half expected to find him with y'all in Tulsa."

"He's not here. Where is he?"

"Don't rightly know, ma'am. I do know we can't do anything here, just yet. If I was a betting man, I'd put money down that your husband's found himself a computer and is out trying to find Patriot."

Kaye couldn't sit down because that would take her out of the cam-era's view. She really needed to sit down. "But he's not ready to get back on the computer. That man's going to kill him." She felt the old fear coming back, like it had been there all along, behind the drapes, just waiting for the moment to pounce. "You've got to help him, Mike! You've got to find him and get him off that computer!"

"I don't know where he went, ma'am."

"Well you find him. You —"

Mr. Simms took his daughter's elbow. "Kaye, honey, go lie down on the sofa."

Gillette pleaded to the camera. "I just wanted her — and you, sir — to know that the FBI isn't like this most of the time. I know you won't believe me right now — I wouldn't believe it, if I were you — but we really are the good guys. I...that is, we don't usually..."

Mr. Simms just stared at the screen.

"But sometimes even the best agent's got to do something he don't like. I know the agents who took your grandson. They're good men."

No response.

"I just...I just wanted you to know."

"I'll be seeing after my daughter now."

"Yes, sir."

Mr. Simms saw the agent's eyes fall. Again he found words coming to his mind that he would prefer not to say. After fifty years of walking with Jesus, he knew that it was best not to use his own words when his Master was giving him others. "Thank you for calling, Mr. Gillette. I won't forget it."

< virtually eliminated >

"You're welcome, sir."

"I hope you don't get into too much trouble for tipping us off."

"Me, too."

"When we pray for Jordan and Ethan, son, we'll be praying for you, too."

Gillette tried to terminate the call before the tear escaped his eye.

When he looked out from under his headset, Jordan saw Ricky on the phone in the doorway to their little office and Paul right at his own shoulder.

"You okay, little guy?"

"Yes, sir."

In GlobeNet Jordan's dad took that as the answer to his question. "Did they say they were with the FBI?"

Paul, for his part, took Jordan's words as if spoken to him. He spoke at the same time Jordan's dad did.

Jordan yanked the helmet off. "What?"

Paul's eyes tracked the helmet. "I said we thought we heard you talking to someone."

"Nope, just talking to mys — I mean, yeah! I saw Patriot. I was talking to him. He dressed up like a Japanese toga man, only his sheet was orange."

"That's strange. We thought we heard you talking to somebody else. Your dad, maybe."

"Did you hear how close Patriot came to getting me again?"

Paul made a face. "We heard your side of it."

"Well, this big statue started to attack me. But I got away. Now I'm talking to this other guy. He's dressed like...he's dressed like Conan." Jordan leaned toward Paul conspiratorially. "But I think it's really Patriot in another disguise. He says he's my dad, but I know it isn't. If I could just talk to him, I bet I can make him tell me where Katie is."

< jefferson scott >

Ethan looked out over the GlobeNet cityscape while his son spoke with the FBI agents. James Bond's inanimate body sat motionless beside him. The simulated city lay frozen in eternal twilight.

For the first time since this whole enterprise began, Ethan wondered about Patriot's spiritual state. He said the Christian God had no effect on him, yet he also seemed quite knowledgeable about Christianity. At least Patriot was an honest non-Christian. Ethan preferred that to the hundreds of so-called Christians who flocked to his church every Sunday morning, and he thought God probably felt the same way. A little persecution might separate the sheep from the goats. For an honest unbeliever there was hope.

So Ethan prayed for Patriot. The words didn't want to come at first. He wasn't sure he wanted someone like Patriot in heaven with him. But something had happened to Ethan after he found out Louis Parks was paralyzed, that he had been paralyzed as a boy. There was an element of compassion mixed in with Ethan's feelings for Patriot.

The man seated beside him, wearing the tuxedo, suddenly came to life.

"I'm back."

"Okay, son. I heard all that. I think I know your situation. We'll just pretend that I'm Patriot for your little audience, okay?"

"Okay, Patriot."

"Good." Ethan faced his son. "Jordan, the men holding you are with the FBI."

"Are you sure?"

Rhatok shrugged burly shoulders. "Pretty sure. But whoever they are, they're holding you illegally. It was against the law for them to take you without the consent of me or your mother. When this is all over we are going to be sure they get into big-time trouble, you understand me?"

"Yes."

"Now, do these guys know much about computers?"

< virtually eliminated >

Jordan giggled. "No way."

"Okay, good. I want you to check for something else. Is there a surge protector on your computer?"

Jordan didn't have to look. "Yes, we had to get one because there's only one outlet in the whole room."

"Is there a surge protector for the phone line?"

"Huh?"

"Look at the back of your computer. Does the phone line go straight from your computer to the wall, or does it go through something else first?"

Jordan looked. "It goes straight into the wall."

Great. Thank you, Mr. "We've got our best people on it" Gillette.

"Okay, Jordan, listen to me very carefully. Your computer is not safe from Patriot, do you understand me? When we get through talking here I want you to take off your VR gear and turn off the computer, okay?"

"But —" Jordan paused. "Wait a minute, Patriot. You can't leave yet. First you have to tell me where you're holding my little sister prisoner."

"Have they taken Katie, too?"

"No. Patriot — *you* took her. You've got her, I mean. And I want to know where. And if you hurt her I'm going to hurt you."

"Jordan, did Patriot tell you he had Katie?"

"Well, not exactly."

"Then why do you think anybody's got her? Did the FBI agents take her when they took you?"

"No. But they told me he — *you* — took her."

"That's what these guys told you?"

"Yes."

"And that's what you're doing, trying to find Katie?"

"Yes. Where is she?"

"Jordan, these men are lying to you. Katie is safe."

"But—"

"No, son, it all makes sense now. The FBI wants to use you to catch Patriot. They want to try to make Patriot take a shot at you so they can

< jefferson scott >

arrest him. All that about Katie, that's just a story they've made up to make you do what they want. Katie's safe, Jordan. You don't have to rescue her, okay?"

"Well…okay, I guess."

"Jordan, take off that gear and do not put it back on. They had to use you, because I said I wouldn't go on the computer anymore."

"But what if —"

"They make you? Like if they put a gun to your head or something? Okay. If they do that, go ahead and get on. But don't sign onto GlobeNet. Just play a VR game — they'll never know the difference. Say, 'Don't do it, Patriot,' every now and then to make them believe."

Father and son, separated by fifteen hundred miles, shared a good laugh.

"And if," Ethan went on, "they somehow figure it out and make you log on to GlobeNet, here's what I want you to do. I want you to go straight to Falcon's Grove, okay?"

"Okay."

"Go there and get about fifty of those silver shields. Pile them up all around you like a fort and just hide. One of those shields saved my life once when Patriot took a shot at me. They'll take care of you, too."

"Okay, D — Patriot."

"Jordan," Ethan said, holding his son's arm for a moment, "you were very brave to come out here trying to save your sister. I have never been more proud of you than I am right now."

"Thanks."

Ethan smiled. "Good-bye, son."

< virtually eliminated >

chapter.30

KAYE PRESSED THE BUTTON to terminate the call. She walked into her parents' brown living room, crossing a name off her clipboard.

Wysiwyg bumped Kaye's heels as she followed her mistress into the living room. She found a spot beneath an end table to lie down. With both Ethan and Jordan gone, no one played with her. Katie loved her kitty, but usually expressed it by slapping Wizzy on the head. Amid this crisis, Kaye, who only tolerated the feline, had quickly gone from calling their pet Wysiwyg to calling her "The Cat."

"Okay, that's Lanny, Dr. Bush, and the Crennas." Henry Simms sat in his blue recliner with Katie asleep on his chest. Shirley Simms sat on the sofa with one of her friends from church. Kaye sat down beside her mother. "Anyone else?"

"Can't think of anyone," her father said softly.

Her mother leaned back in the sofa. "Lucy Kettleman has a brother in Paraguay who she said she could call."

"My goodness." The friend, whose name was Rhona, was impressed. "You have the whole world praying."

"That's right," Mrs. Simms said. "England, China, Argentina…"

< jefferson scott >

"Zambia," Mr. Simms added.

Kaye read from her clipboard the countries they hadn't mentioned. "Burkina Faso, Poland, Australia, Iran, Korea, and Israel."

"And Paraguay," Rhona said.

Mr. Simms nodded. "Don't forget everyone in the U.S."

"Of course, dear. Denver, San Antonio, Fort Worth, Boston, San Francisco, Indianapolis, Orlando…"

"Plus Tulsa, Oklahoma City, and San Diego," Kaye said.

"Chaplain Burris said he would mention it at chapel this evening. That's El Paso."

"Why there must be hundreds of people praying," Rhona said, "what with our church here and your church in Fort Worth and those servicemen in El Paso."

"And all the churches of the people we've called." Mrs. Simms looked at Kaye confidently. "Your family will be all right. You'll see."

Kaye accepted the sentiment. She liked the idea that God could be moved.

Ethan was always saying that God couldn't be coerced into doing anything he didn't want to do, no matter how many people prayed for it. A single prayer, he always maintained, offered in faith, had as much potency as a thousand voices crying to heaven from every continent.

That was fine for him. And when her family was together and everything was calm, Kaye allowed it to be fine for her, too.

But right now she needed to feel like she was doing something. And the only way she could reach her husband and son at this moment was through her heavenly Father. She didn't know the theology of it. She didn't care. Besides, it was invigorating to know that there were people all over the world lifting up her husband and son in prayer. It took the edge off her horror. Ethan could correct her about it later.

Kaye's father put his granddaughter down and eased to his knees. "It's time for us to pray, too."

They joined hands and entered the presence of the Most High.

< virtually eliminated >

"What's the matter?"

Jordan removed his helmet and began unstrapping his gloves. "Nothing."

Ricky glowered at him from a stackable chair in the corner. "What do you think you're doing, kid?"

"Nothing." With both gloves off, Jordan powered down the computer.

Ricky jumped up with a shout. Paul lunged for the power switch.

"Kid," Ricky said, "get back on that computer."

Jordan ignored him. He put all the VR gear on the desk, pushed his chair in, and plopped down on the floor, arms folded.

"I'm done for today."

Patriot was beginning to question his own virility. This Hamilton clan had frustrated his every effort against them. Wolfsbane, silver bullets, and kryptonite. Perhaps he was not the virtual virtuoso he fancied himself. The other explanation for his failures, a notion just as noisome, was that he had sorely underestimated Ethan Hamilton's skills.

Patriot's advisors came to his rescue, as they had throughout his post-adolescent life. Lord Chesterfield, "Take care of the minutes, for the hours will take care of themselves." Benjamin Franklin, "Dost thou love life? Then do not squander time; for that's the stuff life is made of." And of course his beatified Horace, "Seize the day, put no trust in the morrow."

Carpe diem!

Yes. He would remit these Hamiltons no further energy. They had almost caused him to deviate from his chosen course.

He annihilated the Buddhist temple with a snap of artificial fingers.

The voltage he had accumulated for Jordan needed to be discharged. He would have preferred to simply store the energy for the few

< jefferson scott >

remaining minutes, but the technicians at the Novosibirsk power station had finally detected the anomaly and were working to eliminate it.

He activated his outlet-finding macro and sent it off, but not before restricting its search to Japan. If there was property damage to be done at this late juncture, then let it be done on enemy soil. A moment later his macro provided him with the network address of an unused pay vidphone in the city of Akita. He sent the spike there.

A consultation of his status menu showed that both Grant and Yasunari were on-line. Grant was already at the simulated version of Saint Andrews' famous golf course. Yasunari was uploading a file to a number of important servers. His victory speech, no doubt. Patriot initiated the jump to the golf course.

Fifteen minutes to the appointed hour. *Tee* minus fifteen, as it were.

Patriot took a moment to call up his own victory message. It was a large file, replete with full-motion video, stereo sound, and a two-minute animation. This little file, once initiated, would release onto every GlobeNet computer a nondestructive virus with a specific dispatch. While the world watched his message, the program would also trigger an irreversible chain reaction in the high-tech equipment connected to Patriot's computer.

As he waited for the file to preload, Patriot reflected on his last encounter. Of course it had been the elder Hamilton who had emancipated Jordan at the last moment. Who else? But why had he placed his son in danger in the first place if he intended to snatch him out like that? Something seemed suspicious. Another thing that disturbed Patriot was Ethan's newfound ability to fly.

Patriot tore his mind from that subject and onto the task at hand. Slight not what's near, he chided himself, through aiming at what's far.

He arrived at the first tee. For once he allowed himself to focus on the unreality of the virtual world in which he lived. The Royal and Annuitied Old Course was splendid in the imitation early morning light. Artificial grouse uttered throaty cries while manufactured roe deer grazed in the nearby meadow. A synthetic golden eagle perched in a fir

< virtually eliminated >

tree, supposedly scanning for salmon in a simulated stream feeding the counterfeit Saint Andrews Bay.

A forgery, all of it. Yet he bore it no malice. He was like a condemned man surveying his homeland for the last time, loving it despite its manifold flaws.

Invisible as always, Patriot hovered like an evil spirit over the traitorous founder of the last significant American-owned corporation. Grant crouched over his bag of clubs, mumbling to himself.

Patriot shook his head. "Whom the gods wish to destroy," he recited, "they first make mad."

Tee-minus-twelve.

"Holy Guacamole, what was that?"

Monroe didn't take his eyes off his screen. "That, my man Gillette, was discharging voltage."

"Estimate 120,000 volts," Diesel said crisply.

Mike Gillette put his finger on the young man's screen. "You're reading that here?"

Diesel removed the offending finger. "Affirmative, sir. Meaning no offense, sir, but please keep your hands off the equipment."

"Beg pardon." Gillette went to stand over Monroe's shoulder. "That was illegal, wasn't it? 120,000 volts?"

"Nothing illegal about the number, Mr. Gillette." He entered commands into his keyboard. "It's what he did with all that electricity that counts."

"Well, what did he do with it?"

"That's what we're trying to find out. Look, Special Agent, why don't you go up front and get you a sody pop. We'll let you know when we have anything."

"All right." Gillette dragged himself forward.

"You got a fix on location yet?" Monroe asked his partner.

"Pository. Bad news, Monroe."

< jefferson scott >

Gillette craned his neck back. "What?"

"It's foreign soil."

"Where?"

"Looks like our boy Parks popped a payphone in the land of the rising sun."

"So?" Gillette slid back into their working area. "That's illegal, isn't it?"

"Not very nice, sir, but not illegal. Feel sorry for the nip that's got to clean it up, though. That phone's in exactly one trillion pieces right now."

The men in the surveillance van fell silent. After an eternal moment, in which Diesel wiped his monitor with a tissue, Monroe spoke.

"Get on the horn to CIA, boy."

"Why?" Diesel might have asked the question, but he took the mike in hand just the same.

"Got an idea."

Ethan had witnessed many bizarre things in cyberspace. He'd seen a colleague ruin a day's work in an artificial environment by lunging after his spilled real-world Coke. He had even seen a woman choke while in VR gear. Her persona's body convulsed, hands went to throat. Then she rose and shook like a rag doll as someone performed the Heimlich on her.

But he had never seen anyone's hands tremble, as his were doing right now. It made sense, of course. Any movement on the outside would be recreated on the inside. But he wished there was some way he could toggle his shuddering off.

Already he was having trouble remembering what it was about computers that was so terrible. Surely all that had just been a mistake — one of his wife's hysterical fabrications.

"Help, Father, help. It feels so good here. I want it."

Words came to him then. Faintly, as if overheard from a passing car. *My grace is sufficient for you.*

< virtually eliminated >

"I know, but —"

We will never again say 'Our gods' to what our own hands have made.

"Of course not, but you—"

Surely I am with you always, even to the end of the age.

He didn't interrupt this time.

'Not by might nor by power, but by my Spirit,' says the Lord.

"Yes."

Stand still and see this great thing the Lord is about to do before your eyes!

"Yes, Father."

Ethan used to tell his children that God didn't speak out of the clouds any longer because he had already said it all and anybody could read it. He wasn't going to tell them that anymore.

But the Counselor, the Holy Spirit, whom the Father will send in my name, will teach you all things and will remind you of everything I have said to you.

"I need my helpers."

Ethan was immediately surrounded by his artificial friends. Thumper and Meely were absent from the group, but the fireplug was there, as were the chrome ball, the yellow cloud, the cricket with the hiccups, and others. He muted the hiccups.

Two of his minions were predesigned for high-speed GlobeNet searches. These he dispatched with the following command, "Search all news and article databases and Veronica servers; find any event set to begin at—" he calculated the time Patriot's coup was set to begin "— 3:00 P.M. Pacific time. Go!"

Ethan checked his internal clock — 2:50. "Ten minutes! There's no way."

Nevertheless he zipped open two of his other infobots and went to work refocusing their instructions. He might be able to get to one more after these, but there wouldn't be time for any others, not enough to reprogram them and give them any time to search.

A woman's voice startled him. "Stand by, Ethan. I think we might have something here."

< jefferson scott >

It was Dr. Hosokawa. Ethan had almost forgotten her presence. Though her jarring interruption had actually helped him remember that there was a real world.

"Ethan," Hosokawa said, "I'm going to let you speak with Kevin Crowell, one of my doctoral students."

The microphone bumped and scraped before a young man's husky voice came through Ethan's speakers. "Mr. Hamilton, I think I might know what you're looking for."

Ethan didn't catch the import of what he said. He was busy reprogramming his helpers.

Kevin was going on. "...anybody had thought of it."

Ethan jerked back into focus. "Thought of what?"

"The Nanotech takeover."

"The what?"

Kevin answered but Ethan wasn't listening. Nanotech — of course! It would qualify to Patriot as the last important American business. What was it Diesel had said? That Grant had taken Nanotech from zero to sixty but needed a new challenge. So he was selling it to someone.

Ethan knew without asking who Grant was selling to. The nation anyway, if not the person.

Patriot was going to attack at the takeover.

"Come on, guys!" His helpers still present followed him across the GlobeNet cityscape into the business district.

< virtually eliminated >

chapter.31

"YOU SURE YOU'RE REALLY TRYING, KID?"

Jordan looked out from his expensive HMD. "What?"

"I said," Ricky almost yelled, "I don't think you're trying very hard to find him."

"I am trying. GlobeNet's huge. Patriot could be anywhere."

Paul nodded. "It's true, Kidner. Half a trillion people a day."

"There's only seven billion people on the earth, genius." Ricky grabbed Jordan's headset. "I say the kid's doing us dirty." He put the headset on.

"No, wait!" But Jordan's objection came too late.

Ricky laughed.

Paul stood up. "What is it, Kidner?"

"I was wrong, Groves," he said, still laughing. He took the headset off and handed it to his partner. He might be smiling, but the look he shot at Jordan did not agree with the rest of the face.

"What's this?" Paul's voice sounded nasally when he spoke. He pulled the headset off. Both men looked at Jordan.

"What is this, Jordan?"

"You should try it. It's a cool game."

< jefferson scott >

"Come on, Runt, do your stuff."

Ethan had made his fireplug helper green in honor of the one that used to stand in his front yard when his family had lived in San Antonio. This fireplug didn't control the flow of water; it controlled the flow of data. Ethan had surreptitiously attached it to a main lead — he called it a vein—emanating from a Nanotech subnetwork. With the turn of a virtual monkey wrench, Ethan could regulate the data flow. And with a special software filter, he could search for a specific string of characters, panning for artificial gold.

Ethan floated directly above the fireplug's little infiltration, surrounded like the sun by his solar system of helpers. Two minutes before three. Still no sign of his other hunters.

"Hurry up, hurry up. One of you Nanonerds pop off a note about your big daddy Martin."

One minute before three.

A white pulse swept up the fireplug's body.

"Bingo!" Ethan dove for the surface. "Stop, Runt. Capture." He reached his helper and rotated the big wrench clockwise. "Okay, buddy, disengage."

The fireplug glided back from the vein. Ethan moved the wrench to another bolt and rotated. ASCII text poured out at Ethan's feet into a pool of numbers and letters. The word *takeover* stood out in bright yellow. Ethan grabbed the word with an artificial hand. "Come here, Cricket."

The half dozen other helpers made way as the hiccuping cricket hopped forward.

Ethan reactivated its hiccups. "Okay, Cricket, open up." He fed the word *takeover* into the thing's mandibles. "Digest, boy, and make it fast."

This was a trick he'd learned in college. A little gadget to find Internet coordinates and then go there quick. With only slight modification, it worked extremely well in GlobeNet.

And then, with a gulp and a belch, they were off.

< virtually eliminated >

Jordan actually saw his dad go flying by. With all his helpers right behind, he looked like Halley's comet.

Funny, but neither Paul nor Ricky had wanted to play *Galactic Ripper*. Jordan decided that FBI guys needed to learn to have more fun. That, he realized on the spot, would be a great topic for that essay due next Monday.

They hadn't exactly made him go into GlobeNet. Ricky had wanted to, though. He said something about a South American prison. Jordan went back on, in the end, just to get these guys off his back.

Paul had started talking about how Patriot was going to hurt Katie really bad and stuff. Ricky said he'd probably cut her fingers off one by one. Jordan thought it was funny, actually, since he knew they were liars with their pants a-smoking. He had to cover his face not to laugh. But they went on and on about what Patriot was going to do to Katie, and it finally started to get to Jordan. He picked up the headset again and went on into the net, like they wanted. But it was more to shut them up than anything else.

There was no way he was really going after Patriot, though.

He watched his dad go by. He thought about going after him, just to see what was going on. If he got caught, though, he was pretty sure his dad would not be happy.

He decided to send one of his own helpers instead.

This one looked like the HMS *Victory*, Nelson's flagship at the battle of Trafalgar.

"Sail on, *Victory!*" Jordan commanded. Then he gave Paul and Ricky an explanation, "That's GlobeNet code for, uh, 'Go check your e-mail.'"

Jordan wasn't a very good liar.

When the ship's white sails had vanished in the direction of his dad, Jordan continued on his way to his destination.

Falcon's Grove.

< jefferson scott >

A golf course?

Ethan scanned the beautiful fairway. No bombs going off, no lightning striking that he could see. Just two golfers teeing up.

He must have been at the right place. Both golfers had that newest and most expensive VR rage, HIREV — High Imaging Resolution, Enhanced Video.

In HIREV the person still had an artificial on-screen body, but the face was his own. So the men moved around with their computer animated bodies, but where their attending computer generated faces should have been, there was a flickering, live-action video shot of their own kissers. The effect was disconcerting. It reminded Ethan a little of a knight in full plate armor looking out from an upraised visor.

But the technology hadn't been perfected yet. It had no way, for instance, to adjust for changes in the position of the head relative to the rest of the body. When the first golfer bent down to place his tee in the turf, his face remained up and down, though it should have rotated almost upside down with the rest of his head.

Ethan recognized the golfer about to swing. He checked his chronometer: 3:01. By all rights these guys should be dead.

"Excuse me, gentlemen."

The divet from Martin Grant's mis-swing traveled farther than the ball itself.

The nation's richest man turned to Ethan with his driver in his hand. "Who are you?"

Ethan backed away involuntarily, stunned to be able to see the man's face. He also realized he still looked like Rhatok, Barbarian Prince.

The other golfer bowed. "Welcome, Rambo."

This man, Ethan saw in the video projected image, was clearly Oriental. Definitely in the right place.

The Japanese golfer sliced the air horizontally with his gloved hand. "Another ball, Martin. No penalty."

< virtually eliminated >

"Excuse me, gentlemen. I'm sorry to interrupt your golf game, but I think you should know you're in serious danger right now."

Grant turned back to the tee and spoke with his back to Ethan. "The only one in any danger right now is you, Conan. I suggest you leave before I have you ejected from the course." He bent down to place another ball. Head down, face up.

Of all the possible ways Ethan might have imagined this moment, this was stranger than the strangest. He had expected a conference room, not a golf course. He had expected tons of people from both sides sitting on opposite sides of a big table, not the two bigwigs alone. He had expected to be too late, only able to pick up the pieces. He had even expected to catch Patriot in the act and leap to the rescue in the nick of time.

He had not expected to be shooed, unheard, off the premises. He had half a notion just to let them have what was coming to them.

Then there was that Golden Rule thing, causing problems again.

"I know you don't want to hear this, gentlemen. I know you just want me to leave, but I can't. There is a man whose name is Patriot — his real name is Louis Parks — who intends to electrocute you both."

Ethan saw the two golfers trade amused looks. This was not going as he had intended. The Oriental man jutted his chin forward, like an old man who didn't catch that last.

"Electrocuted, Chairman Yasunari," Grant explained. "You know, shocked." He did an imitation of someone in, Ethan supposed, an electric chair. If the situation hadn't been so serious, he would have laughed. The pantomime seemed to work, however.

Chairman Yasunari nodded sagely. Then he looked at Ethan. "Why will this Patriot be wanting to…" he copied Grant's mock-electrocution, "Martin Grant-san and Yuki Yasunari-san, hmm?"

Ethan bit back the words that came to his mouth first. He wanted these men to believe him. Offending one or both probably wasn't the best way to accomplish that goal. "Because Patriot very much dislikes Americans selling things to — if you'll excuse me, Chairman — the Japanese."

< jefferson scott >

Yasunari and Grant traded another live-action look, then both burst out in laughter.

"Well, it's a little too late to start worrying about that now."

"You don't understand. He —"

Ethan saw movement down the fairway, near the first green. A flash of black.

"There he is." He pointed.

The men spun around.

Ethan lost track of the movement. "There!" He pointed to a spot much nearer, where the fairway met the woods. A deer trotted out onto the grass. The laughter this time was worse than before.

"Get out of here," Grant said.

"I'm telling you, if you stay on-line, you will be killed."

Then Ethan saw Patriot, full bodied, unmistakable.

He hovered above them like the Angel of Death.

"Most amusing, Ethan Hamilton."

That calm, refined voice. A chill shot up Ethan's spine. He turned to Grant and Yasunari with a there-you-see look, but they were going on with their game.

"Of course they cannot hear me yet. You see and hear me because I wish it. I must say, I cannot approve of your tailor. Rather medieval, I should say."

"It's been a long time, Louis Parks." He knew Patriot would have his electricity ready. Maybe it had some kind of time limit. Maybe he could buy these ingrates some time.

It had come down to a game of seconds.

"I've been to your house, you know. Seen your yard. You really ought to get someone to look after it better."

Patriot hovered, his black robes billowing elegantly in a whispering wind. "Yes. Truly. I really must. Tell me, Ethan, you are a man of the Book, are you not? Your word can be trusted, yes?"

< virtually eliminated >

"As my Lord Jesus Christ gives me strength."

"Spare me the sermon. If you have seen my house, as you allege, why then have you and your Department of Justice assassins not made an arrest?"

Ethan didn't want to answer, didn't want to give anything away.

"Very well," Patriot went on, "I will tell you why. Because there is nothing for which to arrest me. There are no charges. There is no evidence whatsoever that would lead any district attorney in the country to issue a warrant for my arrest."

"There are also no witnesses to your crimes. And no survivors."

"Very well put, thank you."

"Except me. And Jordan."

"Yes, except you and Jordan. How thoughtful of you to remind me." He glanced at the golfers. They had both teed off and were moving down the fairway. "You will excuse me now, Ethan. It seems my prey has taken flight." Patriot began to veer away.

"Burt Wikowski says hello."

It was astonishing the things one heard when one paid attention. All around the tee cicadas sang their choral lullaby. A grey squirrel chattered in a nearby tree, upsetting a flight of birds. A stream gurgled from somewhere nearby. The voices of the golfers carried lightly across the vibrant Scottish glen.

Patriot's back faced Ethan. "How is Burt?"

Careful, Curly. "He's fine. He...remembers you. Fondly. I don't think he's been the same since you left." Ethan felt that was probably true.

Patriot turned so that he could look at Ethan. "He said that?"

"Yes. Well, not in so many words. But he definitely seemed sad that you gave up."

"I didn't give up! I *grew* up."

"Whatever."

"Old man Wikowski." Patriot's voice took on a wistful tone Ethan had never heard from him before. "You know, I once bit him on the

< jefferson scott >

nose? Spit on him, too. I hated him so much."

"He told us about the spit."

But Patriot wasn't talking to Ethan. "Not hated, precisely. Or else it wasn't him I hated, but myself." His body began drifting upward.

Ethan levitated beside him.

"How could I hate that man? I never could. The only person who never gave up on me, never betrayed me." He turned to Ethan. He didn't seem to notice they were both airborne. "My father left me when I was in the hospital, did you know that?"

"It must have been very difficult for you." *Are you crazy, Curly? Playing chaplain to a maniac?*

"He lives in Idaho now with his new wife and children. Only six hours' drive, but he's never been to see me. Do you know what he named his first son with his new wife? Louis. They named him Louis! Replaced as if I had never existed."

It was not the first time Ethan found himself with mixed feelings toward Patriot, this serial killer, this mass murderer.

"And please do not get me started about my mother." Patriot looked at Ethan for several moments before continuing. "Ethan Hamilton, you are a wonder. In your way you have been just as true to me as Burt Wikowski ever was." Patriot touched him on the shoulder, and Ethan imagined he actually felt the contact. "I envy you, you know."

"You envy me? You're so gifted in VR. I've never seen anyone like you. I'm the one with envy."

"Yes, my matchless skills. Euripides said, 'Along with success comes a reputation for wisdom.' Those vaulted gifts to which you refer — parlor tricks and sleight of hand. In time you could learn every one. What you have I could never imitate. Your wife, your family. I even envy you your faith in the Christian God. One day, you and I shall have to talk on that subject, and you have my permission to testify to me with all vigor how I might save my eternal soul."

Ethan saw, like the sun cresting the horizon, a way out for all of them. "Why don't we have that talk right now?"

< v i r t u a l l y   e l i m i n a t e d >

For a moment Patriot did not answer. They had risen to the clouds. The perfect place for a discussion about heaven.

When he did answer, it was with resignation. "No, my friend. I think not. Had we met seven, even five, years ago, perhaps. No, I must maintain my course to my own Promised Land. I cannot waver."

Why did Ethan feel like he was talking to an old friend? "If you do, you know I'm going to have to try to stop you."

Patriot's shoulders faced Ethan squarely. "You will not succeed. I have a surprise due in thirty seconds — a little gift imported all the way from Paris, Texas. But leave it be, my friend. In ten minutes this will all be over and I will be dead. You can go back to your winsome family in peace."

"You won't be dead. No one's going to hurt you."

Patriot chuckled. "Give my regards to Jordan, will you? He is an exceptional boy, you know? You should be most proud."

"I am."

"It has been amusing, Ethan Hamilton. Content yourself with the knowledge that you have 'fought the good fight.' And allow me to complete the race marked out for me."

Ethan watched him descend back toward the golf course. He was left pensive, unwilling to move. But he knew he must. He plunged through the clouds after his foe. He spotted him downrange, dropping like a hawk on Martin Grant and Chairman Yasunari. Ethan angled his dive to intercept him.

That's when the line went dead.

< jefferson scott >

chapter.32

Edgar Ramirez put away his tools and got back in his truck. He headed for the Sizzlin' to collect his hundred thou. One of their steaks sounded good right now. Maybe he would stay for supper. Maybe he would buy steaks for everyone in the joint.

He had to be careful not to act too rich all at once, though. Maybe he would just pack his family up and move to the city, then he could flaunt it all he wanted. For now, though, he had to keep acting discreet.

He pulled the sun visor down and headed back into Paris, careful to obey the speed limit. He would get his money soon enough. First he wanted to stop at Honest John's Jeep/Eagle. He had to see if the Aztec came in Fiesta Red.

Two weeks later Edgar Ramirez set up his own telecommunications consulting business out of the office in his new Highland Park home. Little Hector got the operations for his eyes, the Ramirez family got out of debt, and Edgar never did anything illegal again. Except drive a little too fast now and again in his bright red Aztec.

< virtually eliminated >

"It's for you, Special Agent."

Gillette took the phone from Diesel. "This is Gillette."

"Mike, Ethan."

"Ethan, buddy, where you been?"

"I'm at Loma Linda. Mike, you've got to do something for me right now."

"I thought you might go there." He took the phone into the cab of the van and spoke softly. "I called your wife. I told her what you're doing."

"Mike — you talked to Kaye? How is she? Is Katie okay, my little daughter? Have you heard anything about Jordan?"

"I can't talk right now. Give me your number and I'll call you from a payphone."

"There's no time. You've got to get me emergency phone access, Mike. Now!"

"What do you need that for?"

"Mike, the phone lines are dead."

"What are we talking on, tin cans?"

"This is a cellular call, Mike. My cell phone calling the cell phone in the van. It's not affected. But the modem in my computer here has to have a land line. You've got to get me on at the lab here. Doesn't the Department of Defense have its own network? I need access to it now!"

"Let me tell you what Monroe here has figured out about how we can bag —"

"Mike! People are about to get fried. Remember Diesel talking about Martin Grant, the richest guy in America? Made the software in the van?"

"Right."

"He's the one who's going to bite the big one if you don't get me that access."

"Okay, partner, I'll do it."

< j e f f e r s o n   s c o t t >

"Fast, Mike. Patriot was going in for the kill when the lines went dead. It's been almost six minutes."

Gillette called back into the body of the van. "He hasn't shot anything yet, has he?"

Monroe called back up. "Not yet."

"Relax, buddy, it's all right. Nothing's gone off yet."

"Mike!"

"Okay, okay. I'm on it."

"And get some people out to the Nanotech headquarters in Portland. Get Marty boy off the computer."

Patriot circled Grant and Yasunari slowly, like a schoolmaster pacing the classroom. Their photo-accurate eyes followed his lecture with apparent fascination, as if consuming every word before it might fall to the Scottish turf.

Their concentration was greatly enhanced by one factor. They believed Patriot's claim that he had kidnapped members of their families and would terminate them if either man so much as yawned. Patriot had produced audio messages to back up his claim. And when Yasunari threatened to disconnect, Patriot supplied video of the chairman's favorite granddaughter with a semi-automatic rifle pointed at her pristine chest.

Thus Patriot held two of the world's richest men on-line as tautly as if he had riveted them to their computers.

"When I was eight," Patriot said, "my father took me to Hawaii on one of his business trips. I was too young to care about the women in their bikinis or to admire the islands. I wanted to see one thing, and one thing only. On the second day my father took me to see it — the Pearl Harbor Memorial.

"My father had not fought in World War II, nor any war, for that matter. Nevertheless I remember him being moved. We sat together over the submerged hull of the USS *Arizona* for, I suppose, a full hour. I only cared for the massive guns and the video of the *Arizona* in flames.

< virtually eliminated >

"He called me 'son' that day more times than he did in the balance of our brief relationship. He said, 'Son, in 1941 the Japanese attacked Pearl Harbor because it was the smartest and fastest way to reach their goal to rule the world.'

"I remember being confused by that statement, since the Japanese had not been militaristic in my lifetime. I recall realizing that I had never in my short life seen a single Japanese weapon of war. Not one tank or submarine or jet fighter. I found it difficult imagining that country — which up to then I had only known for its excellence in electronics — ever mounting a fleet of deadly warships.

"Yet my father remembered. 'The Japanese lost in World War II, son. Hiroshima and Nagasaki settled that. But for them the war's not over yet — they still want to rule the world. World War II took away their weapons. They'll be back, son, mark my words. And they will find the fastest, smartest way to win the war without dropping a single bomb.'"

Patriot planted his feet on the fairway. Grant and Yasunari never took their eyes off him.

"Gentlemen, my father was a fool. Is a fool. There are times when I question how I ever turned out so well, hindered as I was with his genes. When things got difficult, he abandoned my mother and me in less time than it took the *Enola Gay* to destroy Hiroshima. But imbecile that he was, my father was correct in his assessment of the Japanese people. Was he not, Chairman Yasunari?"

"You bear much anger toward my people."

"Oh, do shut up." Patriot was suddenly furious, raving. "Both of you just shut your mouths. Neither of you will admit to Japan's aggression against America, so what is the purpose of continuing this conversation? Japan owns the United States, and the American people do not even realize it."

"You know," Martin Grant said, "I don't remember seeing a Japanese flag flying over the White House any time lately. The last time I checked, our president's name wasn't Connor-asaki."

< jefferson scott >

Patriot stepped between the two golfers, singling Grant out. "You. Great American role model. All-American man. The veritable poster child for the American capitalist system. Of all men, you should be leading the crusade against the yellow menace. Instead, with your betrayal you drive the final nail into your nation's coffin."

"I don't know what you're talking about."

"No? You are prepared to offer Nanotech, the last significant American-owned corporation, to her sworn enemy. You should know, by the way, that Chairman Yasunari is prepared to pay almost three times the amount you plan to name. As you sell your country out, at least have the decency to make the buyer pay dearly for her. She may not mean much to you, but greater men than you have given their lives to make her free. And other men continue their legacy."

Patriot loaded his electrical charges into the palm of each virtual hand.

"What would you have us do," Grant asked, "call off the sale? Would that make you happy? Would that make you release my wife and his granddaughter? Or do you want more? Maybe I should go out and buy back every corporation that's ever been sold to the Japanese — would you like that? I don't know what you've heard about my money, mister, but I don't have that much. The reports of my wealth have been greatly exaggerated."

Patriot was calm again. Grant and Yasunari couldn't know it, but that was a very bad sign.

"You misquote, sir. The correct wording is, 'The report of my death was an exaggeration.' But of course you may be excused for not knowing Mr. Clemens's words very well. He was an American, after all."

And suddenly it was time.

Somehow Patriot had expected to feel something more from this moment. As if it would stand out above all other moments for its brilliance and import. His brave blow for American independence. Poets would vie to compose the most stirring rendering of his heroic knight-errantry.

< virtually eliminated >

Instead, he felt nothing. Nothing besides a mounting distaste for himself.

He viewed himself as if from outside. He saw his black-robed persona standing like a wraith over his two pathetic prisoners. He was no patriot, no hero. He looked more like a withered cripple trying to give his ludicrous life some meaning.

Any meaning.

His moment had come and he had to play it out. The final act in his Theater of the Absurd.

He triggered the subroutine that would, in ten minutes, end his life.

He reached one hand each toward the heads of Martin Grant and Yuki Yasunari.

"Good-bye, gentlemen. I leave you with Emily Dickinson's timeless words: 'Because I could not stop for Death, he kindly stopped for me. The Carriage held but just Ourselves and Immortality.'"

Patriot pressed his hands to their heads.

And found himself on his backside.

< jefferson scott >

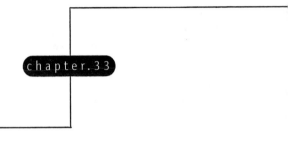

chapter.33

Hamilton, you imbecile!"

Ethan risked taking his eyes off Patriot. He turned to Grant and Yasunari. "You two get out of here now! Jack out."

"Who are you?" Grant said.

Ethan pushed the golfers down the fairway away from Patriot, trying to gain a moment or two more. "I tried to warn you before about this guy, remember? I was Conan then." Ethan had changed to his usual persona, which happened to resemble Ethan's real-world appearance.

"Ah," Yasunari said. "Rambo."

Far up the fairway, Ethan saw Patriot rise to his feet.

"Right. Now get out. I won't be able to keep him off you a second time."

"I cannot," Yasunari said. "He capture my granddaughter, say he going to kill her."

"And my wife!"

"I don't think so," Ethan heard himself say. He saw Patriot then, bounding down the fairway like a black wolf. "Hostages aren't his style.

< virtually eliminated >

Jack out and call your families. They're probably sitting in front of the tube."

Patriot was almost upon them, black robes flowing behind him like a cape.

Ethan could feel the indecision around him, taking them down like quicksand.

Patriot took a final step.

Left his feet.

Pounced on them with a ferocious roar.

And grasped thin air.

Yasunari and Grant vanished with a flicker of blue video.

Patriot stared at his hands. "No!"

At precisely that moment, 1,836,009,214 GlobeNet users worldwide watched whatever they were working on dissolve into the image of an American flag billowing in the wind. A narrator's resonant voice began, in whichever language each user had selected, a survey of American history. Despite all efforts the impostor message could not be overridden. A few users just jacked out. But most stayed on, transfixed.

When the survey reached VJ Day, an animation came on showing the efforts of Japan and Germany to win through industry the war they had lost through military means. The final three minutes of the message covered what little defenses the few Americans who knew of the problem could muster.

"Some," the narrator informed a watching world, "took action against the aggressors, on land" — a photo of the bombed Oklahoma City federal building flashed across the screen — "in the air" — the wreckage of the '03 Delta crash — "and through the airwaves."

Another animation began, showing a user siphoning American goods off to Japan. A second user was shown cutting into the call and sending a bright pulse of light to the offender. When the pulse arrived, the traitor simply blinked out.

"Thus America's few patriots defend her against the enemy, while

< jefferson scott >

kings and princes sleep."

The message concluded with a shot of the American flag. JFK's voice gave the epitaph.

"Let every nation know, whether it wishes us well or ill, that we shall pay any price, bear any burden, meet any hardship, support any friend, oppose any foe to assure the survival and the success of liberty."

"Do you know what you have done?"

"I saved two men you were going to murder."

"No, you fool. You addlepated half-wit." Patriot picked himself off the grass. "You have condemned your own country to oblivion." He shot his arms over his head and sprang into the sky. "No!"

Ethan backed away. He lost sight of Patriot in the clouds. There were about 200,000 volts of electricity in those clouds now, and Ethan had no desire to be caught in the electrical storm.

Patriot's voice boomed down to Ethan like the voice of God, halting him. "Do you fancy yourself a hero, Ethan Hamilton? To me you are anathema. 'Even throughout life,' Browning wrote, ''tis death that makes life live, gives it whatever the significance.' Your rescue has robbed me even of that. Browning's words now course like poison through my heart."

Through a break in the clouds, Ethan caught a glimpse of Patriot. He hung as if crucified, arms extended, face arched to heaven. He laughed, a sound devoid of gladness. "What bitter trick is this that allows me now to feel my toes turn cold when I have been so long deprived of their warmth? Ah, Hamilton, Hamilton, my friend. It has begun. I am almost out of time."

The clouds closed over him. Ethan opened an exit portal and began to key in a destination.

"But not," Patriot said, suddenly at Ethan's shoulder, "before I unburden myself of thee."

< virtually eliminated >

Ethan had never seen the Abu Simbel Temple at sunrise. Or at any other time, for that matter. He'd never even heard of it. If he somehow managed to survive this day, he promised himself he would take his family there.

Four massive statues of Ramses II flanked the entrance to the breathtaking temple. Six-foot tall stone figures of Ramses' family stood at the pharaoh's feet, a picket line stuck like matches in the dirt. The entire edifice was carved out of a sandstone cliff. By design, the sun's first rays reached far down the entrance shaft and illuminated statues of Heliopolis, Memphis, and Thebes, ancient Egypt's most important gods.

When Patriot had materialized at his side, Ethan had panicked. He knew that Patriot need only touch him to deliver his voltage, since once Patriot picked his form of delivery, there seemed to be no way for him to change it. Ethan just dove into the exit portal, not caring where he ended up so long as it was away from there.

He had emerged here. Ancient Egypt. Beside the mighty Nile.

Before Ethan could do more than run like a scalded cat, Patriot had teleported in behind him and given chase.

And now Ethan found himself fighting for his life. He had no plan other than to keep Patriot's hands away from his body. What more could he do against this maestro of cyberspace?

Ethan plucked one of Ramses' wives from her resting place and threw her at Patriot. Patriot dodged the stone projectile and rushed on toward his foe.

Ethan fled headlong, first springing up to sit atop one of Ramses' heads, then, when Patriot slammed into the rock wall after him, diving away into the Nile.

Dr. Hosokawa's RVT contraption helped even the field for Ethan, but it wasn't enough. Patriot was faster and more adept. His task was simpler, too. He didn't have to keep thinking of new ways to get away; all he had to do was chase. And chase he did. In the end, all the RVT

< jefferson scott >

gave Ethan was a few more ways to jump out of danger.

He couldn't evade Patriot forever. One time soon Patriot was going to anticipate Ethan's dodge and the whole thing would be over in a millisecond of fire.

Ethan was getting tired already. Physically, as well as mentally. He didn't realize it, but he was putting his whole body into every lunge. Writhing on a table in a Loma Linda lab. He felt his legs fall off the MRI table once, then get pushed back on by unseen hands.

Ethan bolted down the chamber into the belly of the hillside. It was the only thing he hadn't done yet. Patriot recovered from his last pounce quickly and barreled into the temple, shrieking like an animal.

Bad idea, Curly, Ethan thought, emerging into the inner chamber. Dead end.

Patriot's approaching body blocked out the sun. His shadow danced over the gods like a disembodied spirit.

Ethan leaped straight up.

Patriot struck the wall face first.

Dove up.

Ethan dove sideways.

Black hands swatted the space he'd just vacated.

This was Ethan's dead end, too, unless he could think of something fast. He didn't want to die — that much he knew. But he didn't want anyone else to die, either. If he jacked out now, the game would just go on. Even if Patriot didn't use this voltage to kill someone else, he would be free to kill again. Nothing would have changed.

It had to end now.

Patriot coiled his body and struck.

Ethan opened a portal and dove in.

And found himself in someone's 3D spreadsheet.

Columns of different heights rose from a black floor like stacks of colored quarters. They huddled together, overlapping, to maximize the visual impact of their contrasting elevations. A man's voice resonated through the site in a fast language Ethan didn't recognize. But he knew

< virtually eliminated >

the tone well enough. This was a presentation at somebody's boring business meeting.

Ethan flew to the top of a purple platform and looked back.

Patriot teleported in with the pleasant GlobeNet chime. He saw Ethan and came at him. Was it just Ethan's imagination, or did Patriot's flight seem a little less precise?

This was not a good place to fight it out. There were no obstacles to throw in Patriot's way.

Ethan opened a portal and went through.

Ethan had never gotten into the BattleMech kind of game. Jordan had. But Ethan had never been infected with the fever generated by colossal walking machines standing toe to toe and unloading arsenals larger than those of small countries.

He thanked God for them now.

For here was a site that might save his life. Obstacles galore: hills, buildings, rubble, burned-out mechs. A red haze restricted visibility to the equivalent of less than one hundred yards.

Ethan emerged from his trans-site hop almost under the feet of an armored behemoth. He bounded up to its head and settled on a shoulder like a parrot on a pirate.

Patriot chimed in a moment later, but couldn't locate Ethan right away.

Ethan watched his rival head off in the wrong direction. There was definitely something wrong with Patriot. His movements, once graceful, now seemed ragged and chopped. Perhaps he truly was dying.

The mech Ethan was riding came under attack from two others. The landscape resonated with the sound of battle as the machines engaged each other with guns, rockets, and lasers. The graphics for the explosions were exceptional.

Ethan dropped down beside a burning communications bunker and scanned the scarlet horizon. He saw an explosion in the distance and decided to check it out. Perhaps Patriot was there.

He didn't know what he was doing, exactly. He still hadn't come up with a brilliant way to solve his dilemma. His conscience wouldn't let him jack out, but his sense of self-preservation wouldn't let him think of anything but jacking out.

He prayed for wisdom. And divine intervention, if possible. He took some comfort in something he'd heard his pastor say once, "A Christian is immortal so long as God wants him alive."

And if God wants you dead, Curly, there's not much you can do about that, either.

So he just went with his gut.

All evidence pointed to the notion that Patriot was dying. But he'd been fooled by that ploy before. Ethan determined to find him. And if he found him, then what? He didn't know.

Ethan reached the site of the explosions he had seen. Three mechs lay in smoking ruins. A fourth towered over the scene, motionless, like an armored scarecrow. A white flash to Ethan's right, followed by a *kuTOOM*, told him in which direction the battle had moved.

He sighed. The battlefield was too large. Once he had lost track of Patriot there was little hope of finding him again. Ethan was at once glad that he had lived and frustrated that he hadn't stopped him.

"Okay, Dr. Hosokawa. Looks like I've lost him. Pull me on out and we'll try to think of something else."

There was no response. Ethan reached up to tap his speakers, forgetting that he wasn't wearing any. He felt the wires on his arms grapple across his face. Ethan's fatigue, matched with disappointment, made him irritable.

"Hello? Earth to Loma Linda University. Dr. Hosokawa? Kev? Yoo-hoo, anybody home?"

"They cannot hear you, Ethan Hamilton."

"All agents, move in."

Special Agent Mike Gillette had his warrant. If so much hadn't been

< virtually eliminated >

on the line, Gillette might have laughed at the situation. The warrant wasn't for the arrest of a suspected killer, but for an international litter-bug. Ethan wasn't going to believe it.

If Ethan lived.

"Carruthers and Brown, take the back. Johnson and Householder, you're with me."

Gillette stowed his phone and drew his pistol. He met Johnson and Householder at the curb. Together they strode to the front door of 11187 NE Valley Court.

Ethan spun around. "Where are you?"

There it was — that cold certainty that nothing Ethan could do would give him even a prayer of a chance against this man.

"I have disabled your allies' audio." The voice came from all around.

Ethan walked in a backwards circle. He mustered a brave voice. "That wasn't very hospitable of you."

"The Loma Linda labs. How fitting. Of course my onetime allies have turned against me. It is not the first time. And the infamous Dr. Hosokawa, no less. That at least explains your sudden ability to soar through GlobeNet on the wings of a grackle."

The voice seemed strongest around the leftmost burning BattleMech hulk. Ethan moved toward it cautiously, the command for an exit portal cued in his mind. If Patriot really had cut him off from the outside world, then he would have to fend for himself until he found a way out. He couldn't even tell them to sever the connection and get him out of the machine.

It occurred to Ethan that he didn't have a surge protector on the phone line going into the RVT. All his angst over Jordan not being protected, and he hadn't even bothered to put one on his own machine.

He rounded the billowing mech with audacity. If God wanted him alive, just let Patriot try to kill him.

Patriot lay on the ground before him, his black torso propped up

< jefferson scott >

against an exploded gun turret. "Ah, Hamilton, at last."

Ethan thought he heard a rasp in the silken voice. Patriot looked pathetic, a far cry from his virile self. Nevertheless, Ethan didn't go any closer. This looked too much like the setup back in the virtual library.

"Are you sick?"

Patriot chuckled weakly. "You have no idea. Let us call my affliction world weariness. Too long have I fought to make this a better world, with little or no success. And now, Ethan Hamilton, I am tired." He sat up better against his backrest. "I'm glad to have you with me, Ethan, here at the end. Though I doubt you will believe me."

He indicated the artificial landscape with a sweep of his hand. "A fitting graveyard for me, would you not agree? I shall die where I have lived, adrift on the cybernetic brine. Burial at sea, no less."

"Don't you want to 'unburden' yourself of me first?"

"Alas, I cannot. Whilst I was engaged in pursuing you, engineers at the Panamanian power plant I was using finally detected my charge. It has been dissipated, I fear. Cheers, man, you have saved yourself. Furthermore, it is you who shall shortly be unburdened of me."

"Why is that?"

"A childhood accident has rendered me quite dependent on medical machinery. That machinery has been switched off for almost fifteen minutes, you see. I have, from the beginning, planned to give my life for my beloved America, regretting, as did Nathan Hale, that I have only one life to lose for my country.

"Only now my death will not be seen as being given for my country, will it? Like the rest of my life, my death will amount to nothing at all."

Ethan's compassion overwhelmed his caution. Perhaps it wouldn't hurt anything to sit by this exceptional man as his life drained away. He knelt beside Patriot and looked out over the battlefield. Smoke poured into the scarlet sky from a score of beaten goliaths.

Out of the red haze, Ethan could see a mech running toward their position at full speed. He scanned the horizon, but saw no enemies

< virtually eliminated >

nearby. The approaching mech didn't appear to have anything on its tail. Its earthshaking footfalls became audible. It was definitely on a beeline for their location.

Gillette pushed the door open.

This wasn't strictly by the book. The warrant did not give the issuing agents the right to enter the suspect's house without being let in. But they had knocked three times and rung the doorbell twice. They had reason to believe the suspect was alone and was incapable of rising to let them in, even if he'd wanted to. Besides, the door had been unlocked.

One of the other agents thought he had heard something once. Perhaps it was the suspect shouting, "Come in!"

Gillette didn't think so. None of them did.

They went in anyway.

The front door opened into the living room. Though tidy, the house failed to rise above the poverty which pervaded it like an odor. Behind a sagging sofa Gillette could see part of a white-tiled kitchen. Just before the kitchen, a hallway led off to the right.

A high-pitched noise called to them from down the hallway.

Gillette led the agents through the living room.

Ethan took a stand between the oncoming BattleMech and Patriot's prone body. It couldn't actually damage them in any way, of course, but Ethan wouldn't want to die in the middle of a toy battle game. He didn't think Patriot would want to either.

Ethan walked forward waving his arms. "Go away! Leave us alone."

A voice crackled back. "Get out of the way!"

"You get out of the way." Ethan had to speak between mini-earthquakes. "We're not bothering anything. Just let us —"

The mech halted. Panels opened over weapons bays. Hundreds of

< j e f f e r s o n   s c o t t >

tiny missile points swiveled to aim at Ethan's head. "Move out of the way!"

"I don't believe this."

Behind Ethan's back, directly in his blind spot, a black form rose up like a phantom. Black arms stretched out for Ethan's head.

Gillette shut his eyes. He pressed his ear against the door at the end of the hallway.

This was the room Diesel and Monroe had said was full of machinery. Gillette could believe it. He heard beeps and whirs enough for twenty machines.

And now and then, rising above the din, Gillette could hear a voice.

A voice he knew.

He took his ear from the door and nodded at the other two agents. They tensed themselves for an assault. Gillette dried his hands on his jeans. He flipped his pistol off safety.

Reached for the brass knob.

The door was locked.

Ethan froze. Something was terribly wrong, and it didn't have anything to do with an annoying BattleMech. He looked over his shoulder with nightmare slowness.

Patriot's hands were inches from Ethan's back.

"Wh —"

"Did you actually believe Panamanian engineers could catch me? You are a fool, Ethan Hamilton." He lunged for Ethan's heart.

Ethan lurched backward. Icy hands touched his chest. Warmth sprang into his head. He fell.

The mech opened fire.

< virtually eliminated >

Gillette burst through the bedroom door in an explosion of splinters. The hollow door gave way beneath his charge as if it were made of balsa wood.

Gillette shoulder-rolled on the carpet and came up in firing position. The other agents burst in behind him, shouting, guns out.

"Federal agents, nobody move!"

Patriot disappeared beneath a wave of orange fireballs. Rockets peppered him as from a machine gun. Earth and debris sprang skyward in the deafening bombardment.

Ethan crawled away, clutching his chest. Patriot had touched him, but somehow he wasn't dead. He lifted himself off the ground and hovered just behind the mech's armored head, trying to see Patriot through the nebula of flame.

As abruptly as it had begun, the cannonade ceased. Ethan could hear the missile launchers clicking, still attempting to fire from empty pods. The sound of the final impact rocked out to the hills and back.

When the smoke lifted, Patriot lay prostrate on the ground.

Ethan wasn't going anywhere near him.

The mech driver's voice crackled.

"It's okay. He's really dead this time, Dad."

< jefferson scott >

chapter.34

"I KNEW HE WASN'T AS HURT as he was telling you." Jordan sat on his grandparents' couch, his legs draped over his father's lap.

Ethan patted his son's knee. "How?"

Jordan nodded at the man sitting in a folding chair, brought out of a back closet to handle the overflow. "He called and told me."

Special Agent Mike Gillette tipped an imaginary hat.

"You, Mike?"

"Yessir." He took a sip of iced tea. "The boys in the van told me he hadn't shot yet."

Ethan scratched his head. "Jordan, how did you even know where we were? And where did you get a BattleMech that could shoot energy dampeners?"

The nine-year-old shrugged. "I made it. It's just like your castle helpers, only I made mine a mech."

Kaye's father spoke from his recliner. "Jordan, tell him how you knew where they were." He leaned toward Gillette. "Kid's a prodigy."

"I had one of my infobots, the *Victory,* following you wherever you went."

< virtually eliminated >

"But didn't you lose it when the phone lines went down?" Ethan asked. "You couldn't maintain control. It would've reverted to its anterior command structure, which meant it should've just stopped wherever it was."

Gillette and Kaye exchanged confused looks. Gillette passed a hand over his head. Katie, sitting in her father's lap, between Jordan's knees, copied Gillette's gesture. She smiled at the man, then smashed her face into her father's shoulder.

"Ugh." Ethan looked at his daughter. "She's flirting with you, Mike. Before this goes any further, I want to know your intentions toward my daughter."

"I didn't lose it," Jordan said.

"Lose what, son?"

"They didn't lose the phones in Oklahoma," Gillette said.

Wysiwyg jumped into Ethan's lap with a beseeching meow. Ethan scratched her behind her ears.

"Here's another thing I don't get. Patriot touched me square on the chest, but I didn't get electrocuted. How is that? You said he hadn't used his charge yet."

Gillette shrugged. "Diesel and Monroe said the voltage was going down for some reason. Can't hold that much energy for very long without some of it leaking away, if I understood the kid right. It did hit you — by all counts you should be Cajun chicken — there just wasn't enough left to do you any harm."

Kaye's mother spoke for the first time, seated in the rocker by the fireplace. "There's no question in my mind how it happened. Half the planet was praying. You get that many people petitioning the Father and you can just expect good things to happen."

"Amen, Mother," said her husband.

"Also," Gillette continued, "it looked like Patriot had set some kind of self-destruct on himself. There was nothing wrong with his machines that we could tell. His IV bags were full; all the power was on."

"Are you saying he unplugged himself?" Ethan asked.

< jefferson scott >

"No, he was still plugged in. Maybe he just had his computer tell his medical machines to shut off. Anyway, that's what it looked like to me. It might help explain why his power was getting weaker, since he was fading away at the same time."

"He did have the thing pretty tightly planned," Ethan admitted. "And he told me he had planned to die doing this. Maybe I just delayed him too long and his own shut-down procedure took effect too early."

Kaye cleared her throat softly. "No. It was God."

"Amen, Kaye," her father said.

"Now wait a minute," Ethan said after a moment, "doesn't this mean I ran around GlobeNet scared out of my brain, thinking that if he touched me I was dead, and all the time he didn't have squat for electricity?" Wysiwyg jumped down. "I didn't really save Grant and Yasunari at all!"

"Relax, hero, you did save them. Patriot's zap gun still had plenty of juice when y'all were on together. Monroe said the charge didn't start going down until the last ten minutes or so."

Ethan relaxed a little. He caressed Kaye's shoulder. "You really had half the world praying?"

She rested her cheek on his arm.

"Looks like I owe my life to my wife, my son, God, and the FBI." Ethan looked at his son. "If you hadn't come running up in that BattleMech, I would've been french fried on the spot."

Jordan blushed.

Ethan turned to Gillette. "You and I, Mike, on the other hand, are going to have to have a talk about Special Agents Paul and..." He turned to Jordan for help.

"Ricky."

"Paul and Ricky. And more. I'm still sore about you taking my son and putting him in danger."

"Technically, Ethan, buddy, Jordan did get in the car with the agents of his own free will."

"And when they put him on-line with a killer without any kind of

< virtually eliminated >

surge protection at all, was that of his own free will, too?"

No one moved.

Ethan sighed. "Sorry, Mike. I know you and the other guys were just following orders. Maybe the problem's with the order-givers, not the agents."

"And the order-givers' order-givers."

Mrs. Simms stood up. "Who's for apple pie and ice cream?"

Everyone moved to the kitchen for dessert.

Ethan took Gillette aside. "Mike, aren't you telling me you never caught Patriot doing anything illegal? He never shot at Grant or Yasunari. The one he shot at me was so weak." He paused. "You did raid the house, right?"

"Yessir."

Kaye brought them both pie and ice cream. People were beginning to return to their seats.

"Isn't that kind of against the law? Won't you get in trouble?"

"No. We had a warrant. We hit the house, all right, but not because of the little tickle he gave you."

"Then what was the warrant for?"

"That was something Monroe thought up," Gillette said around a mouthful of dessert. "I couldn't believe it. Best piece of detective work I've ever seen, and he ain't even a detective."

Ethan took a bite. "What was it?"

"You know when Patriot was after Jordan?"

Kaye almost choked. "Which time?"

"Yeah," Jordan said, "which time?"

"The Buddha time."

"The what?" Jordan said.

"Remember the giant statue of the fat man?"

"Oh, yeah!"

"Right. Well, after Ethan came out of the sky and scooped Jordan out of the fire like that, honorable Patriot-san still had all the electricity built up for your son. He finally sent it out to a payphone in Japan. We thought

< jefferson scott >

we were out of luck. But Monroe made some calls to some people, who made calls to some *other* people. Seems a woman happened to be walking by when that payphone exploded. She got some glass in her face and arm. Thanks to Monroe, the CIA got with Japanese intel, and they tracked the lady down and got her to lodge a complaint. The CIA faxed the complaint to Monroe, and I took it to the DA. We got a warrant on the spot."

"For what?" Ethan asked.

"Negligent disposal of a hazardous material. Can you believe it?"

Henry rocked in his recliner. "Makes about as much sense as anything else I've heard."

"So the hostage/terrorist attack team raided Louis Parks's house on a hazardous waste charge?" Ethan said. "Unbelievable."

"We didn't actually call in the hostage boys. What we had — the four other special agents and me — was overkill enough."

"Was he still alive when you got to him?"

"Dead as a post. Wish I would have known that before I knocked his door down, though. It's hard on a man's shoulder. It's not like they show it in the movies."

"You busted a door down, Mike? For me?"

Gillette rubbed his shoulder. "I'm pretty good when the chips are down. You want to know the kicker? The door wasn't locked, after all. The knob was just stuck. Agent Householder made sure I knew it, too."

Ethan smiled. "I appreciate it anyway."

"No problem. Maybe I can talk sweet Liz into giving it a rubdown when I get back in town." Gillette winked at Jordan. "Anyway, we broke into his room, hootin' and hollerin'. But he was already dead. Laying on his bed. Hadn't been gone long, though — he was still pretty warm. His machines were beeping up a storm."

Ethan was confused. "So you called Jordan then?"

Gillette's fork scraped the plate. "Could I please have another piece?"

Mrs. Simms took his plate, smiling broadly. "Why, of course."

"Mike." Ethan motioned with his fork, trying to get him back on track.

< virtually eliminated >

"Hmm?"

"How did Jordan know he was really dead?"

"Oh, yeah. As soon as we figured out he was flatlined, we called Kidner and Groves. And they must have told Jordan."

Jordan drew his knees up to his chin. "What'd he look like?"

Gillette looked at the ceiling. "Real white, Jordan. Like he'd never been outside his whole life. Real skinny legs and arms. I mean *real* skinny. Like a skeleton with skin."

"Gross."

"He's what you call a quadriplegic," Gillette said. "You know what that is?"

Jordan shook his head.

"It means he can't move his legs or arms."

Mrs. Simms brought Gillette his second piece of pie. "Wasn't there anyone with him? How did he eat?"

Gillette took the plate. "Thank you, ma'am. No, nobody was with him. Someone must come by a couple times a day. That's the only thing I can figure. That reminds me of another weird thing we found: a letter to his parents was sitting in his printer. It was real long. We had to keep the originals as evidence, but we made photocopies and sent them along. I hope they read it."

"Where was his mother?" Ethan asked.

Gillette wolfed down a bite. "Mmf! I forgot to tell you. They found his mom. She's in Kingston, Jamaica — get this, in jail."

"Jail?"

"Yep. Something about her visa going bad on her once she got into the country."

Ethan stared into space and smirked.

Katie was getting restless. It was past time for her pill. Kaye whispered into the little girl's ear, and she walked over to Gillette and climbed into his lap. Gillette managed to hold her and still eat his second piece of pie.

"What was he wearing on his face, Mike, some kind of goggles?" Ethan said.

< jefferson scott >

"Looked like cheap sunglasses to me, till I took them off. Skin around his eyes was even whiter than the rest of his face. Little red and blue cables taped all over his head."

"What kind of person would you say he was if you saw him walk down the street?"

"Little bit of a hippie, I guess. Long brown hair, kind of frizzy."

Ethan tried to reconcile Gillette's description with the image he'd formed in his mind. The long hair was definitely out of place. How could someone who quoted Horace and Shakespeare all day long be called a hippie?

"What I don't understand," Mrs. Simms said, "is why he turned mean."

"Maybe because of his condition," Kaye said.

"But there's plenty of people in his condition who don't turn out that way," Mr. Simms said. "It's not like being crippled makes you mean." He turned to his wife. "Mother, what's the name of that Methodist minister in the wheelchair?"

"Noble, isn't it? Jerry Noble. Wonderful speaker."

Jordan folded his legs under him. "Maybe nobody ever told him about God."

The statement ricocheted around the room. The heater came on. Katie drifted to sleep in Gillette's arms. The clock bonged ten.

Ethan sighed. "There were so many things he was angry about. He was mad at his father for deserting him. He was mad at his mother for driving recklessly and causing his injuries — then she deserted him in the end, too. He was mad at the Japanese for what he saw as an ongoing attempt to take over America. He was mad at American businesses for selling out to the Japanese and at the U.S. government for not intervening. He was certainly mad at me — and Jordan — for getting in his way. But I think most of all he was mad at God."

"What on earth for?" Mrs. Simms said.

"For allowing him to be injured. For allowing his parents to divorce. For allowing all the things he was mad at to happen without

< virtually eliminated >

lifting a finger to prevent them, so far as he could see. I even wonder if his murders and executions weren't an attempt to somehow get God to pay attention to him."

"Like when Wizzy climbs on top of bookcases when we've been ignoring her?"

"Exactly, Jordan."

"He got what he wanted then," Kaye said. "God prompted you, Ethan, to get involved."

"I guess he's getting lots of God's attention right now," Mr. Simms said.

"Except why was he so mad at the Japanese?" Jordan asked.

"I don't know, son. Maybe that was just an excuse."

"Well, whatever his reasons were," Mrs. Simms said, "may God forgive him and have mercy on his eternal soul."

Gillette checked his watch. "I'd best be heading out. Plane leaves at eight in the morning, and I'd like to get a full night's sleep for a change."

Ethan walked him to the front door. "Hey, thanks for swinging by Loma Linda for me. I wasn't looking forward to buying a plane ticket to Oklahoma."

"No problem." Gillette offered his hand and they shook. "We sure had us a big time, didn't we?"

"Yes, a big time."

"We've come a long way from the Ol' South Pancake House, huh?"

Ethan laughed at the memory. "We sure have."

"That sounds good, actually. Wonder if Tulsa's got an IHOP anywhere around."

"Don't know."

Gillette pulled out his keys. "So what's your plan now, cowboy?"

"I don't even want to think about it."

He needed to call Ron Dontwell back, for one thing. It seemed ImTech's CEO wanted Ethan to do some freelance work for him on the M7. Certainly an honor, but lots of work. He needed to call Dr. Hosokawa too, out at Loma Linda University. She wanted Ethan to help her refine her RVT.

< jefferson scott >

He was crazy even to consider it. He'd never have enough time to do all that and still be a good employee for DES, no matter what these people wanted to pay him. Might as well just leave DES and hang out his own consulting shingle.

Not a bad idea, Curly.

Gillette pulled his hat and coat out of the coat closet. "I was wanting to ask you something."

"Okay." Ethan thought he saw that dangerous gleam.

"I was wondering if I could count on your help the next time something like this comes up."

"You serious?"

"You betcha. We're a great team, aren't we? Besides, Hamilton, this may be news to you, but we never would have caught Patriot without you. Martin Grant and Yuki Whatshisname would be worm chow right now if it wasn't for you. Face it, Hamilton, you're a hero."

"Let me pray about it, Mike."

"Don't you ever quit?"

"Try not to."

"All right, have it your way. I'll give you a call Monday."

"How about a year from Monday?"

"A year!"

"That is if you can find me in a year. One of the first things Kaye said to me at the airport was, 'Let's move away.'"

"Where to, Dallas?"

"Don't know. Maybe Virginia, or Alaska, or Washington State. Someplace with lots of trees and not much concrete."

"I'll find you."

"That's right — I forgot. You're the FBI; you keep tabs on everybody. Well, better update your files fast."

"Why? You moving already?"

"No, family vacation. I promised myself that if I lived through all this I would take my family to see this unbelievable rock temple in Egypt."

"Egypt! You ever been to Egypt before?"

< virtually eliminated >

"No, but I feel like I know this temple pretty well. Anyway, we're going from there to the Holy Land. I think it'll do me good to do some walking in my Savior's footsteps for awhile. Sit for a week by the Sea of Galilee, that sort of thing."

Gillette opened the door. "Well, Ethan Hamilton, I have to say it's been a pleasure. Hope to work with you again soon." They shook hands again.

"We'll see." Ethan followed Gillette out onto the porch. The wind blew cold.

"Mike."

"Yeah, buddy."

"I've been thinking about some things Patriot told me. You know, about America being owned by a foreign country and citizens not knowing and not even caring."

He left the thought unspoken.

"So what can we do about it, Mike? Or is it already too late?"

Gillette put on his cowboy hat and turned up his collar. "To tell you the truth, buddy, I just don't know." He winked and walked away.

Ethan stood out there a moment after Gillette's rental car had pulled out of sight. He tilted his head back and closed his eyes. The arctic wind stole his breath-clouds away. He could feel the concrete seeping cold up through his feet.

But that was all right.

For this was the real world. And in the real world things hurt.

People hurt. And died.

But in the real world people also lived. And loved. Images of Kaye and Jordan and Katie — and Jesus, seated in the driver's seat — overflowed in his mind.

God had saved his life. Had saved his son and his marriage, too. He had reached down into Ethan's idolatry and pulled him back to his side. There was a line between the real and virtual worlds now. A barricade made by the very finger of God.

Despite chill from the sub-freezing wind, when Ethan turned to go, in his soul there was warmth.